Stepping Stones to Other Religions

Stepping Stones to Other Religions
A Christian Theology of Inter-Religious Dialogue

Dermot A. Lane is President of Mater Dei Institute of Education and Parish Priest of Balally, Dublin 16. He teaches during summer sessions at the University of Dayton, Ohio, and St. Michael's College, Vermont, on alternate years. He is author of several books in theology, including *Keeping Hope Alive: Stirrings in Christian Theology* (1996/2005), *The Experience of God: An Invitation to do Theology* (revised edition 2003), and *Challenges Facing Religious Education in Contemporary Ireland* (2008).

Stepping Stones to Other Religions

A Christian Theology of Inter-Religious Dialogue

DERMOT A. LANE

ORBIS BOOKS
Maryknoll, New York 10545
www.orbisbooks.com

Copyright © 2011 by Dermot A. Lane

First published by Veritas Publications, 7-8 Lower Abbey Street, Dublin 1, Ireland.

Published by Orbis Books, Maryknoll, New York 10545-0302. Manufactured in the United States of America.

Library of Congress Cataloging-in-Publication Data

Lane, Dermot A., 1941-
  Stepping stones to other religions : a Christian theology of inter-religious dialogue / by Dermot A. Lane.
     p. cm.
  Includes bibliographical references (p.   ).
  ISBN 978-1-57075-991-8 (pbk.)
  ISBN 978-1-60833-227-7 (ebook)
  1. Christianity and other religions. 2. Catholic Church—Relations.
  3. Holy Spirit. 4. Catholic Church--Doctrines. I. Title.
  BR127.L345 2012
  261.2—dc23
                                                        2012007635

CONTENTS

ACKNOWLEDGEMENTS

Theology is never performed alone. On a professional level, it must engage in an on-going dialogue of faith seeking understanding in experience, revelation, tradition, the teaching of the Churches, the *sensus fidelium*, and the signs of the times in which we live. These horizons have influenced this book

There are also other sources that shaped the writing of this book. I have been privileged to belong to the academic community of Mater Dei Institute of Education, Dublin City University, especially the School of Theology, for many years. That happy association has enriched my theology in a variety of ways. I have also been fortunate to be part of the Summer Graduate Programmes of St Michael's College, Vermont, and the University of Dayton, Ohio, in alternating years. Both of these institutions provided me with opportunities for research after my teaching responsibilities. I wish to record here my gratitude to Dr Edward Mahoney of St Michael's College and Dr Sandra Yocum Mize of the University of Dayton for their generous hospitality over several summers which facilitated the writing of this book.

In addition to these academic communities, I have also been blessed to belong to the ecclesial community of Balally Parish in which I have ministered as a pastor for many years. The priests and people of Balally Parish have supported me in writing this book. In an important sense, the pastoral and academic have informed and critiqued each other in my experience in ways that have enriched my theology.

I am also indebted to colleagues who have read parts of the manuscript and offered helpful comments. Paul Couture, SSE, and Declan Byrne read individual chapters and made insightful comments. Peter Admirand read the entire script and offered helpful comments on style and content. Terrence W. Tilley, Professor of Theology in Fordham University, long-time friend and colleague, participated in conversations with me over many years. Terry read different drafts, made constructive suggestions, and always offered valuable critiques. To all of these colleagues I am deeply indebted. Whatever flaws remain in the text, remain as mine.

Mention must also be made of my personal secretary, Hazel Rooke, who patiently typed and re-typed various versions of the text. Hazel is more than a typist; she has also been a participant in the dialogue that shaped the final text.

Lastly, I wish to thank my publisher, Veritas, especially Maura Hyland, Director of Veritas, who supported this project from the beginning. Even though the manuscript arrived some years late, Maura kept faith in me and in the project.

Mater Dei Institute of Education, Dublin City University, Dublin 3
Church of the Ascension, Balally Parish, Dublin 16

15 August 2011

ABBREVIATIONS

AG   *Ad Gentes: Decree on Missionary Activity of the Church,* December 1965*

DeV   John Paul II, *Dominum et Vivificantem: An Encyclical Letter On the Holy Spirit in the Life of the Church and the World* (1986)

DI   *Dominus Iesus: On the Unicity and Salvific Universality of Jesus Christ and the Church,* Congregation for the Doctrine of the Faith, 2000

DP   *Dialogue and Proclamation: Reflections and Orientations on Inter-religious Dialogue and the Proclamation of the Gospel of Jesus Christ,* Pontifical Council for Inter-Religious Dialogue and the Congregation for the Evangelisation of Peoples, May 1991

DV   *Dei Verbum: Dogmatic Constitution on Divine Revelation,* November 1965

* Quotations from the Second Vatican Council documents are taken from *Vatican Council II: Constitutions, Decrees, Declarations,* edited by Austin Flannery, OP, a completely revised translation in inclusive language, Dublin: Dominican Publications, 1996. All biblical quotations are taken from the *New Revised Standard Version* Bible, New York: Oxford University Press, 1991, unless otherwise stated.

GS *Gaudium et Spes: Pastoral Constitution on the Church in the Modern World,* December 1965

LG *Lumen Gentium: Dogmatic Constitution on the Church,* November 1964

NA *Nostra Aetate: Declaration on the Relation of the Church to Non-Christian Religions,* October 1965

RH John Paul II, *Redemptor Hominis: The Redeemer of Man,* 1979

RM John Paul II, *Redemptoris Missio: An Encyclical Letter on the Permanent Validity of the Church's Missionary Mandate,* 1990

TI Karl Rahner, *Theological Investigations,* Volumes 1–23, London: Darton, Longman and Todd, 1961–1992

UR *Unitatis Redintegratio: Decree on Ecumenism,* November 1964

INTRODUCTION

We live in a world in which the daily news frequently contains references of one kind or another to Jews, Christians, Muslims, Hindus and Buddhists. These references are often negative, portraying religions as the cause of violence, hatred and intolerance. Many people have given up on the value of religion and increasing numbers are walking away from their particular religious affiliation, especially among Catholics in Europe and the US at this time. While it is true that religions are often the source of social and political unrest in many parts of the world, it is equally true that religions contain within themselves rich resources to bring about justice, peace and reconciliation in the world.

There is now a recognition among many political leaders that religion can be a power for good within society and a basis for the healing of a broken planet. This role of religion is recognised by international bodies like the Council of Europe, the Organisation for Security and Co-operation in Europe, and the United Nations. However, there is a danger that when left to politicians, religion becomes instrumentalised and is often called upon to justify war and violence. Religion has a key role to play in making the world a safer place and also has the capacity to put people in touch with the sacred mystery that 'exists' at the centre of life which Christians name as God, and invoke as Spirit, Son and Father.

Since the beginning of the third millennium there has been a new interest in religion. This new interest has been caused by a number of converging factors: 9/11, globalisation, and the migration of people. Sometimes this interest in religion is superficial and faddish, at other times it is serious and intense. One way or the other, this new interest is challenging people to look again at religion in their own lives and, at the same time, to explore the possibility of a new dialogue among the religious traditions of the world. The drive behind inter-religious dialogue is a drive to understand the other. There is a growing awareness that in the twenty-first century, to be religious will require that one be inter-religious and that to be authentically Christian will necessitate that one enter into respectful dialogue with other religions.

It is against this background that *Stepping Stones to Other Religions* seeks to address a number of issues:

- To outline theological reasons why Christians should enter into meaningful dialogue with other religious traditions;
- To provide guidelines on how this engagement with the other should take place;
- To point towards some of the benefits that come from such encounters for one's own Christian identity;
- To seek common ground between religious traditions, without neglecting to highlight the significant differences that exist between Christianity and other religions;
- To highlight the progress that has been made in the important dialogue between Christianity and Judaism;
- To offer Christians a theological language in which they can engage in respectful and sensitive dialogue with members of other religious traditions;
- To suggest that Christian Pneumatology provides a promising platform for a new dialogue with other religions;
- To summarise the teaching of the Catholic Church on its relation to other religious traditions.

For some people, however, inter-religious dialogue is seen as a new-fangled idea that the world can do without. This view forgets that, historically speaking, dialogue among the religions is as old as the religions themselves. Most religions have come into being through engagement with other religions. For example, Christianity is itself a religion that came to be out of a dialogue internal to Judaism, and Islam is a religion born out of a reaction to Judaism and Christianity. Christians will be mindful that in the Gospels, Jesus engages in dialogue with people from other religious traditions, such as the Syrophoenician woman (Mk 7:25-30), the Samaritan woman at the well (Jn 4:7-26), and the Roman centurion (Lk 7:1-10). Further, Christians will also be aware that there is evidence of engagement with other religions in the Patristic Period and that this continued well into the Middle Ages with Aquinas, Eckhart, Hildegard of Bingen and Francis of Assisi. Indeed, many would hold that the theological synthesis of the Middle Ages was forged by Aquinas partly out of engagement with some of the great thinkers of Judaism and Islam. While *Stepping Stones* does not review the history of engagement between Christianity and other religions, it does map out the debate in the twentieth and twenty-first centuries.

Of books on dialogue among the religions, there seems to be no end! For example, Orbis Books, the publishing wing of the US Maryknoll Missionary Society, has published over sixty-five volumes dedicated to the theme of 'Faith meets Faith'. So why do we need another book on inter-religious dialogue? There is general agreement that we are only at 'the beginning of a new beginning' of dialogue with other religious traditions, and that this dialogue looks set to be a defining feature of the first century of the third millennium. Further, to be Catholic, especially since the Second Vatican Council (1962–1965), carries with it a commitment to dialogue with other religions, not as an optional extra but as an essential part of the definition of what it means to be Catholic. In addition to addressing these particular issues, *Stepping Stones* also seeks to develop the Pneumatological, Christological and Ecclesiological foundations of this new self-understanding of Catholicism.

This book has been inspired by the *Declaration on the Relation of the Church to Non-Christian Religions* issued by the Second Vatican Council in October 1965, commonly referred to as *Nostra Aetate*. *Nostra Aetate* was the shortest document of the Council; it may, however, have the longest effect on the life of the Church. This book is also influenced by other documents from the Council, especially

Gaudium et Spes, *Lumen Gentium* and *Ad Gentes*, which provide the larger theological context for understanding and interpreting *Nostra Aetate*. Further, this book has been shaped by the positive reception of *Nostra Aetate* in the post-conciliar period. While *Stepping Stones* has been written from a Catholic perspective, it draws freely from other Christian theologians, in the hope that it might be of some interest to other Christian denominations.

The methodology implicit in *Stepping Stones* is inductive, following the recommendation of *Gaudium et Spes* that 'the Church carries the responsibility of reading the signs of the times and of interpreting them in the light of the Gospel'.[1] This approach is spelt out in further detail in Article 44 of *Gaudium et Spes*:

> With the help of the Holy Spirit, it is the task of the whole people of God, particularly of its pastors and theologians, to listen to and distinguish the many voices of our times and to interpret them in the light of God's Word, in order that the revealed truth may be more deeply penetrated, better understood and more suitably presented.

Among 'the signs of the times' are the following: the rise of pluralism, the reality of secularisation in the West, and the growing phenomenon of religious fundamentalism. These are developments which are affecting all religions including Christianity.

Among 'the many voices of our times' there exists the World Parliament of Religions, which last met in 2009. There is also the existence of different charters calling religions to a new dialogue. From the Catholic Church there is *Nostra Aetate* (1965). From the Jewish world there is *Dabru Emet – Speak the Truth*, a Jewish statement about Christianity, published in the *New York Times* in September 2000, signed by some 200 Rabbis and Jewish scholars, outlining among other things what Jews and Christians can agree upon. In 2007, 138 Muslim scholars issued 'A Common Word Between Us and You', calling for dialogue between Islam and Christianity, the first agreed statement of its kind in the history of Islam. In January 2011, The World Council of Churches, the Pontifical Council for Inter-Religious Dialogue, and the World Evangelical Alliance issued *Christian Witness in a Multi-Religious World: Recommendations for Conduct.*

Stepping Stones is constructed on three pillars. The first pillar is the teaching of the Second Vatican Council on other religions and the positive reception of that teaching in the post-conciliar period. Coming out of this new teaching of the Catholic Church is recognition that inter-religious dialogue is one aspect of the evangelising mission of the Church in the world. A further insight coming from *Nostra Aetate* and its reception is an awareness that encounter with other religious traditions has the capacity to enrich the particularity of one's own Christian faith and so offers an opportunity to learn 'from' and 'with' the other in a way that can deepen Christian faith and the faith of the other from anthropological, soteriological and theological points of view. The second pillar supporting *Stepping Stones* is the presentation of a theology of the Holy Spirit, both universal and particular, as the foundation for dialogue with other religions. The third pillar is that of Christology which sees Jesus as the Christ, crucified and risen, not as an obstacle but as a source inspiring engagement with other religions.

Chapter One outlines the radically new context in which theology exists in the twenty-first century: 9/11, the rise of multiculturalism, the new but ambiguous visibility of religion in the twenty-first century, and the ongoing tension between modernity and post-modernity.

Chapter Two outlines the teaching of the Catholic Church on its relationship with other religious traditions and the positive reception of this teaching in the post-conciliar period with the support of three different Popes.

Chapter Three maps out the theological debate in the twentieth and twenty-first centuries on the relationship between Christianity and other religions. It summarises the critique of Jacques Dupuis by the Congregation of the Doctrine of the Faith and of Peter Phan by the US Bishops' Committee on Doctrine. In particular, this chapter outlines the basic elements that belong to a theology of dialogue.

Chapter Four discusses Karl Rahner's singular contribution to the development of an inclusive self-understanding of Christianity. It shows how he opens the way for dialogue between Christianity and other religions, and it also notes how the later Rahner recommended Pneumatology as a point of departure for dialogue with other living faiths.

Chapter Five explores how the 'turn to the Spirit' in the twenty-first century could be adopted, with some fine tuning, as a point of departure for dialogue with other religions. However, it notes that this 'turn to the Spirit' as a resource for dialogue with other religious traditions will only succeed if it is reformed. At present, Spirit-discourse suffers from a number of modern prejudices that need to be addressed.

Chapter Six outlines a Pneumatology of Revelation in the light of the *Dogmatic Constitution on Divine Revelation* from Vatican II. Revelation is a key category within inter-religious dialogue. This chapter notes the relationship between Revelation, the gift of the Spirit, and imagination.

Chapter Seven develops a Christian theology of the Holy Spirit that could be used in inter-faith dialogue. In doing this, it highlights the importance of linking Pneumatology and Christology in the service of inter-religious dialogue, moving from a Spirit-Christology to a Spirit-centred Ecclesiology.

Chapter Eight reports on the progress that has been made in Jewish-Catholic dialogue. This final chapter notes how the dialogue between Catholics and Jews has enriched the self-understanding of Catholic identity in a variety of ways.

Stepping Stones is essentially a hopeful book: hopeful in virtue of the progress already achieved in inter-religious dialogue over the last fifty years, hopeful that the emerging new relationship between Christianity and Judaism might be adopted as a model for dialogue between Christians and Muslims, hopeful about the value of inter-religious dialogue for a deeper understanding and praxis of Christianity, hopeful that the religions of the world can work together out of their respective differences in the service of the well-being of the earth, the common good of society, and the possibility of a more peaceful co-existence among the living religions of the world.

NOTE

1. *GS*, a.4

I. THEOLOGY IN A RADICALLY NEW CONTEXT

In this opening chapter, I lay out, in broad strokes, the new context in which a theology of inter-religious dialogue must begin to reconfigure itself in the early decades of the twenty-first century. It is a radically new context, and calls for what some refer to as the re-contextualisation of theology. This new context has many layers to it. I begin with the reality of 9/11 and its implications for a theology of religions. This will be followed by an outline of the ambiguous return of religion to the public square. This return of religion calls for an articulation of some of the questions theology must address as suggested by David Tracy and Charles Taylor. Alongside these questions, I will show how theology in the twenty-first century is caught between the mixed successes of modernity and the wild winds of post-modernity, and how this new location of theology implies the need for engagement with the possibility of a new, second modernity. The chapter will close with some comments on the different kinds of knowledge that exist within modernity and theology, and how these might complement rather than compete with each other, especially when one takes account of the 'intimate relationship' that exists between faith and reason.

1. 9/11 AND THE NEW GLOBALISATION

Christian theology only exists as embedded in the social, cultural and historical forms of the day. When theology neglects or ignores its surrounding context, it ceases to communicate. It is instructive to remember that at the commencement of the Second Vatican Council, John XXIII introduced an important distinction between the deposit of faith and the different ways in which it is expressed. This distinction between form and substance, or between context and content, is echoed throughout the Council and its documents, and it also appears in post-conciliar documents.[1] As John Paul II frequently pointed out, only a faith that is enculturated is truly a living faith. The context of Catholic theology has changed as a result of the Second Vatican Council, becoming experiential, historical, ecumenical and inter-religious. These changes have accelerated significantly in the early years of the new millennium.

a. The Modern Neglect of Religion

The horrors of 9/11 changed the world, and the ill-conceived US response of 'War on Terror' also wrought change. It needs to be noted, however, that President Bush did point out that although 9/11 was enacted by some Muslims, not all Muslims should be associated with this assault on humanity and civilisation.

Prior to 9/11, religion was not always taken seriously by the modern world. For example, in 1979, the US public wanted to know why and how the CIA had failed to anticipate the revolution in Iran. In response, Admiral Stansfield Turner pointed out that the CIA had tracked Iranian markets, cinemas, demographics and publishing houses, and then he went on to admit: 'The only thing we paid no attention to was religion because it had no power in the modern world'.[2] Alastair Campbell, Press Secretary to the former UK Prime Minister, Tony Blair, (in)famously said at a conference: 'We do not do God.' Madeleine Albright, former US Secretary of State during the Clinton administration, in her autobiography, looking back at her public career, regrets buying into the modern assumptions that religion is not important in international affairs.[3] The modern assumptions, inherited from the Enlightenment, are that religions are basically all the same, that they should not be taken seriously in the public domain, that they are a private matter for citizens, that they should be treated in a neutral, detached and objective manner. And yet, when we look around the world, we will notice that most of the war zones are connected to, and often fuelled by, religious differences. The close association of religion with violence in the world is one of the most disturbing realities of the early twenty-first century, and must be one of the factors motivating the much-needed, most urgent dialogue among the religions of the world. On the other hand, there is an increasing awareness that if religion is a source of violence, it is also a powerful force for good, justice, peace and reconciliation in the world. In the 1990s, Hans Küng pointed out, prophetically:

> No peace among the nations without peace among the religions. No peace among the religions without dialogue. No dialogue among the religions without ethical criteria.[4]

b. The Turn to Multiculturalism

In the light of 9/11, governments and politicians have begun to take religion more seriously, realising that it is as much a source of peace and reconciliation as it is a source of conflict and violence. Governments in Europe have promoted programmes of multiculturalism as a way of welcoming and accommodating newcomers into western society. However, engagement with the religions in these programmes was more pragmatic than genuinely religious and to that extent could be described as half-hearted. In the UK, multiculturalism was conceived in terms of integration, seeking to integrate foreigners into British society. In France, multiculturalism was about assimilation, a policy that said, if you want to live in France as a migrant, then you must conform to the French way of being, which includes their philosophy of *laïcité*, not only in relation to education and politics, but also all the way down to the details of religious dress in public.

Such 'politically correct' policies of multiculturalism during the first decade of the new millennium have had very limited success. Many hold that multiculturalism has given rise to the isolation of political extremists and ghettoisation of different ethnic groups. In support of this view, they point to the Madrid train bombings in March 2004, the London bombings of July 2005, the controversy over the Danish cartoons of Mohammed, September 2005, the Paris riots, September 2005, and the bombing and shootings in Norway, July 2011.

As a result of the London bombings, the then Secretary of State in England, Ruth Kelly, established a government 'Commission on Integration and Cohesion'. The speech launching this commission questioned 'the uniform consensus on the values of multiculturalism' and wondered whether multiculturalism in the UK 'is encouraging separateness?' Also at the launch, Kelly perceptively asked the question: 'Have we ended up with communities living in isolation of each other with no common bonds between them?'[5]

In the same year, the UK Muslim scholar, Dr Mona Siddiqui, described multiculturalism as the 'failed experiment of the past and the impasse of the present', mainly because 'multiculturalism has meant nothing and everything at one and the same time.'[6] There is similar evidence for the failure of multiculturalism in France. The 2005 autumn riots in Paris were an indication that the French policy of assimilation was not working. President Nicolas Sarkozy, conscious of the ongoing tension within the French Muslim community sought to promote a 'positive *laïcité*' that goes beyond the negative, traditional and absolute separation of church and state. Sarkozy also sought to promote a better understanding in schools of religion, especially of Christianity, as an integral part of the cultural inheritance of France. In spite of these small steps, the ongoing debate in France about a dress code for Muslim women in public is a further indication that all is not well with multiculturalism.

Part of the reason for this failure of multiculturalism in Europe is that there was no real engagement or exchange between the different cultures. One must move from multiculturalism to the possibility of inter-cultural exchanges that acknowledge diversity, respect differences, and values the other as other. In too many parts of Europe, immigrants were valued primarily for what they might offer to the economy as 'units of labour', in the words of one commentator. Instead, there must be real dialogue between the cultures and this will require at least a moment of inter-ethical exchange and at best experiences of inter-religious dialogue. It is within this larger context that Christians need to have a theology of other religions if they are to contribute to inter-cultural, inter-ethical and inter-religious dialogues.

c. A Post–9/11, New Interest in Religion

There are some signs that governments are beginning to appreciate the importance of religion for promoting social cohesion and political peace at the local, national and international levels. In 2007, the Irish Prime Minister, Bertie Ahern, inaugurated a 'Structured Dialogue with the Churches, Faith Communities and Non-Confessional Bodies'. This initiative sought to initiate dialogue between all denominations that would be respectful of all faiths and those of no faith. In 2009, the French Ministry for Foreign Affairs appointed a panel of six experts to advise its 16,000 strong diplomatic corps on the role of religion in international affairs. In the same year, a similar move took place in the UK through the appointment by John Denham, Communities Secretary, as a policy adviser on faith communities. Further, in the last six years, the Council of Europe, one of the oldest institutions of Europe, has begun to take a new interest in religion, especially in relation to the interplay between religion and education in schools. One other example comes from the Secretary General of the United Nations who appealed to the leaders of world religions to support at local level proposals for the Copenhagen Conference in December 2009 on climate change.

These examples could be described as baby-steps by governments in the right direction of bringing religion into the public forum. They are an indication that politicians are beginning to see religion as a potential force for good in the world, as an important player in promoting civic harmony, social cohesion and justice, and as a way of creating an awareness of the importance of attending to the creation of an ecologically sustainable future.

2. THE AMBIGUOUS RETURN OF RELIGION TO THE PUBLIC SQUARE

In the light of 9/11 and multiculturalism, there has been a resurgence of public interest in religion. This return of religion has been heralded by international magazines like *Der Spiegel*, *The Economist*, and *Time* magazine[7] and is the subject of various books such as *The New Visibility of Religion*[8] and *God is Back: How the Global Rise of Faith is Changing the World.*[9]

a. The Impact of Globalisation

This return of religion to the public forum is not just an after-effect of 9/11. Other forces are also contributing to this new interest in religion such as the movement of peoples through migration, the shrinking of the world through the phenomenon of globalisation, and the revolution in communications through the advent of the internet. The migration of peoples across the globe, but especially from the south to the north, is bringing people of different religions together like never before. The presence of members of other religions as neighbours is now an inescapable social and cultural reality in the west. Globalisation is gathering people of different religions into a new network of social and political relationships. The internet is putting people in immediate contact with each other and giving them access to the texts, traditions and rituals of other religions.

The increasing phenomenon of globalisation is giving rise to a new visibility of religion in the market-place. However, before people rush to see this as a positive development, it should be remembered that globalisation itself is a modern invention, constructed primarily to serve the interests of market-driven capitalism, and operates out of a secularist and supposedly neutral philosophy.

b. The Rise of Vague Religiosities

This return of religion to the public square is found in a variety of different forms. It can be seen in the rise of religious fundamentalisms across the globe. This fundamentalism is found, within Christianity among evangelical movements in America and Pentecostal groupings in Latin America, in certain strands of Roman Catholicism, and among some militant Muslim, Jewish and Hindu groups. In many instances, this fundamentalism is a reaction against western modernisation and the persistent presence of inequalities within society. Another expression of this return of religion is the growing 'commodification' of religion within the new globalised culture. One striking example of this is the extraordinary success of *The Da Vinci Code*, in which religion is made into a source of entertainment. A further expression of the return to religion is the rising tide of vague religiosities among people of all ages. These vague religiosities are expressed in statements like: 'I am spiritual, but not religious', or 'I believe, but I don't belong', or 'I belong but I don't believe', or 'I am a person of faith but I don't practice'. There is in addition a popular turn to spirituality among churches and religions which appeals primarily to the interior sources of significance like self-awareness, self-development and self-fulfilment. A further feature of this new religiosity is the presence of a vague belief 'in something' which seeks to go beyond the endless flow of facts and figures from the information society.

c. The New Visibility of Religion – A Matter of Debate

In the light of 9/11, the crisis within modernity and the ever-increasing phenomenon of globalisation, religion has acquired a new visibility in the public square. It is difficult to assess the significance of this new presence of religion. Is it due to the intellectual limitations of modern rationality, or is it simply the result of post-modern permissiveness, or is it because ethics and morality are in need of resources on fundamental questions surrounding solidarity and social integration? It is possible to discern both a positive and negative assessment of this return of religion to the public square.

There are those who argue that a new dialogue is needed within the public square on the relationship between religion and society, because they believe that religion has a contribution to make to the social and political construction of a post-modern world. Some of those promoting this new dialogue would not describe themselves as religious and in some instances refer to themselves as atheists or agnostics – yet they feel religion has a contribution to make to the needs of society. The names that come to mind here include Jacques Derrida, Jürgen Habermas, and the Slovenian thinker, Slavoj Žižek. Others such as Terry Eagleton, a believer with a critical take on religion, recognise the intellectual resources that religion could bring to a debate about society and politics. Together, these voices suggest that religion has resources, intellectual, prophetic and transcendent, that could stimulate a constructive dialogue within the public square. These voices see religion as offering a critique of the flatness of so much social and political discourse. They are motivated more by an unease with the way the world is than by any personal commitment to any one particular religion.[10]

The reasons put forward by this small group of intellectuals can be summarised in the following way. There is agreement that the non-realisation of the secularisation thesis is a factor prompting their contribution. This thesis, put forward by sociologists and religious thinkers for well over a century, suggested that large sectors of society and culture would become free from domination by religious institutions, that there would be a decline in the religious content of art, of philosophy, and of literature, and that the rise of science as an autonomous and secular discipline would become the yardstick of progress within modernity. This secularisation thesis has not come to pass. Closely connected to this reason for the rise of religion is that the lines of demarcation within modernity between the sacred and the secular, between religion and society, between faith and experience, are far from clear, and that this kind of dualism, exemplified in certain forms of fundamentalism and secularism, does not do justice to either the secular or the sacred.

A second reason is that there is a recognition among these intellectuals that religion offers a potential for individual emancipation and social transformation. For example, Slavoj Žižek suggests that religion should be co-opted as an ally in helping to bring back conflict into politics and also to serve as a critique of the de-politicisation of the public square and the state.[11] In particular, Terry Eagleton argues that the politics implied by theology 'are more, not less, radical than much that is to be found in the more orthodox discourses of leftism today.'[12] Further, according to Eagleton, theology in spite of the implausibility of many of its truth-claims, nonetheless, 'is one of the most ambitious theoretical arenas left in an increasingly specialised world – one whose subject is nothing less than the nature and destiny of humanity itself, in relation to what it takes to be its transcendent source of life.'[13] In other words, for Eagleton, religion deals with questions that go beyond the narrow specialisations of contemporary life and the compartmentalisation of life that is promoted within the modern world.

Echoing Eagleton and Žižek, but in a more explicitly Christian register, US theologian-social critic Cornel West suggests 'secular thinkers ... must become more religiously musical. Too many secular thinkers are religiously tone deaf.' And equally 'Religious persons like myself must be secularly musical ... We must try to get inside other people's view of the world, to understand why people are convinced ... why they are agnostic or why they are atheistic.'[14] To do this, both sides need to have greater empathy and imagination to expand their understanding of each other. Within this exchange, religion offers reservoirs of cultural memory, compendia of utopian yearnings and interruptions, and distinctive moral visions to track the human misery and despair of our modern world.[15]

For these intellectuals, religion may be able to help overcome what many see as a deficit in the perception of what is going on in the world today and further religion has the capacity to shake up and transform political reflection on the world as it is. In brief, religion offers critical and intellectual resources for a more transformative mode of social, cultural and political reflection.

A further reason advanced for a return of religion to the public forum is that it has resources for addressing the ethical vacuum that is a part of the post-modern world. Many point to a moral deficit at the centre of contemporary economics and politics, especially in the areas of social solidarity and community cohesion. This concern about the moral and political discourse of contemporary life has been raised in an insightful way by Jürgen Habermas, to whom we will return later in this chapter.

It should be emphasised that these supporters of the new visibility of religion are not proposing a return to a pre-modern understanding of the relationship between faith and society. Instead, they seek to address secularity itself and call for a more self-critical and self-reflective approach to modern secularity and its exclusion of religion. If anything, this approach is a recognition that religion, especially Christianity, has contributed to the emergence and legitimacy of secularisation and therefore religion should be a participant in the dialogue about the future of modern, secular society.

In spite of this new visibility of religion, and the compelling reasons lying behind this return of religion, there is another view which suggests that this phenomenon should not be taken too seriously. This approach has been expressed by Ingolf U. Dalferth who, after an extensive review of the return of religion to the public forum, concludes: 'Post-secular states differ from secular states in that they cease to define themselves as neutral *vis à vis* religion ... they do not take a stance towards religion or the non-religion of their citizens.' Instead, 'a post-secular state is indifferent to questions of religion ... and not merely neutral.' In other words, the secular state has a position *vis à vis* religion, one of neutrality, whereas the post-secular stance towards religion is one of sheer indifference. Consequently, there is no comfort to be gained for religions in the shift from a secular society to a post-secular society. If anything, the shift is more negative than positive. A prominent exception to this negative assessment of the shift to a post-secular society is the later work of Jürgen Habermas and his dialogues with the then Cardinal Joseph Ratzinger in 2004 and with philosophers from the Jesuit School for Philosophy in Munich in 2007, which we will look at later in this chapter. Dalferth concludes his analysis by pointing out that the challenge facing Christianity, and by implication the religions, is how to address 'the widespread apatheism and indifference towards faith and God that characterise many strands of contemporary society.'[16]

It is this challenge and this particular expression of the challenge that prompts the contemporary need for dialogue among the religions. This dialogue between the religions has the potential to renew the identities of individual religions and at the same time enrich those identities in ways that will enable religions to enter into a more constructive dialogue with the secular world, a dialogue that ultimately could benefit both religion and the world. If this dialogue with the other religions is to bear fruit, and if the further dialogue between religion and the world is to succeed in a manner that is mutually beneficial, then Christianity needs to work out a new theology of inter-religious dialogue. It is this three-fold challenge facing Christianity, namely dialogue with other religions, dialogue between religion and the world, and the need for a theology of other religions, that has prompted this monograph.

3. THEOLOGY CAUGHT BETWEEN MODERNITY AND POST-MODERNITY

Part of the background to this return of religion in the market-place is the ongoing debate about the relationship between modernity and post-modernity. The new visibility of religion is more a cultural phenomenon than a strictly theological one. Lying in the background to this interest in religion is the academic discussion about the philosophical and theological merits of modernity and post-modernity. How does the return of religion fare within the culture of modernity? Is post-modernity a better place for religion? Or, is there some middle position between modernity and post-modernity? This is a debate that the religions ignore at their peril. Some religions exist as if modernity had not taken place, other religions take a hostile view towards modernity, and this helps in understanding the rise of fundamentalisms in the early twenty-first century.

Without rehearsing the history of the Enlightenment which gave rise to the modern era, reference must be made to two highly influential figures who have left an indelible mark on modern culture and theology. The first is René Descartes (1596–1650) who, through a process of methodic doubt, sought to come up with a scientific foundation for clear and distinct ideas. This foundation he found in his famous soundbite, 'I think, therefore I am/*cogito ergo sum*'. This starting point, established by Descartes, issued in the turn to the subject which is one of the defining features of modernity.

After Descartes came Immanuel Kant (1724-1804) who asked: 'What is the Enlightenment?' His answer was, *sapere aude*, which roughly translated means, have the courage to use your own reason without recourse to tradition, authority or religion. With this response of Kant, Enlightenment rationalism emerged over time. In his application of reason alone to life, Kant made a distinction between what he called 'the phenomena' of the external world, which can be known by reason, and 'the noumenon', the hidden and invisible world behind the phenomena, which cannot be known by reason. This distinction has challenged theology and has evoked many different theological responses.

Descartes' *'cogito'* gave rise to the development of the substantial, self-sufficient, sovereign subject of modernity. Kant's *'sapere aude'* produced an emphasis on the autonomy of reason that issued in a cold, clinical and detached rationalism. These two streams of philosophy are largely responsible for the philosophical construction of the modern world with its focus on subjective individualism and scientific, disengaged rationalism. The culture of modernity became the context in which theology sought to find its voice in the nineteenth and twentieth century.

a. Collapse of the Classical Synthesis of God, the Cosmos and the Self

By far the most serious outcome of the influence of modernity upon theology has been what David Tracy describes as 'the break-up of the ancient and medieval synthesis of God, the cosmos and the self'.[17]

As moderns, we privatised religion and God; we stripped the cosmos of divine presence and disenchanted it; we individualised the human self and placed it at the centre of the earth. The consequences for theology have been far-reaching: the modern world has given us a nature-less view of God and a God-less view of nature; the universe has been mechanised and thereby stripped of all traces of transcendence; nature has now been made to serve the needs of humanity.

One of the many troubling expressions of this collapse of the relationship between God, the cosmos and the human is the extraordinary degree of human estrangement, loneliness and isolation that now exists between the self and the earth, and by far the most vivid expression of this is to be found in the ecological crisis of the late twentieth and early twenty-first century. A further expression of this collapse can be seen in the rise of radical secularism that permeates the whole of life, so that if there is a God, that God is no longer present to or mediated by the universe, history or human experience. A further expression of this collapse is the separation that persists within much modern theology between nature and grace, in spite of the gallant efforts made by *la nouvelle theologie* to reunite the natural and the supernatural.

For the moment, however, we will concentrate on what happened to our understanding of God within this culture of modernity. Many today would argue that Enlightenment rationality, namely *logos* understood as scientific reason, has taken over theology at the expense of *Theos*, the mystery of God. There has been too much *Logos* and too little *Theos*. The *logos* in question, the form of rationality operating within modernity, was a rationalism devoid of affectivity, shorn of memory, disengaged from its object, and committed to the totalism of a single paradigm. Human affectivity was put aside in the name of objectivity because it could not be controlled or measured. Memory did not count because tradition and history were suspect and the particular was subordinated to the dominance of universal reason. In its pursuit of rationalism, modernity sought a single paradigm, a scientific and universal paradigm, to which all other disciplines, including theology, had to conform. The role and function of God within this situation was to provide an absolute point of reference and an ultimate foundation for the universal claims of reason. Thereafter the mystery of God was a purely private and personal matter.

Within this picture of modernity, admittedly over-simplified here, two other very significant things were happening in relation to theology, which today are clearer in retrospect than they were in the historical unfolding of modernity. Philosophy, more especially a particular form of rationalism, was using God as a means to ground its own brand of intelligibility. Theology, in turn, if it was to have any credibility, had to conform to the canons of empirical scientific rationality to the neglect of the historical revelation of God in the Bible. Philosophy, which in previous times had been described as the handmaid of theology was increasingly subjected to the norms of the scientific method and was now becoming the dismantler of theology.

A further development within modernity was that God, the mystery of God, was reduced to the level of an item of information, a rational explanation to ground the intelligibility of the world of modern philosophy and science. In consequence, the reality of God was objectified into the category of a being among other beings. The end result of these unfolding influences was the development of what is now called 'onto-theology' which we must review.

b. The Rise of Onto-Theology

The meaning of this strange-sounding term, 'onto-theology', is about 'the conflation of the philosophical notion of being and the self-revelation of God of the Bible'.[18] The God of the philosophers takes over the God of Revelation in a way that identifies God with being, the eternal, immutable, impassable being of philosophy. This God, this absolute being of human reason, is invoked in 'the service of the human project of mastering the whole of reality'.[19] The God of 'onto-theology' is ultimately a being, a super-being, existing alongside other beings and therefore runs the risk of promoting a form of idolatry. A number of difficulties arise with this philosophical God of 'onto-theology'.

The first and most serious issue is the separation between the God of philosophy and the God of Revelation, a separation forced upon modernity by Enlightenment's desire to be rid of tradition and authority.

A second difficulty is that 'onto-theology' reduces God to the level of one more item and one more explanation among many other items and explanations in the world. The effect of this reduction is the inevitable loss of interest in the mystery of God which helps us to understand the stinging observation often made in the post-modern world that 'God is missing but not missed'(J.Vives).

A third difficulty with 'onto-theology' is that it implies that the highest form of knowledge is theoretical reason, a rationality that seeks to control by mastering reality, especially nature. In contrast, it must be countered that Christianity is not simply about knowing the truth, but primarily about doing the truth in love, a lesson we have begun to learn from liberation theology and a careful re-reading of the New Testament. In other words, Christianity is a practical way of being in the world and its credibility is to be judged not only by an appeal to rational norms, but also by its capacity to engender a liberating praxis in the world that serves the well-being of the individual and society.

A fourth difficulty with 'onto-theology' concerns the character of the God it delivers. According to Heidegger, it is a God before whom the individual 'can neither pray nor sacrifice ... can neither fall to his knees in awe nor can he play music and dance.'[20] In spite of this criticism, Heidegger's own attempt to find 'the truly divine God' through the help of the poets failed because it remained too much in the grip of being and did not take sufficient account of the God of the Bible.

A fifth difficulty with 'onto-theology' is that the language used to describe God is one of conceptual clarity and scientific objectivism, a language that forgets about the limits attaching to theological language. In effect, a univocal language replaces the analogical imagination of classical theology and ignores the Jewish prohibition against images of Yahweh. A separation of the God of philosophy from the God of Abraham, of Sarah and of Jesus, took place during the period of modernity with unhappy consequences for theology: a theism untouched by Christology, a deism unaware of the agency of the Spirit in the world and in history, and a fideism blind to the mediations of the divine. Thus the transcendence of God was domesticated by philosophy and the immanence of God controlled by reason alone.

In response to modernity, Christian theology must make clear that the God of the prophets in Judaism is not simply the God of the philosophers, that the God of Jesus in Christianity is not simply the

God of detached reason, and that the God of the Christian tradition is not simply the God of metaphysics but the one God revealed as a Trinity of persons in the life of Jesus.

Of course it would be wrong, indeed it would be a serious misrepresentation, to suggest that Christian theology adopted *in toto* this vision of modernity. To the contrary, we know that much of Catholic theology, right up to Vatican II, shunned modernity and rejected most of its suppositions. Nevertheless, the spirit of modernity did affect and influence the shape of fundamental theology. Consider, for example, the importance given to 'the proofs' for the existence of God, the focus on 'natural theology', and the emphasis placed on the preambles of faith within fundamental theology. In spite of attempts to ignore the Enlightenment, the spirit of modernity did infiltrate, negatively speaking, the method and content of fundamental theology.

c. Charles Taylor's Take on the Gradual Shift from Faith to Unbelief

Paralleling David Tracy's diagnosis of what happened in modern theology is the philosophical analysis of Charles Taylor. In 2007, Taylor published *A Secular Age*, a *magnus opus* which has generated international debate at conferences, in journals and books, and on the internet. Taylor tells the story of secularisation by answering the question: How is it that in the year 1500 most people believed in God and that in the year 2000 most people find it difficult to believe in God? In his answer, Taylor maps out the changing conditions and circumstances surrounding the rise of widespread unbelief. He is quick to reject early on in the narrative what he calls 'subtraction theories of secularisation', that is the suggestion that secularism is the result of public spaces being emptied of God which he calls secularism number i, or the result of the falling-off of religious belief and practice, which he names secularism number ii. Instead the story of secularism and its impact on religion is far more subtle and complicated. The problem with subtraction theories is that they short-change secularism and religion; they also neglect the possibility of a critical engagement between secularism and religion; and they also ignore the ongoing interaction between faith and unbelief.

Instead, secularism is a process in which a number of significant shifts have taken place over the centuries: from an enchanted universe to a disenchanted world; from an understanding of time as *kairos* to *chronos*; from theism to providential deism; from deism to an impersonal order; from transcendence to an immanent frame; from a hierarchical social order to a levelled self-sufficient society; from a moral order with transcendent roots to an order of exclusive humanism.

Anthropology plays a key role in the unfolding of Taylor's narrative. As the author of a major volume on anthropology entitled *Sources of the Self* (1989),[21] Taylor appreciates better than most the centrality of anthropology to the modern project. In *A Secular Age*, Taylor traces what he calls the move from a pre-modern 'porous self' to a modern 'buffered self' as one of the major sources of unbelief. A 'porous self' is one that is open to outside influences, whereas the 'buffered self' is a bounded, autonomous self, master of meaning and creator of purpose. Within this 'modern' anthropology, there is a strong emphasis on the primacy and priority of the individual. The individual comes first, and only then can we talk about the individual's freedom to belong or not belong to community.[22]

Towards the end of *A Secular Age*, he returns to the theme of anthropology, noting that it was the Catholic view of the human as 'part angel and part beast' that led to Walker Percy's conversion, a perspective that stands out in contrast to the scientific view, which sees the human as a 'mere organism in an environment'.[23] And yet, he notes that 'our modern culture is restless at the barriers of the human sphere':[24] a restlessness expressed through the search for meaning, the *ennui* of so much empty time, the lack of human contact with nature, and the dread of death.

A second theme is the debate about the difference between Europe and America in the context of secularism. Is Europe the exception to Taylor's phenomenology of the rise of secularism and its promotion of an exclusive humanism? Most Americans would describe themselves as religious humanists in contrast to the secular humanists of Europe. Taylor explains this difference between Americans and Europeans by noting that America historically did not have to overcome established ecclesiastical institutions in the way that Europe had. The US is founded on the principle of non-establishment.

A third theme running through Taylor is the role imagination plays in shaping the conditions of belief and unbelief. He had previously written an important book on *Modern Social Imaginaries*.[25] In that text, he describes the social imaginary as 'something much broader and deeper than the intellectual schemes people may entertain when they think about social reality in a disengaged mode.' Instead, the social imaginary is about 'the ways people imagine their social existence, how they fit together with others, how things go on between them and their fellows.'[26] The social imaginary is a set of background understandings operative and influential in the way society functions. Taylor singles out three particular areas of the social imaginary that are central to the emergence of secularity, namely the modern economy, the public square, and the sovereignty of the people. What is new and distinctive about these three expressions of the modern social imaginary is the absence of reference to transcendence, a strong sense of autonomy and self-sufficiency, the living out of life within clock-time (*chronos*), and the location of human flourishing or fullness of life exclusively within an immanent frame of reference. The modern social imaginary should not be confused with 'a social theory' about society coming to us from social science. Such social theory is the provenance of the academy and the preserve of elites – and as such can and does change. In contrast, the social imaginary, the way people see their social reality, is the outcome of subtle changes over a period of time which affect the self-understanding of society.

A fourth theme running through Taylor's narrative of the secular age is what he calls the 'great dis-embedding'[27] that took place in modernity. In broad terms, early religions understood themselves as embedded in society and the cosmos, and human well-being was embedded in a relationship of dependency on divinity. This dis-embedding of the modern social imaginary entails the removal of economic, social and public spheres of life from any relationship with transcendence, the separation of the individual from community, and the removal of the immanent frame of exclusive humanism from any external transcendent point of reference because 'flourishing involves no relationship to anything higher'.[28] Because this shift to a secular immanent frame has been inspired by Christian sources, Taylor remains hopeful that this secular frame may be not just the condition of unbelief, but also the condition of a new kind of faith and belief in the twenty-first century.

In summarising what Tracy and Taylor have to say about modernity, it would be wrong and inaccurate to imply that they do not see anything of value within modernity. Quite the opposite, both appreciate the constructive contribution modernity has made to the modern understanding and interpretation of life. Both wish to safeguard the gains of modernity which include the elimination of superstition from religion, the vindication of human rights for all, respect for religious freedom, promoting the values of democracy and the primacy of justice for all, the principle of inclusivity, the importance of human and social solidarity, and the value of secularisation as distinct from secularism. It is against this outline of negative and positive aspects of modernity that we must now examine the rise of post-modernity.

4. A PEEP AT POST-MODERNITY

In mentioning post-modernity, some will react, suggesting it is a passing fashion, one more sideshow, distracting theology from the task of faith seeking understanding. This reaction ignores the cultural tension that exists in the struggle between modernity and post-modernity, and more importantly, the possibility that there are important elements of truth in the criticisms of modernity by post-modernity. There is little agreement about the transition from modernity to post-modernity. Some see the end of modernity and the beginning of post-modernity[29] as something that occurred at the end of World War II, in such events as the Holocaust, Hiroshima, and the Cold War. Others suggest it was in the 1960s that the tide began to turn to post-modernity and that a change of consciousness began to take place through such figures as John F. Kennedy, Martin Luther King and phenomena like Beatle mania, pop culture and the sexual revolution. Post-modernity is often described as a critique of the 'illusions of modernity'.[30]

a. The Mood of Post-Modernity

Part of the post-modern mood can be summed up in the words of Jean-François Lyotard: 'Simplifying to the extreme, I define post-modern as incredulity towards metanarratives'.[31] Lyotard goes on to prompt: 'Activate difference, let us acknowledge incommensurability, advance multiplicity and promote dissensus'.[32] As a reaction to modernity, post-modernity is driven by a desire for the radical deconstruction of all that is informed by the Enlightenment: the deconstruction of the self, history, metanarratives, universal reason, and God. The post-modern deconstruction of the human subject of modernity is particularly fierce, and is summed up rather graphically in the words of Michel Foucault who holds that: 'Man is an invention of recent date' and will be 'erased like a face drawn in the sand at the edge of the sea.'[33] For some post-moderns the self is merely a rhetorical flourish, a linguistic and cultural device to facilitate the interaction of differences. For others, the self is at best a site in and around which speech, transactions of power, and mechanisms of desire play themselves out,[34] a site which in effect has no unified ground or enduring field of identity. Richard Rorty sums up the position of many post-moderns when he says of the self: 'There is nothing deep down inside except what we have put there ourselves.'[35]

Once the human subject is dissolved, then it follows that everything else disintegrates: history is dismantled into disconnected bits, culture is broken down into scattered fragments, metanarratives are reduced to unrelated events, and reality is emptied of reference. This bleak account of post-modernity prompts the question: is there anything of value within the post-modern condition, anything worth salvaging, anything that we can learn? So far, we have given only a rather negative account of post-modernity. There are also some positive aspects of post-modernity that must now be noted.

b. Some Positive Aspects of Post-Modernity

At the centre of post-modern thinking, there is a strong awareness of 'otherness', the other that was all too frequently forgotten, marginalised, or repressed by the master narratives of western modernity. The repressed others of the modern narrative include, according to Tracy, 'the hysterics, the mad, mystics, dissenters, avant-garde artists, subjugated communities of resistance in the past and the present who are allowed to speak on their own terms.'[36]

A second positive feature of post-modernity attracting attention is the emphasis placed on what we do not know. In particular, post-modernity recovers the tradition of negative theology, especially the apophatic and mystical traditions of classical Christianity. In this way, post-modernity retrieves, first of all, the radical incomprehensibility of God but also the hiddenness of God in the suffering, weakness and struggle of others. Within this context, post-modernity offers a radical critique of modern forms of idolatry and ideology.

A third positive feature about post-modernity is its programme of deconstruction. Within every process of deconstruction there is an impulse for reconstruction. Deconstruction is driven by a passion for something better, a restlessness with the status quo, a concern about the future. Of course, not all post-modernists would concede this. Yet, Derrida, one of the most radical deconstructionists of the post-modern movement, openly admits there is something implicit in deconstruction: 'What remains irreducible to any deconstruction, what remains as undeconstructable as the possibility itself of deconstruction is, perhaps, a certain experience of the emancipatory promised.'[37] Part of that emancipatory promise, that messianic expectation, is the possibility of the impossible, the advent of what is unforeseeable and unrepresentable. There is a trace of hope implicit in the radical critique of modernity by post-modernity.

A fourth positive feature about post-modernity is that it has enabled the academy to realise that there is no truly neutral approach to knowledge. All knowledge is contextual, being influenced by location, culture and tradition. Post-modernity has helped to overcome the 'prejudice against prejudice' (Gadamer) and to realise that knowledge is tradition-specific and tradition-based, and that the personal enters into all knowledge and self-understanding. In this way, post-modernity has called into question the so-called objectivity of Enlightenment rationality as normative. In a paradoxical and ironic way, post-modernity points to the legitimacy of an intimate relationship between knowing and believing, recognises that trust is an inescapable dimension of all knowing, and encourages pluralism and dialogue.

c. The Possibility of a New, Second Modernity

What is important about this debate concerning modernity and post-modernity is that it highlights how theology is caught in between the crossfire of two opposing philosophical outlooks. Within this new situation, theology often seeks some kind of safe space in between the ambiguities of modernity and post-modernity. Such a space simply does not exist. The challenge for theology is not a return to a so-called safe haven of pre-modern thought, nor is it the blind embrace of post-modernity. Instead theology must engage more creatively and critically with modernity in the light of the critique coming from post-modernity. Some talk about the possibility of theology engaging with a 'second modernity' or 'a new modernity' or 'a Catholic modernity' that brings about a new synthesis of insights coming from what is best in both modernity and post-modernity.[38] This is part of the radically new context in which theology exists today, and is part of the challenge facing all religions in the twenty-first century. It is, in brief, the new context in which we must construct a Christian theology of inter-religious dialogue.

It was precisely this possibility of a new modernity that Vatican II opened up for Catholic theology. The Council began not only to embrace modernity, but it also took a critical stance towards certain aspects of modernity at the same time. It would be inaccurate to imply that Vatican II resolved this challenge for theology, but it did point theology in a new direction of confronting modernity, both positively and critically. Vatican II did talk about the possibility of the Church contributing to the world, and the world contributing to the Church,[39] and it also talked about the possibility of opening up a new dialogue between Church and the world, faith and culture, Catholics and other churches, Christianity and other religions, in a way that could effect a process of mutual understanding.[40]

This construction of a second modernity will seek to combine elements of continuity and change within theology's self-understanding of other religions. Continuity is essential to understanding, but equally there must be some recognition within a new modernity that there is an element of discontinuity, what Lieven Boeve consistently refers to as 'interruption', and this element of the new is necessary for theology to recognise, respect and learn from and welcome the other into our midst as guest. It is this latter perspective that must shape any theology of inter-religious dialogue among the religions.[41]

In spite of the incredulity of post-modernity towards metanarratives, it must be pointed out that the core of Christianity is structured by a particular narrative which embraces an underlying unity between creation, redemption and consummation; it is this unified story that grounds Christian faith, praxis, worship and dialogue with other religions. The Christian story is more than a construction that can be dismantled at will; it is a personal, existential reality rooted in the ongoing agency of the Spirit of God in creation, in the history of Israel, in Jesus as the Christ, and in the ecclesial community of his disciples and the successors of the Apostles. This does not mean that Christian faith can take for granted the credibility and coherence of this story. Instead Christian faith must continually struggle to articulate the historical particularity and cogency of this narrative in a way that is faithful to the Bible, tradition and the ongoing action of the Spirit of God within the Christian community.

What is important about the debate between modernity and post-modernity is that it highlights the presence of a vacuum, or at least a certain 'in-betweenness', existing between the deep ambiguities of both modernity and post-modernity. This is the primary context in which a new theology of inter-religious dialogue must be formulated in the twenty-first century. This task facing theology, therefore, is one that requires not a return to pre-modern forms of faith, or a naïve embrace of either modernity or post-modernity; instead, it necessitates a rescuing of modernity in the light of some of the critiques coming from post-modernity. In brief, there is no escaping the crucible of modernity within a theology of inter-religious dialogue.

5. KNOWLEDGE, REASON AND FAITH

To conclude this opening chapter, it is necessary to have some sense of the nature of knowledge, the activities of reason, and the praxis of faith that is peculiar to theology and religions. This is necessary in the light of the precarious existence of theology, caught between modernity and post-modernity, and in the light of the suggestion that it may be possible, indeed necessary, for theology to engage with a new, second modernity.

The Enlightenment paradigm of knowledge has had the effect of sidelining religion within public life as already noted. The kind of knowledge that theology offered became suspect in the eyes of modernity, and therefore regarded as of little public consequence in the affairs of modern life. The modern, scientific paradigm of knowledge emphasises the importance of detachment, objectivity and attention to empirical evidence, whereas theology appeared to be focused on the purely personal, the subjective, and the transcendent aspects of life, a characterisation that hardly does justice to theology which must also attend to the data of human experience, history, revelation, texts and rites.

a. There Is More than One Way of Knowing

There can be no doubting the extraordinary advances in knowledge that modern science has brought about since the Enlightenment, especially in the natural sciences, medicine and the cosmologies. These outstanding successes prompted modernity to hold up the scientific method as the norm of all knowing. In response to this claim of modernity, theology argued there is another kind of knowing, an equally valid form of knowledge, based on the personal participation, engagement and involvement of the individual in the subject matter under review that applies to the Arts, Humanities and Religion. Further, theology questions this division of knowledge into such watertight compartments pointing out that the dividing line between the objective and the subjective, between the detached and engaged, between the neutral and participative knowing, is far from clear. In addition, theology suggests that all knowing involves a critically important moment of interpretation and that in truth there is no such thing as detached knowing, nor is there such a thing as simply attending to the facts without some value-laden process of selection and interpretation of the facts. The science of interpretation, known as Hermeneutics, was developed into a fine art by Hans-Georg Gadamer and others in the twentieth century. Hermeneutics highlights that we cannot step outside history, location and culture in the process of interpreting the data, texts, history and religion. The time has come to overcome 'the prejudice against prejudice' within modernity, whether in dealing with the physical sciences or the human sciences, including philosophy and theology.[42] We cannot jump out of history, tradition and location when dealing with science or the religions. We are all shaped and influenced by the complex circumstances of existence, education, history and background. This does not mean we cannot go beyond these circumstances and transform our 'prejudices'; we can and that is precisely the role of dialogue and the value of inter-personal conversation, especially in the area of inter-faith engagement, as will be shown in the following chapters.

An example of a religious thinker who has defended the value of participative knowing is William James (1842–1910), author of the still important work, *The Varieties of Religious Experience,* originally published in 1902.[43] William James is taken as an example because of the critical rehabilitation of James by Charles Taylor in '*Varieties of Religion Today: William James re-visited*', a series of lectures given in 2000 to mark the centenary of the birth of Gadamer and later published in 2002 to commemorate the hundredth anniversary of the publication of James' book on religious experience.

William James makes the case for the validity of other forms of knowledge besides that of modern science. He engages with his contemporary William B. Clifford (d. 1879) who held: 'It is wrong always, and everywhere, and for anyone, to believe anything upon insufficient evidence.'[44] Clifford wants this principle to be applied, not only to science, but also to religion and morality. For William James, this is an example of the 'agnostic vetoes upon faith' which demand that one should not believe anything without compelling evidence. In response to these vetoes against religion from W. B. Clifford, James suggests that there are some domains of life in which truths will remain hidden unless we go at least half-way towards them. More explicitly, James points out that there are 'cases where a fact cannot come at all, unless a preliminary faith exists in its coming.'[45] According to Charles Taylor, William James is building on an Augustinian insight that in some domains of life, love and self-opening enable us to understand what we would never grasp otherwise.[46]

In other words, William James was pointing out over one hundred years ago that it is only in the act of personal participation and self-surrender to a particular experience or event or text that its full meaning and light and truth actually emerges. This experience of discovering new knowledge through personal engagement is most evident in the areas of human relationships which provide an analogy for understanding what happens in religious knowing. To dismiss these areas of life to the margins would be to relegate the drama of existence as expressed in the arts, the humanities and religion to the sidelines of life. Instead, we are dealing here with a form of knowing that must be recognised as having its own validity alongside the knowing that belongs to the scientific method of enlightenment. It is this former mode of knowing, that is participative knowing, that characterises religious and theological knowledge. It would be wrong to polarise or separate these two modes of knowing: instead they should be seen as complementary; indeed it is debatable that one can happen without the other.

This does not mean there is no such thing as detached knowing. Clearly disengaged reasoning takes place in formal logic and mathematical reasoning. In a nearly similar manner, some level of detached knowing appears to takes place in the scientific method of observation, verification and explanation. However, in the case of the scientific method, the matter is not as clear-cut as some suggest. In the process of observation, verification and explanation, certain conceptual assumptions or imaginative frameworks are at work as the philosophy of science has highlighted. These assumptions or frameworks drive the work of science and can hardly be described as detached or disengaged. Further, these assumptions or frameworks change from time to time through paradigm shifts. The difference between scientific knowing and religious knowing is not as great as some would have us believe.[47]

b. Questioning the Self-Sufficiency of Secular Reason: Expanding Horizons

Because these two types of knowing have become separated within modernity, secular reasoning has assumed a sufficiency and independence that has come in for criticism in recent times. This does not mean that anyone wants to deny the intrinsic validity of secular reasoning and its extraordinary success over the centuries. It does mean recognising, however, that the so-called detached pursuits of secular reason are premised on a number of assumptions that cannot be ignored, such as the existence of order, meaning and intelligibility within the natural world. Secular reason should acknowledge these assumptions and recognise that its activities are not nearly as neutral or detached as it would like to think. It is the existence of these assumptions, often unacknowledged, that drives secular and scientific reasoning. This separation of the objective and participative knowing, so characteristic of modernity, has resulted in a narrowing of secular reason that is open to question, not only from theology, but also from within the guild of secular philosophy and especially the philosophy of science.

A striking description of this narrowing of secular reason is given by the French philosopher, Jean-Luc Marion. Marion describes the modern restriction of reason as the 'most profound crisis of our era' and then goes on to talk about 'the dilation, evanescence, perhaps even the disappearance of a rationality that is able to clarify questions that go beyond the mere management and production of objects.' The problem with this restricted rationality is that it has very little to 'say about the human condition: about what we are, what we can know, what we must do, and what we are allowed to hope for.' According to Marion, we are lost in a 'dry desert of rationalism'.[48] A similar concern with this narrowing of secular reason is found in Charles Taylor. For Taylor: 'calculating reason cuts us off from sympathetic union with others', separating secular reason from its 'own desiring nature, from community which thus threatens to disintegrate, and from the great current of life in nature.'[49]

This concern about the role of reason, about the narrowing of secular reason, has been a theme in the work of Jürgen Habermas, and has surfaced in his dialogues with others, especially his dialogue with the then Cardinal Josef Ratzinger in 2004 and the Faculty from the Jesuit School of Philosophy in Munich in 2007. Habermas has described modernity as 'an unfinished project' and therefore has sought to defend modern rationality against attacks from post-modernity.

The young, earlier Habermas held that the task of social integration, once exercised by religion, had been transferred to secular reason, especially in the light of mounting secularisation: 'the authority of the Holy is gradually displaced by the authority of an achieved consensus' through secular reasoning or what Habermas prefers to call 'rational communication.'[50]

Some years later, Habermas, still reserved about the role of religion, nonetheless calls on religions to contribute to our understanding of the human condition: 'Among modern societies, only those that are able to introduce into the secular domain the essential elements of their religious traditions which point beyond the merely human realm will also be able to rescue the substance of the human.'[51] Implicit here is a recognition by Habermas that secular reason needs the insight of the religions to understand better the meaning and possible rescue of the human condition, a task not only for modern secular society, but also for all religions and especially for the dialogue between religions.

The later Habermas, in his dialogue with representatives of the Jesuit School for Philosophy in Munich in 2007, calls for a new dialogue between modernity and the major world religions.[52] For this dialogue to succeed, Habermas puts down a few markers or conditions. We must speak 'with' one another and not merely 'about' one another. For this engagement to succeed, two presuppositions must be fulfilled. On the one hand, 'the religious side must accept the authority of "natural" reason as the fallible results of the institutionalised sciences and the basic principles of universalistic egalitarianism in law and morality.' On the other hand, 'secular reason may not set itself up as the judge concerning the truths of faith, even though in the end it can accept as reasonable only what it can translate into its own, in principle universally accessible, discourses.'[53] Here Habermas is challenging religion to translate its theological insights into a discourse that is accessible and meaningful to all in the public square. In his dialogue (2004) with Cardinal Joseph Ratzinger, he offers as an example of what he has in mind: 'the translation of the concept of "man made in the image of God" into that of the identical dignity of all men that deserves unconditional respect.'[54]

Theologians are not happy with the demand for translation by Habermas. For example, Maureen Junker-Kenny points out that such a demand disconnects religion from its originating context which is the gift of faith inspired by God. Further, she argues that 'reason remains below its potential', especially when the highest hope of humanity is confined to reason alone.[55] Others like Judith Butler point out that when a religious claim is translated into secular reason, the religious part gets left behind and the translation becomes an extraction of the rational element, thereby reducing the religious element to so much dross.[56]

Habermas wants a new dialogue between faith and knowledge to take place in order to overcome some of the inadequacies of modern reason.[57] The motive promoting this dialogue between secular reason and the religions 'is to mobilise modern reason against the defeatism lurking within' itself. For Habermas, something is missing within modern reason and he wants to spell out what this missing dimension might be. As an example, he points to the failure of practical reason 'when it no longer has sufficient strength to awaken, and to keep awake, in the minds of secular subjects, an awareness of the violations of solidarity throughout the world' and it is this he calls an awareness of what is missing that cries out to heaven.[58]

The need for this new dialogue between secular reason and religious convictions becomes all the more important in light of the conflicts between the religions and political authorities around the globe. These conflicts are often sparked by misunderstandings surrounding the neutrality of the state towards religions or the presence of a certain type of fundamentalism within these religions. A key moment within this dialogue is the challenge, according to Habermas, for the religions to translate their core convictions 'into a publicly accessible language'.[59] An equally central moment within this dialogue is the challenge for secular authorities not to treat religions as simply irrational.

In summarising this openness of Habermas to an expansion of secular reason, and in noting his call for a new dialogue between reason and the religions, it would be naïve to think that Habermas is a new apostle intent on promoting the interests of religion or Christianity as such. Instead, Habermas is seeking to widen the range of secular reason and then only in terms of secular reason as such. Habermas is content to use religion in this way in the service of the needs of secular reason, especially in the area of discourse ethics and the challenge this faces in terms of providing motivation for global solidarity and the holding together of community.

Adopting a more critical stance towards Habermas, Stanley Fish points out that the religions are brought in to prevent or overcome social disruptions, and once 'they have performed this service, they go back in their box and don't trouble us with uncomfortable cosmic demands.'[60] In spite of such comments by Fish and others, it must be acknowledged that these dialogues of Habermas, on the nature of reason and the possibility of a new dialogue between reason and the religions, pose a new intellectual challenge for all religions. These conversations of Habermas also offer draft guidelines on how dialogue between reason and the religions might be conducted. The real value of these dialogues by Habermas is the acknowledgement by a secularist of the limits of secular reason and the need for a new dialogue between an enlightened self-understanding of modernity and the theological self-understanding of religions. Furthermore, Habermas's dialogues also highlight the necessity for religions to take more seriously the findings of secular reason, and that raises questions about what kind of relationship can and should exist between faith and reason, which will now be briefly addressed.

c. The Relationship between Faith and Reason

One of the enduring themes throughout the history of Christianity has been the close relationship that exists between faith and reason, and the insistence that this relationship be respected. This emphasis on faith *and* reason can also be found in Greek philosophy. For example, Aristotle suggests that:

Whoever wishes to understand must believe.[61]

Similarly, Isaiah of the Hebrew Scriptures points out:

If you do not stand firm in the faith, you shall not stand at all.[62]

This interplay between faith and reason is given classical expression in Augustine who sums up their relationship in this way:

Believe, so that you may understand (*Crede ut intelligas*)

and

Understand, so that you may believe (*Intellige ut credas*).[63]

For well over a thousand years, one of the principal philosophical questions was working out the proper relationship between faith and reason. An emphasis on this relationship between faith and reason can be found explicitly in the Patristic period, in Augustine and in Aquinas. It is also a permanent theme in Catholic theology and is addressed in the documents of Vatican I, Vatican II, in the 1998 encyclical of John Paul II on Faith and Reason (*Fides et Ratio*), and in the address of Benedict XVI at Regensburg on 'Faith, Reason and the University', 12 September 2006. It was only with the advent of the Enlightenment and the development of a specifically modern version of reason that faith and reason became separated.

The basis of the classical relationship between faith and reason can be found in the congruence that exists between biblical revelation and Hellenistic philosophy. This rapport between philosophy and faith is expressed in the revelation of God in Judaism in the 'I am' epiphany of Exodus[64] and the Johannine theology of the Word (*Logos*) that for Christians enlightens all and is made flesh in Jesus.[65] These pivotal revelations are communicated respectively in the categories of 'existence' and reason/*logos* that have deep resonances in the history of Hellenistic philosophy.

The dynamic of the relationship between faith and reason has been and continues to be a matter of philosophical and theological debate. One important aspect of this debate is how one translates the verb *credo* which, more often than not, is rendered simply as 'I believe'. However, the problem with this English translation is the potential confusion that exists between the personal act of faith and the content of that act as expressed in propositions. A better translation of *credo* would be one which recognises that *credo* is a compound of two words, *cor, cordis* (heart) and *do* which primarily means to put or place, or possibly to give. Thus *credo* is about placing one's heart in the object of faith, namely God, or making a personal commitment rather than subscribing to a series of statements even though statements do spell out that to which one is making a commitment or placing one's trust in. Faith is primarily a personal act of trust and commitment addressed to the Mystery of God as at least not less than personal.[66]

The actual relationship between faith and reason is described as dynamic, reciprocal, convergent and mutually illuminating. The particular theme of mutual understanding between faith and reason, between the Church and the world, between faith and culture, between Christianity and other religions is found in the documents of Vatican II. This model of mutual understanding as a key for interpreting Vatican II is advanced persuasively by John Dadosky[67] who shows among other things how mutual understanding enables a process of mutual self-mediating identities and relations between the churches and in reference to other religions. It is worth noting that this particular way of looking at faith and reason, namely the model of mutual understanding, resonates with some of the proposals put forward by Jürgen Habermas for conducting dialogue between enlightened reason and the religions as outlined above.

In this dialogue between faith and reason, there can be benefits for both sides. The dialectic between faith and reason is a two-way process and when conducted in an open and honest manner can effect a mutually self-correcting relationship. On the one hand, reason protects faith from fideism, idolatry, superstition and ideology. At the same time reason needs faith if it is to go beyond a blind rationalism and political totalitarianism. On the other hand, faith, as already seen, can expand the horizons of reason by insisting there is more than reason alone can deliver. Equally, faith can offer an important critique of various forms of rationalism and the politics of secular self-sufficiency. Likewise, faith, Christian faith, will insist that our grasp of truth is incomplete and unfinished, and that, therefore, there is an eschatological dimension to the truth that reason and faith seek together. It is ultimately the unifying character of truth that keeps faith and reason together.

It is especially important for the religions that this interactive unity between faith and reason be progressed. One way of doing this is to assert, as Newman does, that the act of faith 'is an act of reason, but of what the world would call weak, bad or insufficient reason; and that, because it rests on presumptions more, and on evidence less.'[68] Here Newman is using the idea of reason in an expanded sense in contrast to a purely empirical view of reason restricted to evidence. Further, for Newman the act of reason within faith is more than that which issues in 'paper logic' or 'the smart syllogism'.

What is important here is the statement that the act of faith is an act of reason and that it rests on what he calls 'presuppositions' more than evidence. Newman, some thirty years later in the *Grammar of Assent*, spells out these presuppositions which for him are a part of the rationality of faith without, however, reducing faith to rationality. Among the presuppositions attaching to the act of faith as an act of reason there are at least three moments or phases in the journey of faith. These include the call of conscience, the presence of first principles such as the love of truth, justice and respect for others, and thirdly what he calls antecedent probabilities or instruments of conviction in religious matters.[69] Newman was very clear in his own mind, contrary to the claims of modern rationalism, that there was no such thing as pure reason, no such thing as reason alone, no such thing as thinking without presuppositions because: 'Almost all we do, every day of our lives, is on trust, that is faith' in 'the sense of reliance on the words of others'.[70] In the same sermon he asks: 'After all, what do we know without trusting others?'[71] What this means in effect is that it is impossible to think without presuppositions, and this applies as much to science as it does to theology and in particular to the performance of faith.

NOTES

1. See *Gaudet Mater Ecclesia, GS*, a.62; *UR*, a.6 and a.17, *Mysterium Ecclesiae* (1973)

2. James L. Heft, 'Introduction: Religious Sources for Social Transformation in Judaism, Christianity, and Islam', *Beyond Violence: Religious Sources of Social Transformation in Judaism, Christianity, and Islam*, James L. Heft (ed.), New York: Fordham University Press, 2004, 2

3. Madeleine Albright, *The Mighty and the Almighty: Reflections on America, God, and World Affairs*, New York: HarperCollins, 2005

4. Hans Küng, *Global Responsibility: In Search of a New World Ethic*, New York: Crossroad, 1991, 138

5. Launch of 'Commission on Integration and Cohesion' by Ruth Kelly on 24 August 2006

6. Mona Siddiqui, 'Response to Max Farrar', *Conversations in Religion and Theology*, May 2006, 111

7. *Spiegel Special: International Edition*, No. 9, 2006; 'Special Report on Religion and Public Life', *The Economist*, 3–9 November 2007

8. *The New Visibility of Religion: Studies in Religious and Cultural Hermeneutics*, Graham Ward and Michael Hoelzl (eds), New York: Continuum, 2008

9. *God is Back: How the Global Rise of Faith is Changing the World*, John Micklethwait and Adrian Wooldridge, London: Penguin Books, 2009

10. A helpful review of these different voices is given by Ola Sigurdson, 'Beyond Secularism?: Towards a Post-Secular Political Theology', *Modern Theology*, 26, April 2010, 177–96

11. See discussion of Žižek by Ola Sigurdson, art. cit., 182

12. Terry Eagleton, *Holy Terror*, Oxford: Oxford University Press, 2005, vi

13. Terry Eagleton, *Reason, Faith, and Revolution: Reflections on the God Debate*, New Haven: Yale University Press, 2009, 167

14. C. West, 'Prophetic Religion and the Future of Capitalist Civilisation' in Judith Butler, Jürgen Habermas, Charles Taylor and Cornel West, *The Power of Religion in the Public Sphere*, New York: Columbia University Press, 2011, 92–100 at 93

15. Ibid., 11, 99, 105

16. Ingolf U. Dalferth, 'Post-Secular Society', *Journal of the American Academy of Religion*, 2010, 334–9

17. David Tracy, 'T.S. Eliot as Religious Thinker: *Four Quartets*', *Literary Imagination, Ancient and Modern: Essays in Honor of David Grene*, Todd Breyfogle (ed.), Chicago: The University of Chicago Press, 1999, 269–84 at 278

18. Michael Scanlon, 'Post-Modernism and Theology', *New Theology Review*, February 2000, 70

19. Ibid.

20. Martin Heidegger, *Identity and Difference*, New York: Harper and Rowe, 1969, 70–1

21. Charles Taylor, *Sources of the Self: The Making of the Modern Identity*, Cambridge: CUP, 1989

22. Charles Taylor, *Modern Social Imaginaries*, North Carolina: Duke University Press, 2004, 64–5

23. Taylor, *A Secular Age*, Cambridge: Harvard University Press, 2007, 731

24. Ibid., 726

25. Taylor, *Modern Social Imaginaries*, 2004

26. Ibid., 29

27. Taylor, *A Secular Age*, Chapter 3, and *Modern Social Imaginaries*, Chapter 4

28. Taylor, *A Secular Age*, 151

29. Graham Ward, 'Introduction', *The Postmodern God: A Theological Reader*, Oxford: Blackwell Publishing, 1997

30. David Tracy, 'The Post-Modern Renaming of God as Incomprehensible and Hidden', *Crosscurrents*, Spring/Summer 2000, 240–7 at 240; and Kevin Hart, *Postmodernism: A Beginner's Guide*, Oxford: Oneworld, 2004, 10

31. Jean-François Lyotard, *The Postmodern Condition: A Report on Knowledge*, Minnesota: University of Minneapolis, 1979/1984, xxiv

32. Ibid., xxv, 82

33. Michel Foucault, *The Order of Things: An Archaeology of the Human Sciences*, New York: Random House, 1970, 387

34. Rowan Williams, *Lost Icons: Reflections on Cultural Bereavement*, Edinburgh: T. and T. Clark, 2000, 166

35. Richard Rorty, *Consequences of Pragmatism*, Minnesota: University of Minnesota Press, 1982, xlii

36. David Tracy, art. cit., 241

37. Jacques Derrida, *Spectres of Marx: The State of the Debt, the Work of Mourning, and the New International,* New York, Routledge, 1996, 59. Some twenty years prior to this text, Derrida acknowledged that 'It is totally false to suggest that deconstruction is a suspension of reference.' See Jacques Derrida in *States of Mind: Dialogue with Contemporary Thinkers*, Richard Kearney (ed.), Manchester: Manchester University Press, 1984, 123–4

38. See the Marianist Lecture by Charles Taylor, *A Catholic Modernity* (1996), and the subsequent debate of this lecture in James L. Heft (ed.), *A Catholic Modernity?: Charles Taylor's Marianist Award Lecture*, Oxford: Oxford University Press, 1999. A similar position is found in Robert Schreiter's four-part series of articles in *New Theology Review*, February, May, August and November 2007, and in *On the Way to Life: Contemporary Culture and Theological Development as a Framework for Catholic Education, Catechesis and Formation*, 2005 (published by the Catholic Education Service of the English Bishops and the Heythrop Institute for Religion, Ethics and Public Life), as well as in Dermot A. Lane, *Challenges Facing Religious Education in Contemporary Ireland*, Dublin: Veritas, 2008, 50–4

39. *GS*, a.40-5

40. See John Dadosky, 'Towards a Fundamental Theological Re-Interpretation of Vatican II', *Heythrop Journal*, 2008, 742–63

41. See Lieven Boeve, *God Interrupts History: Theology in a Time of Upheaval*, New York: Continuum, 2007, and more recently L. Boeve, 'Theology in a Post-Modern Context and the Hermeneutical Project of Louis-Marie Chauvet', *Sacraments:*

Revelation of the Humanity of God, Engaging the Fundamental Theology of Louis-Marie Chauvet, Philippe Bordeyne and Bruce T. Morrill (eds), Collegville, MN: Liturgical Press, 2008, 5–23 at 17–20

42. See Hans-Georg Gadamer, *Truth and Method*, New York: Crossroad, 1989
43. William James has been chosen here as an example of the importance of engaged knowledge because he has much to say that is still important for religion, especially his emphasis on religious experience. James has also been selected in spite of the many serious theological deficits within his treatment of religion, such as his disdain for the institutional, ritualistic and sacramental aspects of religious experience
44. This quotation is taken from Charles Taylor's book, *Varieties of Religion Today: William James Re-visited*, Cambridge: Harvard University Press, 2002, 45, which Taylor took from W. K. Clifford, *The Ethics of Belief* (1879)
45. William James, *The Will to Believe*, 1896, 28
46. See Taylor, *Varieties of Religion Today: William James Re-visited*, 47
47. See Taylor, 'Reason, Faith, and Meaning', *Faith and Philosophy*, Vol. 28, No. 1, January 2011, 5–18. For some, the concept of 'detached knowing' is self-contradictory
48. Jean-Luc Marion, *Le Monde*, 11 September 2008, quoted by Stephen England, 'How Catholic is France?', *Commonweal*, 7 November 2008, Vol. 135, No. 19, 12–18 at 15
49. Taylor, *A Secular Age*, 315
50. Quotation taken from Michael Reder and Josef Schmidt, 'Habermas and Religion', *An Awareness of What is Missing: Faith and Reason in a Post-Secular Age*, Jürgen Habermas et al., Cambridge: Polity Press, 2010, 1–14 at 4
51. Ibid., 5
52. Jürgen Habermas, 'An Awareness of What is Missing', in *An Awareness of What is Missing*, 16
53. Ibid., 16
54. Jürgen Habermas, 'Pre-political Foundation of the Democratic Constitutional State', in Jürgen Habermas and Joseph Ratzinger (Pope Benedict XVI), *The Dialectics of Secularization: On Reason and Religion*, San Francisco: Ignatius Press, 2006, 45
55. Maureen Junker-Kenny, 'Post Secular Society and the Neutral State', *Religious Voices in Public Places*, Nigel Biggar and Linda Hogan (eds), New York: OUP, 2009, 80–1. These points are further developed by Junker-Kenny in her book *Habermas and Theology*, Edinburgh: T. and T. Clark, 2011

56. Judith Butler, 'Concluding Discussion', *The Power of Religion in the Public Sphere*, 112

57. Jürgen Habermas, 'An Awareness of What is Missing', 18

58. Ibid., 19

59. Ibid., 22

60. Stanley Fish, 'Does Reason Know What it is Missing?', *Opinionator: Exclusive online Commentary from the* Times (*New York*), 12 April 2010

61. Quotation and translation taken from Raimon Panikkar, *Myth, Faith and Hermeneutics*, New York: Paulist Press, 1979, 220, n. 14. In this footnote, Panikkar discusses this saying of Aristotle and its subsequent influence on people like Augustine, Aquinas and others

62. Is 7:9. See Panikkar, op. cit., 187 for a discussion of the different translations of this text

63. For a discussion of these sayings in Augustine and the possibility of different translations, see Panikkar, op. cit., 188–95 and 220, n. 14

64. Exod 3:13-15

65. Jn 1:1-14

66. For a fuller discussion of this meaning of faith, see Wilfred Cantwell Smith, *Faith and Belief*, New Jersey: Princeton University Press, 1979, chapter 5, and Dermot A. Lane, *The Experience of God: An Invitation to do Theology* (revised edition), Dublin: Veritas, 2003, 77–99

67. Dadosky, 'Towards a Fundamental Theological Re-Interpretation of Vatican II', *Heythrop Journal*, 2008, 742–63

68. John Henry Newman, *University Sermons*, 2004, as quoted by David Burrell, 'Newman in Retrospect', *Cambridge Companion to Newman*, 69, 2009, 256–7

69. See Tom Norris, 'Newman's Approach to the act of Faith in the light of Catholic Dogmatic Tradition', *Irish Theological Quarterly*, 2004, 246–7

70. John Henry Newman, 'Religious Faith Rational', *Parochial and Plain Sermons*, San Francisco: Ignatius Press, 1997, 125

71. Ibid. For a more extensive account of faith in Newman's writings, see Terrence Merrigan, 'Newman on Faith in the Trinity', *Newman and Faith*, Ian Ker and Terrence Merrigan (eds), Louvain: Peeters, 2004, 93–117

II. THE CATHOLIC CHURCH AND OTHER RELIGIONS

A key question for Christianity in the twenty-first century is how and in what way do the churches relate to other religions. Given on the one hand the new visibility of religions, the post-modern interest by some in religion and the failure of modernity to engage constructively with religion, and on the other hand the increasing reductionism of all religions, including Christianity, to the lowest common denominator, it is not only important but imperative to know something of the Catholic Church's outlook towards other religions.

Further, the rise of religious pluralism, the increasing levels of secularisation, the demographic shift in Catholicism from the North to the South, and the rise of Islam in the West challenge the shape of the self-understanding of Catholicism in the twenty-first century. Alongside these trends in religion you have paradoxically increasing levels of secularisation, growing indifference and new levels of institutional disaffiliation from organised religions.[1] The religious voice is less and less articulate in the public square. The closest attention religion gets in the public realm is more often than not in the area of ethics – but religion is more than ethics. Thus in a strange way you have certain sociological currents that almost cancel each other out – but not quite.

We now live in a world that is simultaneously religious and secular, sacred and profane, other-worldly and this-worldly. In spite of these tensions, there is a growing appreciation of the importance of Hans Küng's prophetic pre-9/11 statement:

No peace among the nations without peace among the religions. No peace among the religions without dialogue. No dialogue among the religions without ethical criteria.[2]

1. VATICAN II ON OTHER RELIGIONS

The purpose of this chapter is twofold: to examine the teaching of the Catholic Church on other religions at the Second Vatican Council and the theological challenges it poses for the self-understanding of Christianity today. This will require an examination of the origin and the historical development of the *Declaration on the Relation of the Church to Non-Christians Religion* known as *Nostra Aetate*, its relation to other documents and an outline of the reception of *Nostra Aetate* in the post-conciliar period, with particular reference to the contribution of the late Pope John Paul II. Towards the end of the Chapter One will outline some of the challenges arising from the teaching of Vatican II on other religions.

a. The Gentle but Determined Influence of John XXIII

When Pope John XXIII announced the convening of the Second Vatican Council in January 1959, it was not envisaged that a document dealing with the relationship of the Church to other religions would be issued. As one commentator put it, the production of a document on non-Christian religions 'was an unexpected outcome of the conciliar process' and, as such, it arrived 'almost as an afterthought'.[3]

However, the relationship between Catholics and Jews, or more accurately, the poor relationship between the Church and Judaism, was a matter of considerable concern for John XXIII. The horror of the Shoah in Germany was deeply troubling for many Christians and the ongoing presence of so much anti-Semitism throughout Europe and beyond exercised the consciences of all churches.

Angelo Giuseppe Roncalli had been Apostolic Delegate in Turkey from 1935 to 1944. During that time, he sought actively to prevent the persecution and execution of many Jews. On becoming Pope John XXIII, Roncalli decreed in March 1959 that prayers for what at that time were known as the 'perfidious Jews' in the solemn intercessions on the Good Friday liturgy were to be deleted. In June 1960 he gave an audience to Jules Isaac, a Jewish French historian, who communicated his deep concern about the contempt of Jews found within Christian teaching. In September 1960 John XXIII requested Cardinal Bea to draw up a draft document on the relationship of the Catholic Church to the Jewish people for consideration at the forthcoming Council.

In October 1960, John XXIII received in audience 130 US Jews whom he greeted warmly with the words: 'I am Joseph, your brother', words that deeply touched his audience at the time.

In March 1962, while John XXIII was being driven along the Lungotevere in Rome, he saw a group of Jews coming out of the synagogue; immediately he stood up in the car and offered them a blessing – an event that was subsequently described by a Jewish Rabbi who was there as 'perhaps the first real gesture of reconciliation'.[4]

In the meantime, preparatory work on a document on the Jews was progressing until in June 1962 it was announced in Israel, prematurely, that a Dr Chaim Wardi would represent Jews at the forthcoming Council. This announcement provoked an outburst of protests from the Arab world against the Vatican. Discussions on the Jews came to a halt and the document was not presented at the first session of the Council in the autumn of 1962.

Bea, who was bitterly disappointed, made a passionate plea at the first session for the question of the Jews to be put back on the conciliar agenda. John XXIII agreed to this. However, controversy continued to dog discussions on the Jews:

- The play by Rolf Hochhut, *The Deputy*, was released on Broadway in 1963 which, among other things, drew attention to the silences and inaction of Pius XII in the face of the extermination of so many Jews;
- Strong reaction against the document on Jews came from the Arab world;
- Christian Arabs living in the Middle East also objected;
- Why not just mention the Jews in the Constitution on

the Church or put something into Schema XIII or even
Dei Verbum;

- What about the other religions, especially Islam?

A second draft document was presented as part of the decree on
ecumenism but not debated at the council in 1963 and a further draft
appeared in 1964.

Though each draft was controversial, there was a growing
acceptance of the importance of making a statement on the Jews.
Yves Congar OP, however, remarked in his diary for September 1964:
'Anti-Semitism is not dead.'[5] In spite of this ongoing nervousness
concerning the document on the Jews, a declaration was approved
in October 1965 and promulgated on 28 October with 2,312 in favour
and 88 against. In the light of these controversies and the protracted
birth of the document over three different sessions of the Council,
Nostra Aetate has been dubbed as 'the declaration that almost did not
happen'[6] and 'almost a miracle that it was ever passed'.[7]

b. An Outline of *Nostra Aetate*

The final declaration is made up of thirty sentences in Latin and five
different articles. It was the shortest document of the Council – and
arguably the longest in its implications for the Church.

In Article 1, it points out that all come from one and the same
stock created by God and all share the same common destiny.

In Article 2, it notes first of all that throughout history there is
found a certain awareness of a hidden power and even recognition
of a supreme being, which gives rise to a way of life 'imbued with
a deep religious sense'. Then there are particular religions found 'in
more advanced civilizations' which seek a more exact language to
answer the big questions of life.

Hinduism, in particular, explores the divine mystery and seeks
release from the trials of life by ascetical practices, meditation and
recourse to God.

Buddhism testifies to the essential inadequacy of life in a
changing world and therefore promotes liberation and illumination.

This article states that the Church rejects nothing of what is true and holy in these religions and that these religions often reflect a ray of that truth which enlightens all men and women. The article concludes by 'urging' Christians to enter into 'conversations and collaboration' with the members of other religions. It calls on Christians to 'acknowledge, preserve and encourage the spiritual and moral truths found among non-Christians.' In Article 3, it points out that the 'Church has also a high regard for Muslims. They worship God ... who is one, living and subsistent, merciful and almighty, the Creator of heaven and earth who has spoken to humanity.' They 'submit themselves ... to the decrees of God and they link their faith to Abraham, they venerate Jesus as a prophet; they honour Mary the virgin mother, and they await the day of judgement and the reward of God following the resurrection of the dead.' This article also acknowledges there have been controversies over the centuries between Christians and Muslims; it pleads with all to forget the past, urges 'mutual understanding', and invites Christians and Muslims together to 'promote peace, liberty, social justice and moral values.'

Article 4, the longest, deals with Judaism. It recalls the 'spiritual ties which link the people of the new covenant to the stock of Abraham' and 'acknowledges that in God's plan of salvation, the beginnings of its [Christian] faith and election are to be found in the patriarchs, Moses and the prophets.'

The Declaration acknowledges that 'the pillars on which the Church stands, namely the Apostles, are Jewish, as were many of the early disciples.' It states that the Jews remain very dear to God since 'God does not take back the gifts he bestowed or the choice he made.'

The Declaration encourages 'mutual understanding and appreciation' through biblical and theological enquiry. It notes that 'neither all Jews indiscriminately ... nor Jews today, can be charged with crimes committed during' the Passion of Christ. Further, 'the Jews should not be spoken of as rejected or accursed as if this follows from Holy Scripture.' Lastly, it states that the Church 'deplores all hatred, persecutions, displays of anti-Semitism levelled ... against the Jews.'

In Article 5, it concludes by saying there is no basis for any form of discrimination between individuals and that 'the Church reproves as foreign to the mind of Christ any discrimination or harassment on the basis of race, colour, or religion.'

c. Light on *Nostra Aetate* from Other Documents of Vatican II

It should be remembered that during the discussions leading up to *Nostra Aetate*, it was suggested on several occasions that the question about the Jews and other religions might be inserted into other Council documents. We must now look briefly at what other documents have to say, directly or indirectly, about the relationship of Christianity to the non-Christian religions.

Lumen Gentium (November 1964) is regarded by many as one of the most important documents of the Council, principally because it lays down deep biblical and theological foundations affecting other documents, including *Nostra Aetate*. For example, in Article 13, the Council states that 'all are called by God's grace to salvation' – a clear statement about the universality of God's offer of salvation. Article 16 talks about those who have not yet accepted the Gospel but are nonetheless related to the people of God 'in various ways'. There is, first of all, the Jews, and then the Muslims who hold to the faith of Abraham and adore the one God. A third group are those who 'in shadows and images seek the unknown God.' Then there are those who do not know Christ or the Church, but who seek God with a sincere heart and follow the dictates of their conscience. Lastly, there are those who do not know God explicitly, and yet 'who not without grace, seek to lead a good life.' All of these, in one way or another, have the possibility of attaining salvation through the grace of God. Whatever is good and true among these groups is given by the God who enlightens all. The claim that the salvation of God is offered to these various groups begs the question: how is God's salvation communicated to these different groups?

The beginnings of an answer is given in *Gaudium et Spes* (7 December 1965) which points out that 'the Spirit offers to all the possibility of being made partners, in a way known only to God, in the paschal mystery.'[8] Again, later on, in Article 41, the same document asserts that the Spirit of God stirs the lives of people, both in the past and in the present, and that therefore they will never be totally indifferent.

In the *Decree on the Church's Missionary Activity*, known as *Ad Gentes* (7 December 1965), the Council picks up on the theme of the Spirit and points out that the Spirit was at work in the world before Christ[9] and says later on that the Spirit 'calls all ... to Christ and arouses ... the submission of faith by the seed of the Word and the preaching of the Gospel.'[10] This *Decree* also talks about 'elements of truth and grace ... found among people which are as it were a secret presence of God',[11] acknowledges 'those seeds of the word which lie hidden among other religions',[12] and encourages Christians through dialogue to 'learn of the riches which a generous God has distributed among the nations.'[13]

These three documents provide in general terms a broad theological framework for understanding the positive relationship between the Church and other religions as outlined in *Nostra Aetate*. In brief, the reason why the Church should reach out to other religions and engage in serious dialogue with them is because:

- All are called by God's grace to salvation (LG, a.13);
- The Spirit offers to all the possibility of being partners in the Paschal Mystery (GS, a. 22);
- The Spirit of God was active in other religions before Christ and, by implication, after Christ (AG, a.4 and GS, a.41);
- The seeds of the Word are hidden in these religious traditions (AG, a.11 and 15);
- 'Elements of truth and grace' can be found in other religions (AG, a.9)
- The Church rejects nothing of what is good and true in other religions (NA, a.2);
- Other religions 'often reflect a ray of that truth which enlightens all' (NA, a.2);
- Christians are encouraged to seek out the spiritual

and moral truths found in other religions (*NA*, a.2).

d. Initial Evaluation of *Nostra Aetate*

Looking back from the vantage point of nearly fifty years, the *Declaration on the Relation of the Church to non-Christian Religions* is in one sense quite unremarkable, even bland from a theological point of view, and fairly flat in terms of what we call today inter-religious dialogue. Donald Nicholl says, 'It comes as something of a shock ... to notice how summary is its treatment of other religions apart from Judaism.'[14]

However, we must not assess this document through the eyes of the twenty-first century. Instead, we must situate ourselves historically back in 1965. From that particular vantage point, it must be said, in its favour:

- This is the first time that the Catholic Church reaches out positively to other non-Christian religions and this stands out in stark contrast to the traditional representation of religions prior to the Council.

- This is also the first time that the Church deplores the persecution of the Jews and the presence of anti-Semitism, though it should be noted that Pius XI and Pius XII both had spoken out in favour of the Jews.

- This is the first time the Church acknowledges that God does not take back his gifts, and that the Jews, in the past or in the present, cannot be held responsible for the death of Christ.

- This was the first time, according to Jewish commentators like Rabbi Abraham Heschel, that a statement of the church does not refer to or express hope for the conversion of Jews.[15]

How then are we today to evaluate the historical and theological significance of this document on the relationship of the Church to non-Christian religions?

On the positive side, Michael Barnes SJ says that *Nostra Aetate* 'represents a watershed in the development of a theology of religions.'[16] Although a modest document, '*Nostra Aetate* inaugurated a wide-ranging reappraisal within Catholicism of Christianity's relationship with Judaism.'[17] Further, *Nostra Aetate* 'provided possibilities for dialogue between Jews and Christians that had never before existed in the history of these two great religions.'[18] For some, *Nostra Aetate* ushered in a 'doctrinal revolution' and effected 'a radical upheaval in relation to the traditional representation of non-Christian religions.'[19] John Oestereicher, one of the architects of the Declaration, describes it as 'a deeply theological' document.[20]

From a negative point of view, however, it must be pointed out that *Nostra Aetate* remained silent on the question of whether other religions could be regarded as vehicles of salvation. Further, it removed the word 'deicide' from the final text;[21] it failed to repudiate the atrocities inflicted on the Jews in Germany; it neglected to mention the Shoah, the State of Israel and the post-biblical Jewish tradition. In addition, *Nostra Aetate* did not spell out the theological implications of the Church's positive evaluation of non-Christian religions. From a Muslim point of view, it is disappointing that no reference is made to the Prophet Muhammad or to the Qur'an.

Nostra Aetate, however, when read in conjunction with the other documents of the Council, marks a significant shift in the theological awareness of the Catholic Church. God is now understood to be active through grace, through the Spirit, and through the seeds of the Word, not only within Christianity, but also outside the Christian reality within other religions. While this nw vision is present only in embryonic form in the Council, and largely in documents other than *Nostra Aetate*, nonetheless there is a significant shift, a theological awakening present at Vatican II, which paves the way for major developments in the post-conciliar period.

2. THE RECEPTION OF *NOSTRA AETATE* IN THE POST-CONCILIAR PERIOD

It would be impossible to summarise the many documents issued by the Church in its reception of *Nostra Aetate*.[22] All we can do here is signal some up of the more significant documents that have been issued to open up a new path in the Catholic Church's relationship with other religions.

In the immediate aftermath of Vatican II, most activities focused on other documents of the Council. Pope Paul VI gave many addresses encouraging respect and dialogue among other religions.[23] It should also be remembered that in 1964 he wrote an important encyclical entitled *Ecclesiam Suam*, and established, before *Nostra Aetate* was adopted, the Council for Dialogue with Non-Christians, two initiatives which in their time were significant stepping stones in facilitating a positive reception of *Nostra Aetate*.

a. Encyclicals of John Paul II Promoting Dialogue with Other Religions

With the election of Karol Wojtyła as Pope John Paul II, the subject of inter-religious dialogue began to receive close attention. In his first encyclical, *Redemptor Hominis* (1979), he points out that the beliefs of other religions are an 'effect of the Spirit of truth operating outside the visible confines of the mystical body' of Christ in the world.[24] He notes that religions are a witness to 'the primacy of the spiritual' and are 'reflections of the one truth, seeds of the Word'.[25]

In a later encyclical, entitled *On the Holy Spirit in the Life of the Church and the World*, known as *Dominium et Vivificantem* (1986), there is an explicit emphasis on the importance of the role of the Spirit as a 'source of ... religious questioning' which influences the course of history, peoples, cultures and religions.[26] In the same encyclical, he says, echoing *Ad Gentes*, that the Spirit of God is active in the world before Christianity. Referring to the action of the Spirit in the world, he goes on to say: 'We cannot limit ourselves to the two thousand years since the birth of Christ. We need to go further back, to embrace the whole action of the Holy Spirit even before Christ ... from the beginning, throughout the world, especially in the economy of the Old Testament.'[27]

In another encyclical entitled *An Encyclical Letter on the Permanent Validity of the Church's Missionary Mandate* called *Redemptoris Missio*

(1990), he talks about the presence and activity of the Spirit in the Church, in 'individuals ... society and history, peoples, cultures and religions.'[28] It is this same 'Spirit who sows the seeds of the Word ... who blows where He wills ... who holds all things together and leads us to broaden our vision.'[29] Further, there is a recognition of the 'universal action of Spirit': 'we need to go further back to embrace the whole action of the Spirit even before Christ ... in every place and at every time ... in every individual.'[30]

b. *Dialogue and Proclamation* (1991)

An important non-encyclical document coming from the Church during the pontificate of John Paul II was *Dialogue and Proclamation: Reflections and Orientations on Inter-Religious Dialogue and the Proclamation of the Gospel of Jesus Christ*. This document was issued jointly by the Pontifical Council for Inter-Religious Dialogue and the Congregation for Evangelisation of People in May 1991, to commemorate the twenty-fifth anniversary of *Nostra Aetate*. It is regarded as the clearest expression of the Church's teaching on inter-religious dialogue. The primary purpose of *Dialogue and Proclamation* is to spell out the complementary relation between these key tasks.

It says dialogue and proclamation, meaning inter-religious dialogue and the proclamation of the Gospel, though not on the same level, are authentic elements in the Church's evangelising mission; both are legitimate and necessary; both are intimately related but not interchangeable.[31] *Dialogue and Proclamation* outlines four forms of dialogue:

1. There is 'the dialogue of life', where people strive to live in open and neighbourly spirit, sharing their joys and sorrows, their problems and preoccupations;

2. There is 'the dialogue of action', in which Christians and others collaborate for the development and liberation of people;

3. Then comes 'the dialogue of theological exchange', where specialists seek to deepen their understanding of their respective religious heritages and appreciate each other's spiritual values;

4. Finally there is 'the dialogue of religious experience', where persons rooted in their own religious tradition share their spiritual riches in prayer and contemplation, faith and ways of searching for God.

This document, one of the most significant during the pontificate of John Paul II, talks about 'the active presence of the Holy Spirit in the religious life of members of other religions', and states 'all ... who are saved share, though differently ... in the mystery of salvation in Jesus Christ through the Spirit. The mystery of salvation reaches out to them ... through the invisible action of the Spirit of Christ.' How? '... through the practice of what is good in their own religious traditions and by following the dictates of their conscience ...'[32] This document is one of the most explicit coming from the Church on the action of the Spirit in and through other religions offering them the possibility of salvation. One should note here the increasing emphasis on the role of the Holy Spirit, which we will develop later in other chapters.

c. *Dominus Iesus* (2000)

One other document that must be mentioned is *Dominus Iesus: On the Unicity and Salvific Universality of Jesus Christ and the Church*. This document was issued by the Congregation for the Doctrine of the Faith in 2000 – a document that sparked off controversy because it seemed to call into question the progress of the previous thirty-five years and came in the midst of discussions taking place between Jacques Dupuis and the Congregation for the Doctrine of the Faith. The spirit of *Dominus Iesus* for some seems to go against the positive outlook of Vatican II towards other religions: it appeared to neglect the real gains made in the post-conciliar period, it failed to recognise the special relationship that exists between Christianity and Judaism, it drew far too sharp a distinction between theological faith and the beliefs of other religions, and it offended other religions by describing their position in life as 'gravely deficient'.

It was argued that *Dominus Iesus* provided on the one hand clarity on the uniqueness of and universality of the Christ-event and on the other hand it highlighted the differences between Christianity and other religions. According to *Dominus Iesus*, inter-religious dialogue is a part of the evangelising mission of the Church and 'requires an attitude of understanding and a relationship of mutual knowledge and reciprocal enrichment.' This emphasis on 'mutual understanding and enrichment' continues a theme found in the documents of Vatican II and in *Dialogue and Proclamation*. *Dominus Iesus* notes that in the practice of dialogue between Christian faith and other religions, 'new questions arise that need to be addressed through pursuing new paths of research' and discernment.[33] In that context, *Dominus Iesus* seeks to set forth the 'doctrine of the Catholic Church' that should inform these discussions. This doctrine is set forth in six different chapters, dealing respectively with the fullness of revelation in Christ; the unity of the economy of the incarnate Word and the Holy Spirit; the uniqueness and universality of the salvific mystery of Christ; the unicity and unity of the Church; the inseparability of the kingdom of God, the kingdom of Christ and the Church; the Church and other religions in relation to salvation.

It is the last chapter of *Dominus Iesus* on 'The Church and Other Religions in relation to Salvation' that is of most interest to us here. *Dominus Iesus* emphasises that 'the Church ... is necessary for salvation' and as such is the 'universal sacrament of salvation'.[34] This doctrine of the Church should not be set up against the universal saving will of God. Instead, 'it is necessary to keep these two truths together, namely the real possibility of salvation in Christ for all mankind and the necessity of the Church for this salvation.'[35] It notes that according to Vatican II, the saving grace of God comes to individuals in 'ways known to [God] Himself'.[36] It encourages theologians to explore this question. In doing this, care must be taken not to reduce the Church as simply one way of salvation alongside other religions, or simply to see other religions as complementary to the Church.[37] Yet, it acknowledges that 'various religious traditions contain and offer religious elements which come from God.' However, it says one cannot attribute to these a divine origin '... which is proper to the Christian sacraments.'[38]

In relation to other religions, *Dominus Iesus* points out that 'objectively speaking they [other religions] are in a gravely deficient situation in comparison with those who, in the Church, have the fullness of salvation',[39] a point of view that triggered negative reactions from Christians and members of other religions. The Catholic Bishops' Conference of England and Wales in their document *Meeting God in Friend and Stranger: Fostering Respect and Mutual Understanding between the Religions* (2010) offers an interesting gloss on the phrase 'gravely deficient': 'It is not the people whom *Dominus Iesus* sees as "deficient", but their situation.'[40]

It must be noted that over and above these documents on the relationship of Christianity to the other religions, a series of other documents on the specific issue of Catholic-Jewish relations have also been issued since *Nostra Aetate*. Again we can only mention these without going into any real detail here. We will return to these documents in Chapter Eight.

d. Post-Conciliar Documents on the Jews

The first follow-through on *Nostra Aetate* dealing with the Jews specifically was the establishment by Pope Paul VI of the Commission for Relations with the Jews in 1974. This Commission quickly set about publishing various documents. In 1974 'Guidelines and Suggestions for Implementing the Conciliar Declaration "*Nostra Aetate*" (n.4)' were published. These guidelines picked up themes outlined in *Nostra Aetate* and presented them in a way that would promote better relationships between Jews and Catholics.[41]

In 1985, 'Notes on the Correct Way to Present Jews and Judaism in Preaching and Catechesis in the Roman Catholic Church' appeared. This document was intended to put into ecclesial practice the recommendations contained in *Nostra Aetate* and the 1974 guidelines. It talked about the dialogue between Jews and Christians 'as favouring a better mutual knowledge' and demanding 'respect for the other as he is ... for his faith and his religious conviction.' The 'Notes' are significant for being very practical and for making reference for the first time in a Vatican document to the State of Israel, the extermination of Jews in Europe during 1935–1945, and for emphasising the permanence of Israel as a sign to be interpreted within God's design.

The 'Notes' in turn were followed by another document entitled 'We Remember: A Reflection on the Shoah' in Mark 1998. This document, though widely welcomed, was criticised for distinguishing too sharply between Christian anti-Judaism and Nazi anti-Semitism, and for making a distinction between the responsibility of the Church and the responsibility of individual Christians. Previous documents, issued by the French Bishops (1997) and the German Bishops (1988 and 1995) were more explicit on the link between Christianity and Nazi anti-Semitism. The French Bishops claimed that anti-Judaism in the Christian Churches provided soil that 'nurtured the poisonous plant of contempt for the Jews'.[42]

A further document, issued in 2001 by the Pontifical Biblical Commission, entitled *The Jewish People and their Sacred Scriptures in Christianity*, highlights the intrinsic links between Judaism and Christianity.

While these documents are important benchmarks, there have been a number of significant symbolic and prophetic actions by John Paul II that perhaps speak louder than any document.

e. Prophetic Gestures of John Paul II

1. These include a visit by the Pope to the members of the Central Council for Jews in Germany in Mainz in 1980, during which he stated that the covenant with the Jews 'has never been revoked by God'.

2. This was followed by a historic visit to the synagogue in Rome in April 1986, the first visit made by a Pope in history to a synagogue. During this visit, John Paul II referred to the Jews as 'our elder brother' and said that discrimination against Jews over the centuries was deplorable. He also referred to his abhorrence of the genocide visited upon Jews during the last war.

3. This action was followed by a ground-breaking invitation to the leaders of the world religions to a gathering in Assisi to attend a World Day of Prayer for Peace. This event took place in October 1986 and may turn out to be his most original and creative action towards the promotion of good relations between the religions of the world and Christianity. A second gathering at Assisi took place in 1993 to pray for peace in the Balkans. In the aftermath of 9/11, a third meeting in Assisi was convened in January 2002 to pray for peace and to reject the use of violence in the name of religion.

4. In the Jubilee Year of 2000 there was a Mass of Pardon on the first Sunday of Lent during which Apologies were issued to seven different groups, including Jews, with a view to effecting a cleansing of memory. The prayer of repentance in relation to the Jews stated: 'God of our fathers, you chose Abraham and his descendants to bring your name to the nations. We are deeply saddened by the behaviour of those who in the course of history have caused these children of yours to suffer, and, asking your forgiveness, we wish to commit ourselves to genuine brotherhood with the people of the covenant.'

5. Again, in this same Jubilee Year of 2000, there was the visit of John Paul II to the Holy Land, with striking moments at Yah Vashem, the memorial in Jerusalem to

the six million Jews who died in the Holocaust, and the placing of a prayer in a crack in the Western Wall pleading pardon for offences against Jews, a gesture that deeply touched Jews and Christians alike.

These prophetic gestures by John Paul II opened up new bridges of trust between Christianity and other religious faiths. In particular, his outreach to the Jews retrieved an important line of continuity between Judaism and Christianity. This continuity has been broken for the past two thousand years and needed to be recovered. By highlighting the intrinsic relationship that exists for Christians with Jews, the following issues should be noted. From now on, in the light of *Nostra Aetate* and the prophetic actions of John Paul II, Christian self-definition and self-description must include explicit reference to Judaism. Christianity cannot be fully understood without formal reference to Judaism. This has far-reaching implications for the future of Christianity since, for the last two thousand years, Christians sought to understand themselves in isolation and separation from Judaism. A further point emerging from the dialogue of theological exchange is that there is growing agreement among Christian scholars that Christianity began as a reform movement within Judaism, and that for several decades, certainly up to the year 70 AD, Jews and Christians were more united than separate and distinct entities.[43]

There is now a new awareness of the Jewish character of the whole of Christianity and that, as John Paul II put it in 1982, Judaism and Christianity are linked together at the very level of their identity. This can be seen first and foremost in a new appreciation of the Jewishness of Jesus and his life, an appreciation which has important implications for the way we construct Christology. Further, this Jewish character of Christianity can also be seen in the earliest Christian communities made up of Jewish Christians who continued to worship in the Temple while devoting themselves at the same time to the Apostles' instruction and communal life, to the breaking of the bread and prayers.[44]

This in turn necessitates that great care be taken if one persists in presenting Christianity as the fulfilment of Judaism. Classical fulfilment theories over the centuries have had a negative impact on the Christian perception of Judaism and need to be qualified when used in reference to Jews in the light of *Nostra Aetate* and subsequent documents. The language of fulfilment should be qualified by the language of convergence, mutuality and respect because of the long association of the language of fulfilment with theories of replacement and supersessionism.

This new awareness of the Jewishness of Christianity also requires Christians to develop a post-supersessionist understanding of Christology, that is a Christology not over and against Judaism, not at the expense of Judaism but in a way that respects the originality and integrity of Judaism. A further requirement in the light of these developments is the necessity for Christians to develop what Johann Metz and others refer to as a post-Shoah theology, that is a Christology done not with our backs to the Shoah, but rather facing the Shoah.

3. BENEDICT XVI ON INTER-RELIGIOUS DIALOGUE

At the time of his election there were concerns expressed about Pope Benedict XVI's approach to ecumenism and inter-religious dialogue, given that over the years as Prefect of the Congregation for the Doctrine of the Faith he had taken a tough line in both ecumenism and inter-religious dialogue, especially in the well-known and controversial document, *Dominus Iesus*. It is quite striking that within a week of his election as Bishop of Rome, Benedict asserted formally his commitment to ecumenism and inter-religious dialogue as laid out in the Second Vatican Council, and developed by John Paul II, in an early address to representatives of different churches and world religions.

Some months later, at the World Youth Day in Cologne in August 2005, in the presence of representatives from the Muslim community, he pointed out, 'inter-religious dialogue and inter-cultural dialogue between Christians and Muslims can not be reduced to an optional extra.' In early September 2006, he sent a message of support to the spiritual leaders who were meeting in Assisi to commemorate the twentieth anniversary of the meeting convoked by John Paul II in 1986, even though he had absented himself from the original Assist meeting in 1986.

a. Benedict XVI and Catholic-Jewish Relations

Cardinal Ratzinger, prior to becoming Pope, had a good record on promoting positive relations between Jews and Christians. He had signalled, after the publication of *Dominus Iesus*, by way of correction to a misunderstanding in relation to Jews, the unique relationship between Judaism and Christianity. In addition, he wrote a positive introduction to *The Jewish People and The Scriptures in the Christian Bible* (2001), which spoke appreciatively of the importance of Judaism for Christianity. Further, he had written positively about inter-religious dialogue and Jewish-Christian relations in the international journal known as *Communio* in 1998.

Conscious of the singular contribution that John Paul II made to Jewish-Catholic relations, Benedict XVI, on assuming office as the new Bishop of Rome, indicated more than once his 'intention to continue on this path' and 'his determination to walk in his [John Paul II's] footsteps.'[45] Benedict XVI is aware on the one hand that he is clearly committed to following in the footsteps of his predecessor, and on the other hand he is conscious of some of the theological questions surrounding the Jewish-Christian dialogue opened up by Vatican II and John Paul II. These questions include prayer for Jews, the issue of supersessionism, mission to the Jews, and the Holocaust. These are questions addressed by Benedict, and his treatment has sometimes given rise to controversy and at times offence to Jews. On other occasions his addresses have been well received by Jews. These questions will be taken up in more detail later on in Chapter Eight.

A number of statements and actions by Benedict, however unintentional, have made some Jews less than enthusiastic when comparing Benedict with his predecessor. For example, Benedict's authorisation of the 'use of the pre-conciliar liturgical form' in his

Apostolic Letter *Summorum Pontificium* in July 2008 took some by surprise. This particular authorisation caused concern among Jews because it brought back the pre-Vatican II Good Friday Prayer for Jews which prayed that: 'God may take the veil from their hearts' and 'the blindness of that people'.

Further, his re-writing of the prayer for the restored liturgical form also caused concern for Jews. In addition, the lifting of the excommunications on members of the Pius X Society created turmoil, and as a result Benedict apologised for misunderstandings caused by this well-intentioned gesture towards unity within the Catholic Church.

On the other hand, in an address to the Jewish community in January 2008, Benedict spoke positively about Jewish-Catholic relations and reflected movingly on the Shoah. Also of importance are his two volumes on *Jesus of Nazareth* (2008 and 2011). In Volume 1, he presents Jesus as a follower of the biblical and Rabbinic tradition, presenting Judaism in positive terms. In Volume 2, he clearly acknowledges, echoing *Nostra Aetate*, that the Jews are not responsible for the death of Jesus. Even more significant is the statement in that book that Christians should not be trying to convert Jews – an issue that has caused much controversy in the past which we will take up in Chapter Eight.

Benedict's position on the question of the conversion of Jews will be welcomed, though it should be noted that this question did come up at Vatican II during discussions surrounding the composition of *Nostra Aetate*. References to the conversion of Jews were excluded in the final text, due, by all accounts, to the influence and intervention of Abraham Joshua Heschel.[46] It is too early to decide whether Benedict has moved beyond what was taught at Vatican II, and by his predecessor John Paul II, concerning Jewish-Catholic relations.

b. Benedict XVI and Islam – A Shift in Focus

On 12 September 2006, Benedict XVI gave a public lecture in Regensburg University, his former university and family home. This lecture caused a lot of international controversy, generated serious misunderstanding within the Muslim world and damaged Catholic-Muslim relations. However, in spite of this, or indeed because of this, Catholic-Muslim dialogue has moved to the centre of inter-religious relations.

The first thing to note about the Regensburg lecture is its title: 'Faith, Reason and the University: Memories and Reflections.'[47] The title indicates that this lecture was not formally about Islam or the Catholic-Muslim dialogue. Benedict did, however, use a quotation from a fourteenth-century Byzantine Emperor's critique of Islam, causing offence to Muslims throughout the world and provoking some violent reactions.

Benedict XVI apologised at least twice in regard to the reception of this lecture. In the first instance, he pointed out: 'I wish also to add that I am deeply sorry for the reactions in some countries to a few passages of my address at the University of Regensburg which were considered offensive to the sensibility of Muslims. These in fact were a quotation from a medieval text, which do not in any way express my personal thought' (September 2006). Subsequently, at a general audience on 20 September, he said: 'In no way did I wish to make my own the words of the medieval emperor. I wished to explain that not religion and violence, but religion and reason, go together.'

It is important to point out that the primary import of this lecture was to show that faith and reason belong to each other, that they are complementary, and that this unique relationship between faith and reason goes back to a rich encounter between biblical faith and Hellenistic philosophy. It was in this sense that he said: 'Not acting according to the *logos* is contrary to God.'

In broad terms, his paper was intended as 'a critique' of the narrowing of modern reason and the need to broaden our understanding of reason beyond the confines of mathematical and empirical reason. Only when this happens, he points out, can we have a genuine 'dialogue of cultures', a phrase preferred in this lecture over 'inter-religious dialogue'. Otherwise there will be an exclusion of the Divine from the universality of reason in its dialogue with culture.

This particular emphasis on the relationship between faith and reason is set out in stark contrast to the relationship emerging today of the connectedness between religion and violence. Benedict's talk in Regensburg seeks to uncouple the link that now exists in the public domain between religion and violence. He emphasises that violence can never be justified by reference to religion or to God.

When we hear religion and violence mentioned together, we all too frequently think of Islam, without taking sufficient account that religion and violence can be found in the other two monotheistic religions, namely Judaism and Christianity. It is unfortunate that reference to Judaism and Christianity and the presence of violence within those two world religions did not receive any mention within his lecture.

In spite of this controversial talk in Regensburg, or more accurately because of it, the Catholic-Muslim dialogue has taken some very significant steps forward. In late November 2006, Benedict travelled to Turkey and part of his mission was to overcome the misunderstandings created between Catholics and Muslims arising from the Regensburg talk. He visited the Blue Mosque in Istanbul, paused in silent prayer alongside the Mufti of Istanbul and the Iman of the Blue Mosque. He also reaffirmed the positive teaching of *Nostra Aetate* about Muslims and acknowledged that Catholics and Muslims worship the same God.

On 13 October 2007, one year after the Regensburg letters, the Muslim world issued an open letter entitled 'A Common Word Between Us and You', addressed to Benedict XVI and the leaders of other Christian churches.[48] This document was signed by 138 Muslim scholars and it was the first time in history that the Muslim world issued a global statement talking in one voice. 'A Common Word' holds that the Bible and the Qur'an teach the importance of the love of God and the love of neighbour. This open letter also points out that over half of the world's population is made up of Christians and Muslims, and that without peace among Christians and Muslims there can be no meaningful peace in the world. This open letter has been well received by other Christian leaders, such as Archbishop Rowan Williams of Canterbury. Also notable was an enthusiastic response by theologians at the University of Yale, known as the 'Yale Response', which was published in the *New York Times* on 13 November 2007 with 130 signatures of Christian leaders and scholars. A Vatican response was slow in coming – but when it did come it was significant, giving rise to the establishment of a new Catholic-Muslim forum, headed by Cardinal Jean-Louis Tauran in 2008. The first meeting of this Catholic-Muslim forum took place on 4–6 November 2008 and issued a joint declaration at the end of its deliberations.

On 9 May 2009, Benedict visited the King Hussein Mosque, Amman, Jordan, and urged the continuation of the dialogue between Catholics and Muslims. On 12 May 2009, Benedict visited Jerusalem's Grand Mufti Muhammad Ahmad Hussein at the Dome of the Rock and the al-Aqsa Mosque, which is regarded as the third holiest site in Islam after Mecca and Medina.

Many hold that a shift is taking place within Catholicism in the area of inter-religious dialogue, a shift towards a greater concentration on Catholic-Muslim relations. This shift has come about as a result of Benedict's talk in Regensburg in 2006, the letter from the Muslim world on 'A Common Word Between Us and You' (2007) and the establishment of a new Catholic-Muslim forum (2008). Moreover, some detect an additional shift within this move, a shift from inter-religious dialogue to inter-cultural dialogue. It may be premature to read too much into this particular emphasis on inter-cultural dialogue. In one sense, all inter-religious dialogue entails a necessary moment of inter-cultural dialogue on the way to inter-religious dialogue. Not all inter-cultural dialogue, however, leads to inter-religious dialogue. It would be difficult to deny the legitimacy of inter-religious dialogue with Muslims, given that *Nostra Aetate* states that: 'The Church has also a high regard for Muslims. They worship God who is one living and subsistent, merciful and almighty, creator of heaven and earth, who has also spoken to humanity.'[49] Further, John Paul II at a meeting with Muslims in Paris (June 1980) refers to 'our brothers in faith in the one God'. In focusing on inter-cultural dialogue, it may well be that Benedict is emphasising those areas of life in which Catholics and Muslims can work together in the first instance. These areas would include the importance of creating 'a culture of peace', an 'alliance of civilisations' (2009), the working together of Catholics and Muslims for justice, the initiation of a process of reciprocity in relation to human rights, addressing the challenges of relativism and secularism.

It would be naïve to think that the dialogue between Catholics and Muslims will be easy, no more than the dialogue between Jews and Catholics has been easy. Further, there will be bumps along the road. Nonetheless, extraordinary progress has been made in the Jewish-Catholic dialogue, and there is no reason to doubt that progress over time will be made in Catholic-Muslim relations. The dialogue between Jews and Catholics is of a different order to the dialogue with Muslims, just as the dialogue between Muslims and Catholics is of a different order to the dialogue of Catholics with non-monotheistic faiths.

In spite of these important areas within inter-cultural dialogue, in which Catholics and Muslims are called to work together, it should not be forgotten that inter-religious dialogue does have resources to promote mutual understanding, enrichment and esteem that inter-cultural dialogue *per se* may lack. Inter-religious dialogue contains a built-in dynamism towards the other that arises from religious principles of justice, compassion and love. These religious principles in many religions expand the range of the other to include not only friends, families and neighbours but also the stranger, the forgotten, the oppressed and even the enemy in some instances. Further, inter-religious dialogue, can draw on the possibility of repentance for past actions towards the other, in a way that inter-cultural dialogue cannot. Thirdly, in many forms of inter-religious dialogue, appeal can be made to the ultimately Real or the transcendent dimension of life as a reality external to the participants that motivates dialogue and engagement between the religions of the world. This reference to the ultimately Real can effect change and transformation among the participants in the dialogue.[50]

c. Benedict XVI and Assisi 2011

In early 2011, Benedict XVI invited leaders of other religions and non-believers to a meeting in Assisi on 27 October 2011 to commemorate the twenty-fifth anniversary of the Day of Prayer for Peace initiated by John Paul II in 1986. The event was billed as a 'Day of Reflection, Dialogue and Prayer for Peace and Justice in the World'. The overall theme of the day was 'Pilgrims of Truth, Pilgrims of Peace'.

In his address at Assisi 2011, Benedict spoke of the different faces of violence in the world today. There is first of all religiously motivated violence, which 'should be profoundly disturbing to us all as religious persons'. This kind of violence raises questions about the true nature of religion: 'Is there such a thing as a common nature of religion?' He described this question as 'a fundamental task for inter-religious dialogue'. Religiously motivated violence has existed in Christianity as well as in other religions and as such calls for a purification of faith for all religions.

A second type of violence comes from the denial of God, which diminishes humanity and leads to a cruelty that knows no limits. As examples of this kind of violence, he mentioned 'the horror of concentration camps' and the trading in drugs targeted at young people.

In between these two extremes there is 'the growing world of agnosticism', which has a distinctive contribution to make to dialogue: it removes the false certainty of militant atheists and 'challenges the followers of religion not to consider God as their own property'.

Clearly Benedict was putting his own stamp on what has come to be known as 'the Spirit of Assisi'. In the run-up to Assisi 2011, there was a series of articles in *Osservatore Romano* by members of the Curia seeking to remove any ambiguity around Assisi 2011, and Benedict himself shared in private correspondence with a Lutheran Pastor his intention to 'do everything I can to make a syncretistic or relativistic interpretation of the event impossible'.

Perhaps the most noteworthy feature of the gathering in 2011 was that it commemorated Assisi 1986, that it took place *in* Assisi, and that the commemoration was presided over by Benedict XVI.

Many will welcome the question posed by Benedict about the true nature of religion, the inclusion of non-believers in the dialogue, the recognition of the contribution that agnostics can make to dialogue, the clear separation of religion from violence, and the appreciation that *all* are *pilgrims* of truth and of peace

On the other hand, there were notable differences between Assisi 2011 and Assisi 1986: non-believers were invited, there was no prayer in public (though there was an opportunity for reflection and prayer at the end of the day in separate rooms). Assisi 2011 was more a spiritual event than an exercise in inter-religious dialogue. In brief, Assisi 2011 was a low-key event with no headlines in the way that Assisi captured the imagination of the media and the world.

4. CHALLENGES ARISING FROM VATICAN II REGARDING OTHER RELIGIONS

How are we to face the future in the light of the teaching of Vatican II on other living faiths, in the light of the ambiguous return of religion, and in the light of the unsatisfactory outcomes of multiculturalism in the West?

a. *Nostra Aetate* as a Theological and Pneumatological Event

While it is generally agreed that Vatican II was about ecclesiological and liturgical reform, it is also equally true and perhaps more important to recognise that Vatican II and especially *Nostra Aetate* was 'a theological event'.[51] *Nostra Aetate*, and the post-conciliar documents, have in effect brought about a new theological awareness in the life of the Church. As seen, the Church now speaks about the seeds of the word of God in other religious traditions, talks about the action of the Spirit of God in the world, points to the secret presence of God in the word, refers to rays of the truth that enlighten all, and calls attention to elements of 'truth and grace' as present in varying degrees in other religions.

A new vision of God's providential relationship with all peoples is straining to come into view in various documents of the Council. This new vision requires a re-imagining of God's presence in the world, in other religions and in Christ Jesus. Vatican II, especially *Nostra Aetate* and the theology of John Paul II, require an enlargement of the theological imagination. This expansion of theological imagination will have an impact on many areas of Christian life such as Christology, ecclesiology and the conduct of inter-religious dialogue.

How, for example, are we to articulate a theology of the Spirit of God active before and after the Christ event? Both the Council and John Paul II talk about the universal action of the Spirit of God in the world in a way that pushes back the boundaries of the theological imagination.

Moreover, in *Nostra Aetate*, there is a tilting towards a theology of general or universal revelation, when it talks about all human beings coming from the one God and sharing a common destiny, that God's providential and saving designs extend to the whole of humanity, and that often a ray of the truth which enlightens all can be found in other religions.

b. The Council as a Christological Challenge

A second challenge emerging from the Council, influenced by the enlargement of the theological imagination at Vatican ll, is a renewed understanding of the person of Jesus as the Christ. How do we express the connection between the universal agency of the Spirit in the world and the particularity of the Christ event? How do we re-locate the Christ-event within world history? What is the connection between the universal action of the Spirit of God in the world and in the historical reality of Jesus as the Christ? Is it possible to develop a Spirit-Christology within a unified economy without separating the action of the Spirit from the action of the Word Incarnate in Jesus? How is it possible to affirm God's unrevoked covenant with Israel as recognised by *Nostra Aetate* and the teaching of John Paul II, and at the same time affirm the uniqueness and universality of the Revelation of God in Christ? Is it possible to construct a Christology in the presence of the other without falling into some form of supersessionism? How does one talk about the inauguration of the reign of God in Christ and respect at the same time what is yet to come in the future for Jews and the world, that is, how does one retain the tension between a realised eschatology in Christ and a futurist eschatology awaited by Jews and the world?

In brief these questions can be summed up in the following way: how then are we to relate the new theological awareness of Vatican II and the expansion of the theological imagination this implies with the key issues of the Spirit of God, the person of Christ and the Church as the eschatological community of disciples? If we are to take seriously the thesis that Vatican II was 'a theological event', then it seems we must reformulate our theologies of the Spirit, of Revelation and of Christ so that Christians can encounter the richness of other religious traditions. These issues will be addressed in the chapters to follow.

c. *Nostra Aetate* as an Ecclesial Call to a Dialogue of Mutuality

If it is true that *Nostra Aetate* requires an expansion of the theological imagination – and we have seen some evidence for this in Section 4 a. above – then it follows that *Nostra Aetate* also demands an expansion of the ecclesiological imagination. This shift in the role of the Church in the world is signalled, in principle but not in detail, in the *Pastoral Constitution on the Church in the World*. The relationship between the Church and the world is described in the Council documents as one of dialogue. The dialogue envisaged is a two-way process: the Church contributes to the world, and the world contributes to the Church. *The Pastoral Constitution on the Church in the World* talks explicitly in Chapter 4 about a 'mutual relationship' between the Church and the world. It outlines what the Church offers to individuals, society and human activity.[52] Then the document goes on to talk about the 'Church receiving from the world', and how the Church 'profits from the experience of past ages, from the progress of the sciences, and from the riches hidden in various cultures.'[53] *The Pastoral Constitution on the Church in the World* also acknowledges that the 'Church ... has benefited and is still benefiting from the opposition of its enemies and persecutors.'[54] Here we have an understanding of the Church as one of teaching and learning, giving something to the world and receiving from the world, a Church genuinely in dialogue with the world.

This dynamic understanding of the Church is applied in particular to the relationship that can and should exist between the Church and other religions as outlined in *Nostra Aetate*, *Ad Gentes*, as well as the relationship between the Catholic Church and other churches as indicated in *Unitatis Redintegratio* and *Lumen Gentium*. The overriding principle, as already seen in this Chapter, is a new emphasis in Vatican II and subsequent documents on the mutual understanding, the mutual appreciation, and the mutual enrichment between the Church and other religions.[55]

The language of mutuality in relation to the world, other cultures, other religions and other churches is new in the self-understanding of the Catholic Church and as such calls for an enlargement of the ecclesiological imagination. The Church teaches in relation to other religions but it is also taught by other religions; the Church offers good news to others but it also receives spiritual and religious news from other religions. This vision of Vatican II is being realised only very gradually in the life of the Catholic Church and is at times resisted, to the impoverishment of the Church.

The overriding ecclesiology of Vatican II was that of a communion ecclesiology/*communio* ecclesiology, and this particular ecclesiology was formally recognised at the International Synod of Bishops in 1985 as the primary understanding of the Church at Vatican II. According to the *Dogmatic Constitution on the Church*, 'the Church, in Christ, is a sacrament – a sign, an instrument, that is of communion with God and of the unity of the entire human race.'[56] This communion of people in Christ is continued and enlivened by the gift of the Holy Spirit, and as such mirrors the life of the triune God, holding together diversity within unity. This self-understanding of the Church as a *koinonia* has been well received and enriched by other Christian churches. This ecclesiology of *communio* has served the life of the Church *ad intra* – but it is insufficiently developed *ad extra* in relation to other churches, other cultures and other religions. This distinction between the Church *ad intra* and *ad extra*, suggested by Leon Joseph Suenens at the Council, should not become a dualism – but all too frequently the Church *ad intra* has lost touch with the Church *ad extra*, to the great loss of the life of the Church *ad intra*. It is doubtful that the Church *ad intra* can exist effectively without engaging *ad extra* in relation to the world, other religions, secular culture and other churches. And likewise the Church *ad extra* needs the activities of the Church *ad intra*. Many would hold that a dimension to the crisis in the Catholic Church at present, caused by sexual abuse of children by clergy and failure of institutional governance, is the relative neglect of the activities of the Church *ad extra* and the enrichment that comes from the mutuality of engagement between the Church and the world as suggested by the *Pastoral Constitution on the Church in the World*.

Given the emphasis of Vatican II and subsequent documents on the mutuality of understanding, enrichment and esteem, the encounter between Christianity and other religions is an urgent issue, especially in the first instance between Christianity and the monotheistic faiths. Further, the encounter between the religions and the world is also a pressing task. What might the religions together have to offer in the dialogue between faith and society, the sacred and the secular, between religion and politics? The dialogue between the religions and modernity has only begun to take place for some religions – not to mention the necessary encounter between religions and late modernity/post-modernity, between religions and science, between religions and aggressive forms of secularism.

Religion must engage critically and imaginatively with the secular world, especially with the closed and hostile forms of secularism. In doing this, religion might discover that the secular is the site of the sacred, that it is in the world of an open secularity that religion can best flourish, and that, as we shall see later on in Chapter Five, it is in the depth of material secularity that spirituality emerges to reveal the gift of the Holy Spirit who broods over our broken world, bringing order out of chaos and light out of darkness.

It is within this expansion of the ecclesiological imagination that the Church is called by Vatican II:

- To be not only the light of the world but also the source of joy among the nations;
- To be an agent of peace and justice and reconciliation in collaboration with other religions;
- To be a sign and symbol and sacrament of the sacred in the world.

This will only happen if the Church as a *communio* looks not only 'in' but also 'out', allowing itself to be enriched by this ability to look in both directions. The churches together could become a forum of dialogue promoting mutual understanding, mutual enrichment and mutual esteem between Christianity and the religions of the world.

To sum up and bring this chapter to a conclusion, let me try to highlight some of the main points. *Nostra Aetate* did effect a most significant breakthrough at Vatican ll and this breakthrough is best understood as 'a theological event', an event pointing to the action of the Spirit of God outside Christianity and uniquely in the Christ-event. The Council also talks of the presence of the seeds of the Word in other religions, the existence of elements of truth and grace in other faiths, and a ray of the truth that enlightens all. These emphases of the Council when taken together represent a theological shift and a new theological awakening; this shift is based ultimately on a theology of the universality of the grace of the Spirit of God as active in the world. This development requires an expansion of the theological imagination, with particular reference to a theology of the Spirit, Revelation, Christ and the Church. Most of all, this theological shift puts Christians into a new relationship with other religions and provides a basis for new levels of dialogue, mutual understanding and enrichment. This process of dialogue and mutual enrichment has only just begun and will exercise the pneumatological imagination of all religions in the coming decades. In the meantime, Christians are discovering through the gift of other religions new ways of being Christian, and that to be Christian requires that we be inter-religious. In this way, the Christian imagination will not only be enlarged, but will also be enriched by the encounter with other religions.

NOTES

1. At present there is widespread disaffection in many parts of the Catholic Church in the western world due to abuse of children by clergy and the failure of the institutional Church to deal with this crisis in an open and transparent manner. Clearly this complex subject is beyond the purview of this book, except to note in passing in the final section of this chapter some of the ecclesiological reasons why the crisis is as bad as it is

2. Hans Küng, *Global Responsibility: In Search of a New World Ethic*, New York: Crossroad, 1991, 138

3. Donald Nicholl, 'Other Religions (*Nostra Aetate*)', *Modern Catholicism: Vatican II and After*, Adrian Hastings (ed.), Oxford: Oxford University Press, 1991, 126–7

4. J. O. Beozzo, 'The External Climate', *History of Vatican II*, Vol. I, Giuseppe Alberigo and Joseph A. Komonchak (eds), New York: Orbis Books, 1995, 395

5. Yves Congar, 28 September 1964

6. Lawrence Nemer, 'Mission and Missions', *New Catholic Encyclopaedia*, second edition, New York: Thomson/Gale in association with the Catholic University of America, 2003, 683–9 at 686

7. Franz König, 'It Must be the Holy Spirit', *The Tablet*, 21/28 December 2002, 4–6 at 6

8. *GS*, a.22

9. *AG*, a.4

10. *AG*, a.15

11. *AG*, a.9

12. *AG*, a.11

13. *AG*, a.11

14. Nicholl, 'Other Religions (*Nostra Aetate*)', op. cit.

15. See John Wilkins, 'The Beginning of the Beginning: How Vatican II changed Jewish-Christian Relations', *Commonweal*, 18 January 2008, 14–18

16. Michael Barnes, *Theology and the Dialogue of Religions*, Cambridge: Cambridge University Press, 2002, 31

17. Mary Boys, 'The Enduring Covenant', *Seeing Judaism Anew: Christianity's Sacred Obligation*, Mary C. Boys (ed.), New York: Sheed and Ward/Rowman and Littlefield, 2005, 17–25 at 22

18. Donald J. Moore, 'A Catholic Perspective on *Nostra Aetate*', *No Religion is an Island: The* Nostra Aetate *Dialogues*, Edward Bristow (ed.), New York: Fordham University Press, 1998, 13

19. See Claude Geffré, 'The Crisis of Christian Identity in an Age of Religious Pluralism', *Concilium*, 3, 2005, 13–26 at 17

20. John M. Oestereicher, 'Declaration on the Relationship of the Church to Non-Christian Religions', *Commentary on the Documents of Vatican II*, Herbert Vorgrimler (ed.), Vol. 3, London: Burns and Oates, 1969, 1

21. There is at least one plausible explanation why the charge of deicide against the Jews was not explicitly mentioned. By all accounts, Maximos IV Saigh, Patriarch of the Eastern Rite Melkites, had indicated he would walk out of the Council Hall if the charge of deicide against the Jews was withdrawn. Thus a compromised wording was agreed which pacified Maximos IV Saigh. See Wilkins, art. cit., 15

22. An indication of the vast array of such documents can be found in *Inter-Religious Dialogue: The Official Teaching of the Catholic Church from the Second Vatican Council to John Paul II (1963–1995)*, Francesco Gioia (ed.), Boston: Pauline Media Books, 1997, and *John Paul II and Inter-Religious Dialogue*, B. L. Sherwin and H. Kasimow (eds), New York: Orbis Books, 1999

23. See Gioia, *Inter-Religious Dialogue*, op. cit., 69–93

24. *RH*, a.6

25. *RH*, a.11

26. *DeV*, a.28

27. *DeV*, a.53

28. *RM*, a.28

29. *RM*, a.28–29

30. *RM*, a.5

31. *DP*, a.77

32. *DP*, a.25 and 29 respectively

33. *DI*, a.2 and 3 respectively

34. *DI*, a.20 quoting *LG*, a.48

35. *DI*, a.20

36. *AG*, a.7

37. *DI*, a.21

38. *DI*, a.21

39. *DI*, a.22

40. Catholic Bishops' Conference of England and Wales, *Meeting God in Friend and Stranger: Fostering Respect and Mutual Understanding between the Religions*, London: CTS, 2010, p. 35, n.31

41. The Guidelines are available in *Vatican II: The Conciliar and Post-Conciliar Documents*, Austin Flannery (ed.), Vol. 1, New York: Costello Publishing Group, 1975, 743–9

42. Quotation taken from Wilkins, 'The Beginning of the Beginning', 14–18

43. John T. Pawlikowski, 'The Christ event and the Jewish People', *Thinking of Christ: Proclamation, Explanation, Meaning,* Tatha Wiley (ed.), London: Continuum, 2003, 103–21

44. See Acts 2:42

45. 26 October 2005

46. A fuller account of this debate can be found in Wilkins, 'The Beginning of the Beginning', 14–18

47. This text is available on the Vatican's website: www.vatican.va

48. Text, with responses, is available online: www.acommonword.com

49. *NA*, a.3

50. On these points, see David Tracy, 'Western Hermeneutics and Inter-Religious Dialogue', *Inter-Religious Hermeneutics: Inter-Religious Dialogue Series (2),* Catherine Cornille and Christopher Conway (eds), Oregon: Cascade Books, 2010, 1–43 at 16–17

51. Barnes, *Theology and the Dialogue of Religions,* 50 and also 49, 54, 58, and Oestereicher, 'Declaration on the Relationship of the Church to Non-Christian Religions'

52. *GS*, a.41–43

53. *GS*, a.44

54. *GS*, a.44

55. See *NA*, a.3, 4; *GS*, a.44, 58; *DP*, a.9, a.44; *UR*, a.4 and 7

56. *LG*, a.1

III. MAPPING THE DEBATE IN THE TWENTIETH CENTURY AND EARLY TWENTY-FIRST CENTURY

Debate about the relationship of Christianity to other religions moved to the centre of the theological stage in the second half of the twentieth century in the light of the teaching of Vatican II, documents from the World Council of Churches, and globalisation. It is difficult to see how Christianity could survive or indeed remain credible without engagement with other religions. The very nature of Christianity, its doctrines, and its inner dynamism demands dialogue with other religions. The self-understanding of the Catholic Church as outlined in the last chapter requires the church to enter into 'conversations and collaboration' with other religions. There are a number of other factors that have influenced this necessary dialogue between Christianity and other faiths.

Foremost among these have been the rise of historical consciousness and the application of this new awareness to theological understanding. All knowledge is historically situated and socially structured, but this does not imply the adoption of non-realism or relativism. An equally important element in the dialogue between religions is the ever-increasing phenomenon of globalisation. Globalisation, in itself a highly ambiguous development, especially from a religious point of view, is also changing our consciousness. On the one hand it promises a seductive form of planetary unity and on the other hand it seeks to effect a homogenisation of all religious differences. It should be remembered that globalisation is largely a market-driven and capitalist-inspired system with very little interest in religion. A third factor inducing inter-religious dialogue is the challenge of inculturation. All religions are culturally conditioned and historically mediated, including Christianity. As Christianity moves from predominately western forms of expression to other cultural forms, it is brought into direct contact with other religions. The 1998 Asian Synod of Bishops in Rome struggled with the question of how to proclaim the Gospel of Jesus Christ in cultural forms that made sense to the people of that continent without at the same time offending native religions.[1]

These particular influences, namely historical consciousness, globalisation and inculturation, have given rise to new questions about the relationship between Christianity and other religions: Where do the other religions fit into God's plan of salvation revealed in Christ? What is distinctive about Christianity in relation to other religions of the world? How can a loving God allow two-thirds of humanity to fall outside the good news of Jesus Christ? What does religious pluralism tell us about God's plan for humanity? How does one present the uniqueness and universality of Christ without offending the founders of other religions?

These questions are often answered by working out a specifically Christian theology of religions. This response develops a theology of other religions by drawing on the revelation of God in Christ as expressed in the central doctrines of the Incarnation, Trinity and redemption. One example of this approach can be found in the work of Jacques Dupuis, especially in his magnus opus *Towards a Christian Theology of Religious Pluralism*, followed by his more popular text, *Christianity and the Religions: From Confrontation to Dialogue*.[2] In these significant texts Dupuis draws on the classical doctrines of the Trinity, Christology and soteriology and applies them to the reality of religious pluralism to construct a distinctive Christian theology of religions.

Another response can be found in the work of Peter Phan, especially his trilogy: *In Our Own Tongues: Perspectives from Asia on Mission and Inculturation* (2003), *Christianity with an Asian Face: Asian American Theology in the Making* (2003), and *Being Religious Inter-religiously: Asian Perspectives on Interfaith Dialogue* (2004).[3] We will report later on in this chapter on the work of Dupuis and Phan.

Clearly the way one understands Christology will influence one's theology of religions. Until recently most Christologies were premised on a negative evaluation of world religions. The positive appreciation of the other religions given by the Second Vatican Council makes new demands on Christology, as we have seen in the last chapter. Some see this new demand as a threat to the integrity of Christology whereas others such as Rahner see it as an opportunity to develop a truly radical Christology and recover a Christology that operates *in tandem* with Pneumatology. This new situation requires an expansion of the terms of reference of Christology. The range of reference of Christology will have to include religions before Judaism, as well as religions after the Judaeo-Christian dispensation. For example, Christology will have to enter, experientially, historically and pneumatologically, into a respectful dialogue with other religions without losing contact with the content of classical Christology.

The purpose of this chapter is not to work out the details of such a new Christology. Instead the purpose is more modest: to summarise the debate about the relationship of Christianity to the other religions in the twentieth century, to critique the three-fold typology surrounding the debate in the twentieth century, to propose some guidelines on the dynamics of dialogue, to outline the importance of maintaining a dialectical relationship between the particularity and universality of Christian faith, and to report briefly on observations by the Congregation for the Doctrine of the Faith on the work of Dupuis and the US bishops on a book by Phan.

1. OVERVIEW OF THE DEBATE IN THE TWENTIETH CENTURY AND EARLY TWENTY-FIRST CENTURY

Alongside the teaching of the Catholic Church on other religions, a rather intense theological debate has been taking place in the academy. The language adopted initially by most participants to describe their location in this debate has been that of exclusivism, inclusivism and pluralism;[4] the underlying thrust of these positions is the search for salvation.

a. The Three-Fold Typology

Exclusivists claim that salvation is only available to those who embrace explicit faith in Christ Jesus and that this faith comes from hearing the Gospel of Christ (*fides ex auditu*). For exclusivists, Christianity is the one true religion and all others are in error. There is a strong emphasis on Christ (*solus Christus*) and this emphasis finds expression in the statement 'outside the Church there is no salvation' (*extra ecclesia nullus salus*).

The exclusivists' position is based on a variety of New Testament texts. For example, in Acts of the Apostles, Peter 'filled with the Holy Spirit', preaching about Christ to the rulers, elders and scribes in Jerusalem, points out:

> There is salvation in no-one else, for there is no other name under heaven given among mortals by which we must be saved.[5]

Equally explicit is the first letter (of Paul) to Timothy:

> There is one God; there is also one mediator between God and humankind, Christ Jesus, himself human, who gave himself as a ransom for all.[6]

These texts are also confirmed by Paul in his First Letter to the Corinthians where he points out that: 'As in Adam all died, so also in Christ all should be made alive.'[7] Likewise John's Gospel attributes to Jesus the following words: 'I am the way, the truth and the life. No-one comes to the Father except through me.'[8]

Inclusivists, on the other hand, hold that while Christ is the unique, absolute and universal Saviour of the world, nonetheless salvation is also available, in various but limited forms, outside Christianity. Inclusivists appeal to the universality of God's grace in the world to justify their position: salvation in Christ through grace is offered to all and is present implicitly in other religions. This inclusivist position, it is argued, is based on the Bible which talks about the universal will of God 'who desires everyone to be saved' (1 Tim 2:4) and offers salvation to all through Christ (Mk 9:40; Jn 3:16; 1 Jn 2:2; 1 Jn 4:12; Acts 17:22; Rom 5:18, 1 Cor 15:28, Col 3:11). There is also growing evidence throughout the Bible that God's salvation is available to others outside Judaism and Christianity and this evidence has been gathered by various authors such as Giovanni Odasso and Gerald O'Collins.[9]

Pluralism is a relatively recent phenomenon and is influenced by the assumptions of the enlightenment. It argues that salvation is available equally among all religions and that basically all religions relatively have the same goal of introducing human beings into the Real and offering them salvation.

Another expression of this typology can be found in terms of ecclesiocentrism, christocentrism and theocentrism. More recently Paul Knitter has described this typology in the following way: The Replacement Model ('Only One True Religion'), the Fulfilment Model ('The One Fulfils the Many'), the Mutuality Model ('Many True Religions called to Dialogue'), and the Acceptance Model ('Many True Religions: So Be It').[10]

b. Discussion among Theologians

In 1986, the year in which the religions of the world gathered in Assisi at the invitation of John Paul II, a symposium was held in California and most of the papers were subsequently published as *The Myth of Christian Uniqueness.*[11] The thesis put forward in this collection was one of radical pluralism: all religions are equally valid and important; Christianity is one among many religions; the salvation offered by Christ is equally available in other religions; and Jesus is presented simply as one Saviour among others. The argument advanced in favour of this thesis is three-fold. It is suggested, due to the culturally conditioned character of religions, it is impossible to evaluate the truth-claims of different religions. Second, the mystery of God is incomprehensible and therefore no religion can claim to have the final word. Third, the existence of so much suffering and injustice in the world today, sometimes caused by the exclusivist claims of different religions, is a direct challenge to all religions of the world. By adopting a pluralist understanding of religions there is a better opportunity for religions to work together towards the elimination of so much suffering and injustices in the world.

In 1990, a critique of this position was offered in a collection of papers edited by Gavin D'Costa entitled *Christian Uniqueness Reconsidered: The Myth of a Pluralistic Theology of Religions*[12] The contributors to this collection express dissatisfaction with the pluralist proposals put forward in *The Myth of Christian Uniqueness*. The argument against radical pluralism comes from Trinitarian Theology, Christology and hermeneutical theory. Many contributors note that the case in favour of pluralism often ends up being just as imperialistic as the criticised positions of inclusivism and exclusivism. While this controversy continues within the academy, there is growing concern among all Christian Churches about the relationship between Christianity and the world religions.

In 1996, Cardinal Joseph Ratzinger, then prefect of the Congregation for the Doctrine of the Faith (hereafter CDF), suggested that there is a direct connection between relativism and the pluralistic theology of religion put forward by John Hick and Paul Knitter.[13] Cardinal Ratzinger notes a growing presence of relativism in biblical exegesis, in liturgical celebrations, and in attitudes towards dogma today. He finds certain parallel between relativism and the emphasis on praxis in liberation theology and New Age religions. John Hick claims that Ratzinger has misrepresented him.[14] Some months after Ratzinger's article, the International Theological Commission published a wide-ranging document entitled 'Christianity and World Religions'.[15] This document acknowledges the importance of inter-religious dialogue within theology today and seeks to critique different expressions of religious pluralism while defending the uniqueness of Christ and the mission of the Church in the world.

c. Interventions by the Catholic Church

In 2000, the CDF issued *Dominus Iesus: On the Unicity and Salvific Universality of Jesus Christ and the Church*. This document, as seen in the last chapter, while controversial from an ecumenical and inter-religious point of view, did call for further reflection on dialogue with other religions. According to Cardinal Ratzinger, who signed the document, *Dominus Iesus* is a response to 'the growing presence of confused and erroneous ideas and opinions both within the church generally and in certain theological circles concerning the universality of the salvific event of Jesus Christ, the unicity and unity of the church.'[16] In particular, the document addresses 'errors' and 'ambiguities' in the area of inter-religious dialogue, and speaks out against the dangers of religious relativism: 'If it is true that the followers of other religions can receive divine grace, it is also certain that, *objectively* speaking, they are in a gravely deficient situation in comparison to those who, in the church, have the fullness of the means of salvation.'[17]

In January 2001, the CDF issued a short 'Notification on the book *Towards a Christian Theology of Religious Pluralism* by Jacques Dupuis'. In the Preface, the CDF acknowledges 'the author's willingness to provide necessary clarifications, as evident in his responses, as well as his desire to remain faithful to the doctrine of the Church and the teaching of the Magisterium.' The Notification then goes on to say the book contains 'notable ambiguities and difficulties on important doctrinal points which could lead a reader to erroneous or harmful opinions' (Preface). The Notification lists five areas of concern:

i. *On the sole and universal salvific mediation of Jesus*
    It states that 'the salvific action of the Word is accomplished in and through Jesus Christ, the Incarnate Son of God, as mediator of salvation for all humanity' (a.2). It rejects any 'separation between the Word and Jesus, or between the Word's salvific activity and that of Jesus' (a.2) or any 'activity of the Word as such in his divinity, independent of the humanity of the Incarnate Word' (a.2).

ii. On the unicity and completeness of the Revelation of Jesus Christ

Here it affirms 'that Jesus Christ is the mediator, the fulfilment and completeness of salvation' and 'is therefore contrary to the Catholic Faith to maintain that Revelation in Jesus Christ is limited, incomplete or imperfect' (a.3). It does acknowledge, however, that full 'knowledge of divine Revelation will be had only on the day of the Lord's Coming in Glory' (a.3). In the meantime the historical Revelation of Jesus Christ offers 'everything necessary for man's salvation, and has no need of completion by other religions' (a.3). It notes that the seeds of truth and goodness in other religions 'are a certain participation in truths contained in the revelation of or in Jesus Christ' (a.4).

iii. On the universal salvific action of the Holy Spirit

The Holy Spirit, working after the resurrection of Jesus, is always the Spirit of Christ sent by the Father, who works in a salvific way in Christians as well as non-Christians. Thus, the action of the Holy Spirit is exercised through the one universal salvific economy of the Incarnate Word (a.5).

iv. On the orientation of all human beings to the Church

The Church is the sign and instrument of salvation for all people and therefore other religions cannot be regarded as ways of salvation complementary to the Church.

v. On the value and salvific function of religious traditions

Whatever the Spirit brings about in the hearts of other people and religions 'serves as a preparation for the Gospel' (*Lumen Gentium*, a.16). While the Holy Spirit may accomplish salvation in non-Christians through elements of truth and goodness, it cannot be held that these religions, as such, are ways of salvation, or that they 'can be considered as complementary to the Old Testament, which is the immediate preparation for the Christ-event' (a.8).

In June 2007, the Committee on Doctrine of the US Conference of Bishops issued a statement entitled 'Clarifications required by the book *Being Religious Inter-religiously: Asian Perspectives on Interfaith Dialogue* by Rev. Peter C. Phan'. This particular book is one of a trilogy on inter-religious dialogue by Peter Phan. The Statement from the US Bishops seeks to 'identify problematic aspects of the book and provide a re-statement of Catholic Teaching on relevant points' (a.3). However, a summary of the statement by the Bishops may help to locate the on-going debate about the relationship of Christianity to other religions.

It would be impossible to do full justice to the statement of the US Bishops' Doctrinal Committee or indeed the contents of the book by Peter Phan.

The statement addresses three areas of concern:

i.   *Jesus Christ as unique and universal Saviour of Humankind*
     The Doctrinal Committee claims that Phan's book 'could leave readers in considerable confusion as to the proper understanding of the uniqueness of Christ' (a.9). To counter any misunderstanding in this area, the statement summarises the teaching of the Church pertinent to Phan's book, especially as laid out in *Dominus Iesus*.

     On the Christological level, the statement notes that any suggestion that Jesus is merely one among many historical figures who reveals the Mystery of God is rejected. It is 'necessary ... to reassert the definitive and complete character of the Revelation of Jesus Christ ... In the Mystery of Jesus Christ, the Incarnate Son of God ... the full Revelation of Divine Faith is given' (*Dominus Iesus*, a.5).

On the soteriological level, the statement says that 'Jesus Christ ... is God the Father's definitive and universal means of salvation' (a.13). Further, quoting the encyclical of John Paul II, *Redemptoris Missio*, the statement notes that 'Christ's own universal mediation ... is the way established by God himself ... although participative forms of mediation of different kinds and degrees are not excluded, they acquire meaning and value only from Christ's own mediation, and they cannot be understood as parallel or complementary to his' (*Redemptoris Missio*, a.5). The salvation offered by Christ is 'unique and singular, proper to him alone, exclusive, universal and absolute' (*Dominus Iesus*, a.5). Whatever salvation comes through other religions 'is always accomplished in the same way through Christ' (a.14).

ii. *The salvific significance of non-Christian religions*

The document acknowledges, following the teaching of Vatican II, that there are elements of goodness and truth in the religions, and sees these as preparatory to the Gospel of Jesus Christ. It then criticises Phan's view that 'non-Christian religions possess an autonomous function in history' (a.17) and that the non-Christian religions are alternative ways of salvation and, therefore, are part of God's providential plan of salvation (a.19). Two issues arise here. On the one hand, by affirming the autonomy of non-Christian religions, their relatedness to Christ is called into question. On the other hand, by seeing other religions as ways of salvation, the idea of Christian mission is put in jeopardy (a.21).

The Committee also criticises Phan's proposal on 'multiple-religious-belonging' as something 'not only possible but also desirable' (a.25). Equally, the Committee reacts against the suggestion that there is a two-way relationship of complementarity and correction between

Christianity and other religions. The suggestion that other religions can complement or correct Christianity is rejected.

These views of Phan on the saving significance of other religions, it is claimed, are caused by his adoption of a universal perspective on religions at the expense of a specifically Christian view, even though the Committee acknowledges that Phan repudiates the possibility of constructing a universal theology of religions (a.25).

iii. *The Church as unique and universal instrument of Salvation*

In this section, the document criticises Phan's suggestion that the doctrine of the uniqueness and universality of the Church, in view of its history of light and darkness, 'should be abandoned altogether'. The document acknowledges that the Church is a human institution, but it also asserts that it is a divine institution. It notes that 'Jesus, the Incarnate Son of God, in accordance with his Father's will, instituted the Church through his life, death and resurrection' (a.28). Further, 'Jesus sent the Holy Spirit ... upon the disciples and from that moment the Spirit became the source of the Church's life and holiness' (a.28). The holiness of the Church is defined not by its members but by the holiness of her head, the Lord Jesus Christ who 'imbues the Church with his Holy Spirit' (a.29). The Church, as divinely instituted, is 'the universal sacrament of Salvation' and, as such, 'all grace flows from our Lord and Saviour through his Church' and therefore the Church cannot be presented as just one way of salvation alongside other religions (a.31).

The document concludes by noting that while *'Being Religious Inter-religiously* addresses a number of issues that are crucial in the life of the contemporary Church, it contains ambiguities and equivocations that could easily confuse or mislead the faithful, as well as statements that, unless properly clarified, are not in accord with Catholic teaching.'

This thumbnail sketch of the debate about the relationship between Christianity and the world religions simply serves to highlight the theological urgency of the issues at stake. Questions about Christian identity in the presence of other religions will not be resolved merely by reaffirming the Christological tradition, nor will progress be made by ignoring that particular tradition. Instead account must be taken of the new historic context in which these questions arise.

2. A CRITIQUE OF THE THREE-FOLD TYPOLOGY

There can be no doubt that the three-fold typology of exclusivism, inclusivism and pluralism has helped to sharpen the focus of this debate in the last three decades. However, many hold the time has come to move beyond this stage of inter-religious dialogue, which might be labelled as 'phase one', into a more flexible framework. Most commentators hold that these categories have outlived their usefulness. Gavin D'Costa, who once defended them and later described them as 'redundant',[18] now says they have been 'useful, like a raft crossing a river, to get to where we are now' but that we now need to change the angle on them.[19] Charles Matthews refers to them as 'the tired trio of essentially parochial responses'.[20] One of the most serious difficulties with these models is that they advance only marginally the dialogue between religions because they have created premature parameters among participants in the debate. These parameters, each in their own way, have claimed too much.

The problem with exclusivism is that it ends up excluding others, without realising that otherness is an important ingredient in the creation of human identity. On the other hand, inclusivism runs the risk of reducing the other in practice to a mirror image of oneself, even though inclusivism in theory claims to be open to other religions. According to Terrence Tilley, some forms of inclusivism are 'an exclusivism with a happy face'.[21]

a. Critique of Religious Pluralism

The category causing most confusion within the three-fold typology is radical pluralism as proposed by John Hick, Wilfred Cantwell Smith and, to a lesser extent, Paul Knitter. Different versions of radical pluralism have been put forward. John Hick's pluralism, probably the most influential, is based on the Kantian distinction and separation between the noumenal and the phenomenal worlds. The noumenal world cannot be known and yet Hick insists on calling it the Real/Ultimate Reality, whereas the phenomenal world is made up of 'our conceptual frameworks' which merely represent a human response to the Real.[22] Hick does not countenance any formal theology of revelation or any form of personal communication from God to humanity and as a result ends up reducing the Incarnation of God in Jesus to the level of a 'myth'. Consequently all religions are treated as more or less equally valid responses to the Real. As James Fredericks concludes, differences among the religions become 'religiously ..., and theologically insignificant' and end up being domesticated.[23]

Another version of pluralism is found in Wilfred Cantwell Smith's writings who takes an historical and existentialist approach to pluralism. Underlying the continuum of all religions is the fundamental presence of faith and a variety of different belief systems. These different religious belief systems are expressions of one and the same fundamental faith. It is questionable that it is possible to make such a sharp dichotomy between faith and belief or indeed that Cantwell intends such a dualism. It is impossible to have faith without some content.[24]

A third type of pluralism is found in the work of Paul Knitter. According to Knitter, religions are eco-ethical responses of one kind or another designed to promote the praxis of peace, justice and liberation in our world. Knitter's position, however, is continuously refined through ongoing engagement with other theologians and other religions.[25]

These philosophical, historical and ethical versions of pluralism represent explanations of what different religions are all about.

These different theories of radical pluralism amount to one and the same vision. They put forward a meta-theory of religion which is heavily indebted to the enlightenment critique of Christianity. This meta-theory presumes a God's eye view of all religions, a superior, detached and independent perception of what takes place beyond the particularities of various historical traditions. In the light of this view of religions, participants are invited to cross a 'theological rubicon' and to engage in inter-religious dialogue on what is often referred to as 'a level playing field'.[26] This radical pluralism has provoked serious criticism from many different theologians. For example, Terrence Merrigan finds religious pluralism guilty of a certain 'elitism', claiming 'a privileged vantage point from which it is able to pronounce on any and every religious tradition.' Further, Merrigan argues that religious pluralism 'can provide no convincing account of why one should commit oneself to any particular religious disciplines.'[27]

The invitation to dialogue on 'a level playing field' is hardly an invitation to dialogue but rather the imposition of one particular view of religion – a view which seems to ignore the history, theology and sociology of religions. The only reason participants want to be on the same 'playing field' is because it contains such interesting religious valleys and theological peaks – and not because it is level, which would be a rather dull place to be!

One of the principle difficulties with radical pluralism is the way it reduces all religions to some nondescript, lowest common denominator or universal essence which has no direct relationship to the particularities of historical religions. Stephen Duffy points out that this radical pluralism melts down all religious differences and filters out the dense particularities of religions which have fired passions and energised the wills of believers down through the centuries.[28] Gavin D'Costa notes that the logic of this radical pluralism is ironically the creation of a new kind of exclusivism because it depends on 'tradition specific criteria' taken from the enlightenment.[29] David Cheetham argues that the real problem with this pluralistic theology of religions is that it lacks personal passion, feeling and commitment in the name of objective detachment whereas it is precisely these elements that make religion something worth living and dying for.[30]

According to Lieven Boeve and others, the problem with radical pluralism is that it relativises the particular truth-claims of Christianity and reduces the historical Incarnation of God in Jesus to the level of 'a myth' in the perjorative sense of that word. In effect, the Incarnation is absorbed into or reduced to a general religious truth determined by pluralism such as the unbridgeable gap between the Noumenon and the phenomena. The historical specificity of the Christ-event is subordinated to a more universal view of religion.[31]

b. The Legitimacy of Theological Pluralism

In rejecting the radical pluralism put forward by Hick, Smith and Knitter, it is important not to reject all pluralism. Pluralism is a self-evident, given reality of life that derives from the uniqueness of every human being, the historicity of human existence, and the diversity of human understanding. Not all differences are necessarily conflictual or contradictory. Many differences can be complementary and enriching. One of the most significant moments at the Second Vatican Council was the movement beyond a conceptual monolith to a recognition of theological diversity as a positive value.[32] This breakthrough has been followed up in a variety of Church documents,[33] culminating in the 1985 Extraordinary Synod of Bishops in Rome which talked about 'the true theological principle of variety and pluriformity in unity' as 'a genuine richness' inviting 'true catholicity'.[34] A distinction therefore must be made between radical religious pluralism which ends in relativism and theological pluralism that is grounded in the underlying unity of God's revelation in history and the living tradition of Christianity. This latter pluralism is a pluralism-within-unity, or as some prefer, diversity-within-communion. There is a difference between relativism and pluralism. Relativism, often invoked in the name of tolerance, does not require people to know anything or to do anything new; it leaves the human situation as it finds it and frequently leads to indifferentism. In contrast, pluralism demands an understanding and appreciation of difference and otherness within the praxis of dialogue. Pluralism, in contrast to relativism, challenges people to struggle with otherness and differences.

3. MOVING BEYOND THE IMPASSE

There is an emerging consensus around the need to move beyond the three-fold typology. Some degree of flexibility and fluidity between Exclusivism and Inclusivism and Pluralism is recommended. All three contain grains of truth and not a little distortion of each other. For example, it should be recognised that all religions, not just Christianity, see themselves as unique, exclusive and superior to other religions; they would hardly exist otherwise. Equally, religions see themselves as somehow related to other religions, but ultimately they regard themselves as different.

Further, we must begin to recognise that there is an element of irreducibility within most religions and that, therefore, the other cannot be reduced to more of the same, with merely a different external coating. Pluralism is a reality that exists both within particular religions and between religions. Not all forms of pluralism lead to relativism. In discussing pluralism, a distinction must be made, as already noted, between theological pluralism and the radical religious pluralism of John Hick. It also needs to be recognised that there is no such thing as a religious Esperanto and that therefore religions have their own linguistic forms and that religions only exist as embodied in particular historical, cultural and linguistic forms.[35]

a. Inclusive Pluralism

Christianity has the inner resources to move beyond the current impasse in dialogue by drawing on the teaching of the Second Vatican Council summarised in Chapter Two, namely that there are elements of Truth and Grace in other religions, that the seeds of the Word are, as Justin Martyr put it, scattered in other cultures and religions, that the Spirit of God is present in the world and religions, that a ray of the Truth that enlightens all can be found in other religions. In moving beyond the impasse, we do well also to remember that the Bible recognises the existence of other covenants besides the Jewish and Christian covenant, such as the more universal covenant with Noah. For Christians, it should be noted that discipleship of Christ requires the praxis of dialogue if we are to follow in his footsteps. Moreover, for Christians, while the Christ-event is God's final and definitive self-communication of God to the world, nonetheless there is something still outstanding and unfinished about the Christ-event. This was recognised by the earliest Christians in their prayer, *Maranatha, Come Lord Jesus*, and was spelt out by Paul in his theology of the dynamic that exists between the 'already' and the 'not-yet'. In addition, it is worth observing that this early eschatological consciousness was formulated by the early Church in its creedal statement about the Second Coming of Christ. As David Tracy reminds us, the Incarnation must be balanced by an equal emphasis on the *Parousia*.[36]

Jacques Dupuis sought to go beyond the current impasse by proposing what he calls 'inclusive Pluralism'. This category is intended by Dupuis to combine two fundamental affirmations which, though apparently in contradiction, must be seen as complementary: 'the universal constitutive character of the Christ-event in the order of salvation and the saving significance of religious traditions in a plurality of religious traditions within the one manifold plan of God for mankind.'[37] Dupuis is happy to have his position described by his reviewers as a *via media* between Inclusivism and Pluralism, or as one reviewer puts it, 'a *via media* between the pluralist position (irreconcilable with Christian faith and Catholic doctrine) and the pluralist position of Catholic theology before and after the Council (cf. Karl Rahner).'[38]

Dupuis develops his framework of 'inclusive pluralism' by insisting, in his books, articles and his review of the reviewers that he holds together in unity the action of the Word of God in creation and history alongside the action of the Word Incarnate in Jesus, and that these two actions belong to the unity of the one economy of salvation revealed in Christ. He further insists that the work of God continues to be active in creation and history after the Incarnation – but always in virtue of the Word Incarnate in Jesus.[39] In arguing for 'inclusive pluralism', Dupuis moves from a position of *de facto* pluralism to a position of pluralism in principle, that is a pluralism *de iure*, which prompts him to see pluralism as a part of God's plan of salvation. According to some reviewers, it is the word 'pluralism' within 'inclusive pluralism' that gave concern to some of his critics.

b. Universal-Access Exclusivism

A second proposal for going forward beyond the three-fold typology is recommended by Gavin D'Costa in his book *Christianity and World Religions* (2009). D'Costa's proposal, while different to that of Dupuis, is what he describes as 'Universal-access Exclusivism'. D'Costa is concerned to address questions about what happens to the large numbers of people who are unevangelised. D'Costa sees his position as 'required to preserve the truth of Revelation'.[40] This position, says D'Costa, is governed by four different rules.

The first rule says that those who have not heard the Gospel will be given a chance to hear the Gospel of Christ and to respond to it at the point of death or in a post-mortem state or through reincarnation or through purgatory. The second rule is that God knows in advance who would or would not accept the Gospel among the unevangelised and therefore God applies that Gospel even if the person never knew the Gospel during his or her lifetime. A third rule states we cannot and do not know how God will reach the unevangelised who are to be saved, and this is ultimately a matter of mystery. A fourth rule is that explicit faith and baptism are the normal means to salvation. Other means may act as a preparation to salvation such as natural Revelation or the voice of conscience or even different elements within other religions – all of which can lead to salvation.

Having stated these four rules relating to 'Universal-access Exclusivism', D'Costa expresses his own reservations about rules two and three. Basically, D'Costa's position is summed up in rules one and four. He believes his position represents 'the official Catholic position' and can be found in 'a wide number of Catholic, Orthodox, Reform and

Protestant theologians'.[41] Further, he argues his position holds 'together a wide range of doctrinal teachings that constitute orthodoxies'.[42] D'Costa believes that his position allows for the salvation of the evangelised without affirming other religions as a means to salvation. And yet, he claims it can recognise positive elements within other religions.[43]

A third proposal for going beyond the impasse of the three-fold typology is presented by Paul Griffiths. Griffiths wishes to develop the inclusivist approach by distinguishing between what he calls an 'open inclusivism' and a 'closed inclusivism'. An 'open inclusivism' recognises that other religions may 'teach truths of religious significance for the Church; and that some of these are not explicitly taught or understood by the Church.' On the other hand, 'closed inclusivism holds that all alien religious truths, should there be any, are already known to and explicitly taught by the Church.'[44]

4. THE DIALOGICAL IMPERATIVE OF VATICAN II

One of the most striking themes permeating the documents of the Second Vatican Council is that of the call to dialogue. The word 'dialogue' more than any other captures the spirit of the Second Vatican Council.

a. Paul VI on Dialogue and Vatican II

The adoption of dialogue came about through the influence of Paul VI at the council. At a fragile time, between the first and second session, when Paul VI took over after the death of John XXIII (June 1963), many Council documents were unfinished. In his opening address to the Second Session (1963), Paul VI encouraged the bishops to engage in dialogue with the world. A year later he wrote his first encyclical, *On Dialogue* (*Ecclesiam Suam*, November 1964). In that encyclical, Paul VI gave decisive direction to the Council at a time when it needed new direction. Commentators are agreed on the importance of this encyclical for understanding the documents of Vatican II. For example, according to Riccardo Burigana and Giovanni Turbanti, Paul VI intimated to Pierre Haubtmann at a meeting in February 1965 that the 'inspiring principle [in *Gaudium et Spes*] should be dialogue, and the entire document ought to be almost a continuum of the dialogue with the world that he had begun in his encyclical *Ecclesiam Suam*.[45] Others have described *Ecclesiam Suam* as 'a programmatic encyclical' of 'historical value' that had its most direct influence on *Gaudium et Spes*.[46] According to US historian John O'Malley: 'The encyclical had a direct impact on the Council in one important regard, the remarkable prominence it gave to dialogue ... the encyclical infused the word [dialogue] into the Council's vocabulary.'[47]

The influence of *Ecclesiam Suam* is most evident in *Gaudium et Spes,* which advocates dialogue between the church and the world, between the church and society, between the church and culture, between the church and atheism, between the church and non-believers. Of particular interest is the way in which *Gaudium et Spes* discusses what the church has to offer the world and what the church receives from the world, recognising that the 'church ... has benefitted and is still benefitting from the opposition of its enemies and persecutors.'[48] This broad framework between the church and the world was to influence the equally important dialogue between the Catholic Church and other churches and between the Church and other religions.

The theme of dialogue, including the dialogue that promotes a mutuality of understanding between the church and the world,[49] is continued in the post-conciliar period as seen in Chapter Two. In the context of dialogue with other religions, over and above *Nostra Aetate*, reference must be made to *Dialogue and Mission* (1984), *The Permanent Validity of the Church's Missionary Mandate* (1991), and *Dialogue and Proclamation* (1991). If there is a tension surrounding the reception of Vatican II and the proper interpretation of Vatican II, it is partly due to the fact that insufficient attention has been given to the development of a theology of dialogue, and in particular to the hermeneutics that should inform the practice of dialogue.

A number of issues stand out that require clarification: the nature of dialogue, how do we model dialogue, does dialogue lead to relativism. What is needed is a theology of dialogue in the first instance, and then the application of that particular theology to inter-religious dialogue.

b. Elements within a Theology of Dialogue

The first step in working out a theology of dialogue is to recognise the anthropological foundations of dialogue. It is only in and through dialogue that we come to know who we are. The human self is thoroughly dialogical in origin and destiny. We do not come into the world with a ready-made self. The self emerges out of dialogical engagement between parents and that dialogue in turn gives rise to the birth of a child who is shaped by dialogical engagement between parents and offspring. Over time, a human self emerges who continues to depend on dialogue. The self is a dialogical work-in-progress.

One of the most fundamental points about dialogue is that it is only in and through dialogue that we come to know who we are. It is through encounter with the other, especially the otherness of the other, that we come to understand who we are. This applies to both human identity and religious identity. The human is, at its most primordial level and its most developed stage, essentially a dialogical reality. The development of a sense of self is a work-in-progress which is only completed in death. Walter Kasper points out that 'It is the countenance of the other, in confronting the otherness of the other, that we discover ourselves. Not only do we undertake dialogue, we are dialogue.'[50] Dialogical interaction is at the foundation of human existence.

The second foundation in developing a theology of dialogue is to recognise the dialogical character of revelation, which will be developed in Chapter Six. It is sufficient to note here that revelation is the story of God's dialogue with humanity, initiated through the gift of the Spirit poured out on all flesh in the story of creation (Gen 1:1), a dialogue that for Christians reaches a point of completion in the Christ-event and continues in the light of the Christ-event to take place through the agency of the Spirit in the Christian community and the world. This dialogue between God and humanity is apparent 'in many and various ways' through the plurality of religions. What is key in this second step of a theology of dialogue is that the Being/Self of God is dialogical, not only reaching out to humanity in history, but also disclosing the nature of God as dialogical in terms of Father, Son and Spirit.

In the context of inter-religious dialogue, it needs to be stated that God has initiated a dialogue between God and humanity in history through the religions. This divine dialogue is inaugurated in the gift of creation and human existence: through the grace of the Holy Spirit given to all and the unfolding of God's self-revelation in history. The self-communication of God to humanity is found in the 'law written in the heart', in the voice of conscience, in the seeds of the Word of God scattered though out creation, in the action of the Spirit in the history of the religions of the world. Within this dialogue in history, there is respect for otherness, freedom from coercion, and enrichment from difference

The third step in shaping a theology of dialogue is the recognition of how dialogue is a key element in the self-understanding of the Church at Vatican II: *ad intra* in terms of the call to the collegiality among bishops and the Bishop of Rome, collaboration between theologians and bishops, co-responsibility with laity, and *ad extra* in terms of engagement with other churches, members of non-Christian religions, and non-believers.[51]

A fourth foundation in developing a theology of dialogue is to recognise the pneumatological grounds of dialogue. As we will see in Chapter Seven, all have been graced by the gift of the Spirit, poured out on all flesh in creation and history. The biblical tradition testifies to numerous individuals 'filled with the Spirit'. Part of the legacy of John Paul II to inter-religious dialogue was his articulation of the universal gift of the Spirit offered to all: 'not only individuals but also society and history, peoples, cultures and religions.'[52]

What is missing in the understanding of dialogue at Vatican II and in the post-conciliar period is a grasp of the implications of what authentic dialogue demands of the participants. A seed is sown on the nature of dialogue in *Gaudium et Spes* when in discussing dialogue with others, including other religions, it employs the image of 'conversation'.[53]

c. Dialogue as Conversation

The image of dialogue as 'conversation' has been developed extensively by Hans-Georg Gadamer, and taken up in turn by David Tracy and Charles Taylor. For Gadamer, the best way to understand a text, a work of art, an event in history, another person, and by implication another religion, is through the analogy of conversation. There is a movement back and forth between the participants that leads to new understanding. The conversation is led by the subject matter and not by the individuals. According to Gadamer:

> Conversation is a process of coming to an understanding. Thus it belongs to every true conversation that each person opens himself to the other, truly accepts his point of view as valid and transposes himself into the other to such an extent that he understands not the particular individual, but what he says.[54]

Within this exchange it is important at some stage for Gadamer that the participants in the conversation examine the role 'prejudices' play in understanding, and if needs be that these 'prejudices' be reviewed in the light of the conversation through further engagement.

David Tracy, influenced by Gadamer, likens good conversation to a 'game' in which 'we free ourselves from ourselves, however briefly'[55] and thereby become absorbed in the search for truth. In authentic conversation 'we are freed from epistemological solipsisms for a dialogical life with others and with all classics.'[56] According to Tracy, 'without conversation' there is 'no manifestation' of truth.[57] This manifestation of truth can take place in a variety of dialogical encounters: 'in watching a film, in listening to music, in looking at a painting, in participating in a religious ritual, in reading a classical text, in conversation with friends, or in finding oneself in love.'[58] Tracy readily admits that authentic conversation is difficult to achieve, indeed quite rare. For conversation to be authentic, there must be openness, a willingness to risk one's present self-understanding in the face and presence of the other.

Charles Taylor summarises Gadamer's contribution to a philosophy of dialogue under three headings: understanding as bilateral, as party-dependent, and as requiring a renewed understanding of ourselves.[59] Dialogue as bilateral seeks to go beyond the kind of objective understanding that takes place in science: controlling, detached and 'objective'. In contrast, dialogue seeks to effect a process of mutual understanding that impacts on both parties. This kind of conversation is premised on the spirit of openness on both sides, and this openness is driven by a search for truth.

Second, Taylor emphasises that dialogue is party-dependent. This means that it is necessary to clarify the underlying assumptions and 'prejudices' that exist among both participants in the conversation. Only when these are allowed to surface will real understanding take place.

Third, Taylor highlights the need within authentic conversation for participants to be open to the possibility of changing perspectives. This will only happen when what Gadamer calls a 'fusion of horizons' takes place, which enables participants to move to a new place. Taylor sums up this with his own particular slogan: 'No understanding the other without a changed understanding of the self.'[60]

If these perspectives on dialogue as conversation highlight some of the challenges involved in inter-religious dialogue, they also indicate the fruits that can be derived from authentic conversation: transformation of personal 'prejudice', mutual understanding, personal enrichment, two-way respect, new learning, insight into the identity of the other, and a deepening of one's own religious identity. If there is to be progress in the dialogue among religions in the service of peace, mutual respect and appreciation, it will be informed by the principles outlined by Gadamer, Tracy and Taylor. In the light of the commitment by the Second Vatican Council to dialogue for mutual understanding between Christianity and the other religions, the Catholic Church must now learn the art of good conversation. If fruitful conversation is to take place, there should be some guideline for participants. The following represents what these guidelines might look like.

d. Guidelines for Dialogue

A first, introductory guideline for dialogue is respect for the integrity of the religious tradition of the other. There should be an acceptance of the good will of the other, unless there is compelling evidence to the contrary. Equally, there should be an acknowledgment of the intrinsic value of the religious commitment of the other. One of the goals of dialogue is to get some insight into the integrity of the other's religion and discover what it is that drives and motivates the commitment of the other. The document *Dialogue and Proclamation* points out that 'Christians must remember that God has also manifested himself in some way to the followers of other religious traditions. Consequently, it is with receptive minds that they approach the convictions and values of others.'[61] This underlying respect for integrity of the other's position is of course mutual.

A second guideline for dialogue is that there must be a genuine openness to the other and an acceptance that this openness can lead to new understanding. David Tracy suggests 'we must allow the truth of the other to become … a genuine possibility for oneself.'[62] To ignore otherness is to close oneself off from one of the primary sources for understanding the otherness of God in the world. Lying behind this openness to the other is a growing awareness that we are not all the same and that many of the differences that exist, especially religious differences, need not be conflictual or divisive but rather dialectical and analogical.

Openness to the other will only happen if there is awareness that every religious tradition, including Christianity, has within itself a certain ambiguity and incompleteness and absence. Such awareness can act as a check against inflated claims. Christians would do well to remember that at the very centre of Christianity there is an eschatological tension between what is and is not, between the already and the not yet, between what is given in Christ and is yet to come symbolised in the doctrine of the second coming of Christ.

There is, therefore, an important sense in which it must be said that Christianity defines itself as much by what it lacks as by what it has, or as much by what it is not as what it is, or as much by what is absent as what is present. There is an awareness within Christian faith and practice that there is something missing, and it is this that drives the passion of Christian faith for more in its religious relationships with others, the stranger and the religions. As Michel de Certeau, the French Jesuit, notes: 'Rather than the presence, it is the absence which makes things happen; actions occur because of what is lacking.'[63]

This does not mean that Christianity abandons its claim or waters down its conviction about the fullness of God's self-revelation in the Christ-event. Rather, it is in virtue of the unique revelation of God in the Christ-event that Christian faith seeks to make up what is missing and to complete what is unfinished in the Christian narrative. Jesus of Nazareth inaugurated the reign of God, realised that reign of God through his death and resurrection, and established the reign of *God in embryo* at Pentecost through the outpouring of the Holy Spirit. It was in the midst of this unfolding experience of the reign of God that the first Christian prayer uttered was *Maranatha*, Come Lord Jesus, and the Church today continues to proclaim that insight by announcing in its celebration of the Eucharist that 'Christ has died, Christ is risen, and Christ will come again'. The Christian narrative is an open narrative, and as *Nostra Aetate* puts it: 'The Church awaits the day, known only to God alone, when all people will call on God with one voice and "serve Him shoulder to shoulder" (Soph 3:9; cf. Is 66:23; Ps 65:4; Rom 11:11-32).'[64] Our knowledge and understanding of the Christ-event continues to grow and develop, conscious that there is always more to the mystery of Christ than we can grasp in this life. Similarly the practice of discipleship of Christ, of the crucified and risen Christ, now present as the Spirit of Christ in the Church as sacrament, seeks continuous clarification and deeper understanding:

121

'it is vectored towards a not yet' all the time.[65] It is the experience of new life in Christ and the vector towards the not yet that drives the dialogue with other religions.

A third guideline for participants in inter-religious dialogue is the need to adopt a greater sense of theological humility in approaching other religions. What we know about God is extremely limited. Augustine reminds us that if we have fully understood, then it is no longer God. Aquinas states starkly, 'we cannot know what God is, but only what God is not.' Rahner speaks frequently about the sheer incomprehensibility of God. Panikkar is right to insist that theological discourse 'is radically different from discourse about anything else' and as such 'completes itself ... in a new silence.'[66] This does not mean that we should enter into religious dialogue with a purely negative theology but it does demand we begin with a greater degree of humility on all sides which will guard participants from adopting inflated claims in their points of departure. It is salutary for Christians to recover this forgotten dimension of their tradition. All too often the claims of Christianity are misunderstood as much from the inside as from the outside. A delicate balance must be maintained between what we know and do not know about God, between a theology of divine presence and absence, between a vision about the transcendence of God and the immanence of God. This means, in effect, that genuine inter-religious dialogue will include an important moment of mutual insight summed up in terms of a learned ignorance (*docta ignorantia*) which is the beginning of wisdom.

Another way of expressing this awareness of ambiguity and incompleteness within one's own tradition is to admit the presence of a 'holy unrest' or dissatisfaction with all theological statements. There is a sense in which every statement about religion/the ultimate/God is inadequate and it is this among other things that drives religious dialogue in the hope of purifying, deepening, and transforming theological understanding. Awareness of the incomprehensibility of God does not necessarily lead to the relativism implicit in the radical pluralism of John Hick. To the contrary there can be no appreciation of incomprehensibility of God without some theological understanding.

A fourth guideline is that the conduct of inter-religious dialogue should not be reduced to a polite cultural exchange as if religion were simply just another cultural creation – a view that seems to be lurking in the background of radical pluralism. Religion is at least a response to something that is given in life, something that is not created but found, something not invented but discovered, something that is prior to personal interpretation or projection. Further this 'something' should not be pitted against the human or set up in conflict with the human or presented as opposed to the human. Instead religion, in spite of so much historical evidence to the contrary, is ultimately that which constitutes the human in existence. Religions seek to defend human dignity, to enable human beings to flourish, and to bring out what is best in humanity in ways which would not otherwise happen. To this extent it can be said that most religions if not all seek to promote/liberate/save the *humanum* and therefore lay claim to some form of healing and wholeness. The search for salvation therefore is one of key themes animating inter-religious dialogue.

A fifth guideline is that it should be borne in mind that dialogue is driven by different ideologies and prejudices, and that these should be brought to the fore, acknowledged and purified at some stage in the dialogue. For example the specifically modern ideology of claiming scientific neutrality and a value free stance within dialogue is something that has been called into question and is seen to be itself a particular claim – a view now accepted by many philosophers of science. Genuine dialogue does not require participants to abandon deeply held religious convictions; rather it is the existence of deeply held commitments that motivates dialogue. As Stephen Duffy points out so accurately, we do not come to the dialogue with empty heads or vacant hearts but rather with clear commitments.[67]

e. Dialogue – A Shared Search for Truth

Inter-religious dialogue seeks to promote a shared search for the truth among the participants. In the encounter with the other there is always the possibility of discovering new truth about oneself and one's religious commitment as well as new truth about the other and their religious commitment. Of course the idea of truth, especially religious truth, is notoriously difficult to describe. Yet the search for truth remains central to dialogue. Without pretending to resolve the question of truth it must be possible to say something about the quality of the truth we seek in dialogue.

All truth, especially religious truth, is one, relational, transformative and dynamic. As one, truth has the capacity to unify people. As relational, truth establishes bonds between people that transcend their differences. As transformative, truth, especially the truth that comes from the other, has power to change people. As dynamic, the truth which emerges within inter-religious dialogue seeks to be universal. This universality of religious truth is bifocal: it embraces an understanding of what is truly human as well as an understanding of the centre of religion variously described as the Ultimate, a 'nothing', the Holy, the Sacred, the *mysterium tremendum et fascinans*, God.

A further quality of religious truth is that it is practical: it arises out of the practice of dialogue and leads to freedom and the praxis of the liberation of others. Religious truth, therefore, is never just another piece of information, never just a mere explanation of the world in which we live, never just a theory about life. The truth of religion therefore is not the truth of empiricism or of science or of 'pure' propositions or geometric statements. Instead religious truth is relational, dynamic and above all participatory. The truth of religion is not available for chemical inspection or clinical observation, but only in and through the experience of personal participation.

Closely related to this last point about personal participation is the link between religious truth and action. Documents from the Catholic Church emphasise that the goal of dialogue is not simply mutual understanding among religions but also the proclamation of the truth of one's faith. There comes a moment within inter-religious dialogue when one must proclaim the truth of one's own faith. This responsibility applies not only to Catholics but also to other participants in dialogue. However, proclaiming the truth of one's faith is more than the assertion of propositional statements of the truth; it is also about witnessing to the truth in word and action. The truth of one's faith is not found only in statements or conceptual systems or particular theological positions but also and more importantly in the power of the truth of one's faith to effect personal change, social transformation and liberation from idolatry. The truth of religions, including Christianity, is ultimately found embodied in the praxis of liberation and salvation.

Another point about religious truth is the need to make a distinction between historical truth and eschatological truth. There is a constant temptation among all religions to confuse the historical truths of their faith with the fullness of truth that awaits all religions at the end of time. There is an important sense in which, as Aquinas puts it, we tend towards the truth without actually controlling or capturing the fullness of religious truth.[68] To be sure, religious truth has been given in the history of Revelation and the truth about God for Christians is given in Jesus as the Christ/the Word made flesh, and this glimpse of God in Christ serves to deepen the search for the fullness of truth about God.

It needs to be stated over and over again that religious truth is not something I find, but rather it finds me; is not something I create, but rather it seizes me; is not something I project, but rather it grasps me; is not something I control, but rather it controls me; is not something of my own making, but rather something that is received; and, therefore, comes ultimately as gift and grace, given and disclosed, manifested and revealed in many and various ways: in creation, in history, in Israel, in the person of Jesus, in the Christian community, in prayer and ritual, in human relationships, and in other religions. David Tracy sums up this point in the following way:

> The realised experience of the truth character of the religious classic is an experience of its purely given character, its status as an event, a happening manifested to my experience, neither determined by nor produced by my subjectivity. Insofar as I honour experience itself, I may accord this experience the

status of a claim to truth as the manifestation of a 'letting be seen' of what is, as it shows itself to experience.[69]

One other point about truth which follows from the last point about religious truth as gift. David Tracy emphasises that 'the truth of religion is, like the truth of its nearest cousin, art, primordially the truth of manifestation.'[70] The value of 'truth as manifestation' is that it approximates more closely with the ideas of 'revelation' or 'enlightenment' or 'luminosity' as found in many religions. In this way it becomes apparent that religious truth is different from truth as correspondence or coherence or empirical verification or falsification. Thus, truth as manifestation reminds us that the revelation of religious truth is often closer to the dynamics at play in aesthetics, coming as a disarming gift, often in surprising ways.

f. Dialogue between the Particular and the Universal

It is important in the context of inter-religious dialogue to keep in mind the following epistemological principle. There is no such thing as religion in general, or the universal essence of religion unalloyed, or pure religion. Religion only exists as embodied in particular historical events and specific cultural forms and interpretations of experience. It is these particular events of history and their cultural expression that catches and communicates one or other universal aspect of religion. A close interplay exists in every religion between the particular and the universal, between the concrete and the absolute, between the local and the global, between personal experience and the interpretation of that experience. It was this particular insight that prompted Paul Tillich to point out that 'culture is the form of religion and religion is the content of culture.'[71]

The more religions move away from their historical particularity, the more likely they are to make exaggerated and inflated claims. As Stephen Duffy notes: 'A faith can survive only if its particularity and universality do not cancel one another as they do in deism and fideism.'[72] The core truths of religion are only available in particular narratives and practices of religion.

This means that the conduct of inter-religious dialogue must attend to the historical evidence, not as an end in itself, but as a vehicle of the universal significance of religion. The historical evidence for most religions, including Christianity, is only available in the fragile memories of religion as embodied in particular texts, traditions and rituals and their contemporary expression. It is important in maintaining this dialectical and self-correcting relationship between the particular and the universal that we go beyond the polarised positions of historicism on the one hand, and religious positivism on the other. Instead, the historical and the theological must be kept together in a balanced relationship that connects with contemporary experience and interpretation. There must be some degree of continuity between history and religion, between the past and the present, between experience and interpretation in the faith and practices of religion.

One of the lessons to be learnt from post-modernity is its appreciation of the importance of the local and the particular. This emphasis arises out of a reaction against the universal claims and the meta-narratives of modernity. However, post-modernity on its own is of limited value since it never gets beyond the particular and the local. What is needed is a critical correlation between the modern and post-modern approaches to religion, an interaction between the Enlightenment and contemporary experience that moves towards the possibility of a second modernity, or a critical modernity.[73] If this move to a new modernity is to succeed, it will need to be more conscious of the structural injustices that afflict modernity. These particular principles have a direct bearing on the self-understanding of Christianity. They have come into play in the many quests, old, new and ongoing, for the particularity of the historical Jesus. In the light of these quests, it can be said that the historical Jesus, the Jesus remembered, is only available in the New Testament proclamation of Jesus of Nazareth as the Christ who is the Word made flesh, and is now embodied in the living tradition and faith practices and teachings of the Christian Church. It is only in the historical particularity of Jesus as remembered in the New Testament witness that Christianity can make claims about the definitive revelation of God in Jesus of Nazareth. It is by attending to the particular historical humanity of Jesus that Christians can begin to talk about the divinity of Jesus. Assertions about the divinity of Jesus are only possible in and through a concentration on the particular humanity of Jesus of Nazareth. It is in the light of the concrete, particular historical life of Jesus that Christian faith confesses the eternal Word of God was uniquely and irrevocably made flesh in Jesus. It was and is this extraordinary claim that prompted theologians in the early centuries to talk about 'the scandal of particularity' that attaches to the doctrine of the Incarnation. This 'scandal of particularity' must continue to shock and disturb. For many of the critics of Christianity such as Jean-Jacques Rousseau and Aldous Huxley, it was the scandal of particularity that forced them to give up on Christianity. The claim that God sought to reveal God's self to the world in a particular figure, at a particular historical time, in a particular place, was too much to accept. What these critics failed to grasp was that the particular could assume universal significance. In seeking to maintain this dialectical relationship between the universal and the particular, Paul Tillich, as one would expect in the light of the above principles, talks about Jesus as the Christ who is 'the concrete universal' of history.

NOTES

1. Gerard O'Connell, 'Doing it the Asian Way', *The Tablet*, 16 May 1998, 647–9
2. Both published by Orbis Books, New York, 1997 and 2002 respectively
3. All three are published by Orbis Books, New York
4. These categories were introduced initially by Alan Race, *Christians and Religious Pluralism: Patterns in the Christian Theology of Religion* (London: SCM Press, 1983) and were adopted very quickly – some would say too quickly – by mainstream theologians
5. Acts 4:12
6. 1 Tim 2:5; see also Tt 3:6-7
7. 1 Cor 15:21; see also Rom 3:23-5
8. Jn 14:6; see also Jn 1:16-17

9. See Giovanni Odasso, *Bibbia e religioni: Prospettive bibliche per la T.* *delle religioni*, Rome: Urbanania University Press, 1998; and Gerald Salvation for All: God's Other Peoples, New York: Oxford Universit

10. Paul Knitter, *Introducing Theologies of Religions*, New York: Orbis Books, 2002

11. Edited by John Hick and Paul Knitter and published by SCM Press, London, 1987

12. Published in 1990 by Orbis Books, New York. An equally telling critique of radical pluralism is offered by S. Mark Heim in *Salvations: Truth and Difference in Religion*, New York: Orbis Books, 1995

13. Cardinal Joseph Ratzinger, 'Relativism, the Central Problem for Faith Today', *Origins*, 31 October 1996

14. John Hick, 'A Response to Cardinal Ratzinger on Religious Pluralism', Reviews in *Religion and Theology*, February 1998, 7–9

15. Available in *Origins*, 14 August 1997, 149–66

16. Joseph Ratzinger, 'Letter to Bishops' Conferences', *Origins*, 14 September 2000, 220

17. *Dominus Iesus*, a.22; italics in original

18. Gavin D'Costa 'The Impossibility of a Pluralistic View of Religions', *Religious Studies*, 32 (1996), 223–32 at 223

19. Gavin D'Costa, *Christianity and World Religions: Disputed Questions in the Theology of Religions*, Oxford: Wiley-Blackwell, 2009, 34

20. Charles Mathewes, 'Pluralism, Otherness, and the Augustinian Tradition', *Modern Theology*, 14, January 1998, 83–112 at 86

21. Terrence Tilley, in Terrence W. Tilley et al., *Religious Diversity and the American Experience: A Theological Approach*, New York: Continuum, 2007, 88–91

22. John Hick, *An Interpretation of Religion: The Challenge of Other Religions*, Oxford: Oxford University Press, 1989, 246

23. James L. Fredericks, *Faith Among Faiths: Christian Theology and Non-Christian Religions*, New York: Paulist Press, 1999, 113

24. See Dermot A. Lane, *The Experience of God: An Invitation to do Theology*, revised edition, Dublin: Veritas, 2003, Ch. 3

25. See Knitter, *Introducing Theologies of Religions*, and *Without Buddha I could not be a Christian*, New York: Oneworld Publications, 2009

26. *The Uniqueness of Jesus: A Dialogue with Paul Knitter*, Leonard Swidler and Paul Mojzes (eds), New York: Orbis Books, 1997, 7, 81

27. Terrence Merrigan, 'Ecumenism and Interreligious Dialogue: The Foremost Challenge for the Churches at the Dawn of the Twenty-First Century', *Louvain Studies*, Spring/Summer 2008, 159–78 or 172–3. See also Merrigan's critique

of the epistemology of many pluralists in 'Religious Knowledge in the Pluralist Theology of Religions', *Theological Studies*, 1997, 686–707

28. Stephen J. Duffy, 'Christianity in Dialogue: Jesus at the Circumference or Centre?', *The Living Light*, Winter 1995; 'Mission and Dialogue in a Pluralistic Global City', *Ecumenical Trends*, 25, April 1996, 11

29. Gavin D'Costa, 'The Impossibility of a Pluralistic View of Religions', 226. D'Costa develops his critique in *the Meeting of Religions and The Trinity*, New York: Orbis Books, 2000

30. David Cheetham, 'Religious Passion and the Pluralistic Theology of Religions', *New Blackfriars*, May 1998, 229–40

31. Lieven Boeve, *God Interrupts History: Theology in a Time of Upheaval*, New York: Continuum, 2007, 168–72

32. See, for example, *GS*, a.62; *UR*, a.4, 6, 17

33. See the document of the International Theological Commission on 'Theological Pluralism' of 1972 in *International Theological Commission: Text and Documents, 1969 to 1985*, San Francisco: Ignatius Press, 1989, 89–92, and the document of the Congregation for the Doctrine of the Faith on *Mysterium Ecclesiae*, 1973, *Vatican Council II: More Conciliar Documents*, Austin Flannery (ed.), Dublin: Dominican Publications, 1982, 428–40

34. *Synod Report: The Final Report and Message to the People of God*, London: CTS, 1986, Section C, 2

35. Boeve, *God Interrupts History: Theology in a Time of Upheaval*, 173

36. See Scott Holland, 'This side of God: a conversation with David Tracy', *Cross Currents*, 52, 2002, 58–9

37. Jacques Dupuis, *Christianity and the Religions*, 95

38. See Jacques Dupuis, '"Christianity and the Religions" Revisited', *Louvain Studies*, 28, 2003, 363–83 at 370

39. Ibid., 372–4; Gerald O'Collins, 'Christ and the Religions', *Gregorianum*, 84, 2003, 347–62; 'Jacques Dupuis' Contribution to Inter-religious Dialogue', *Theological Studies*, 2003, 388–97 at 390–3

40. Gavin D'Costa, *Christianity and World Religions*, 29

41. Ibid., 30

42. Ibid.

43. Ibid., 32

44. Paul Griffiths, *Problems of Religious Diversity*, Oxford: Wiley-Blackwell, 2001, 53 and 63. A somewhat similar distinction is also found in the work of Gavin D'Costa in the late 1990s in an article entitled 'Trinitarian "Difference" and

World Religions', *Faith and Praxis in a Postmodern Age*, Ursula King (ed.), London: Cassell, 1998, 37–8. However, this distinction does not seem to be present in D'Costa's book of 2009

45. R. Burigana and G. Turbanti, 'The Intercession: Preparing the Conclusion of the Council', *History of Vatican II*, Vol. 4, Giuseppe Alberigo and Joseph A. Komonchak (eds), New York: Orbis Books, 2005, 527

46. Evangelista Vilanova, 'The Intercession (1963–1964)', *History of Vatican II: The Mature Council, Second Period and Intercession, September 1963–September 1964*, Vol. 3, Giuseppe Alberigo (ed.), Louvain: Peeters, 2000, 448 and 456

47. John W. O'Malley, *What Happened at Vatican II*, Cambridge, MA: Harvard University Press, 2008, 204

48. *GS*, a.44

49. See *GS*, a.41 and a.44

50. Walter Kasper, 'Jews, Christians and the Thorny Question of Mission', *Origins*, Vol. 32, No. 28, 19 December 2002

51. See Bradford Hinze, *Practices of Dialogue in the Roman Catholic Church: Aims and Obstacles, Lessons and Laments*, New York: Continuum, 2006, 4

52. *RM*, a.28

53. *GS*, a.3, and a.92. *DP* also, as seen in Chapter Two, gives some indication of what is demanded of dialogue among the participants

54. Hans-Georg Gadamer, *Truth and Method*, second edition, New York: Continuum, 2006, 385

55. David Tracy, *Plurality and Ambiguity: Hermeneutics, Religion, Hope*, New York: Harper and Rowe, 1987, 17

56. Ibid., 28

57. Ibid.

58. Ibid., 29

59. Charles Taylor, 'Understanding the Other: A Gadamerian View on Conceptual Schemes' in *Gadamer's Century: Essays in Honor of Hans-Georg Gadamer*, Jeff E. Malpas, Ulrich Arnswald and Jens Kertscher (eds), Cambridge: Massachusetts Institute of Technology Press, 2002, 279. This article is also available in *Charles Taylor, Dilemmas and Connections*, Cambridge, MA: Harvard University Press, 2011, 24–38

60. Taylor, 'Understanding the Other', *Dilemmas and Connections*, 25

61. *DP*, a.48

62. Tracy, *Dialogue with the Other: The Inter-Religious Dialogue*, Louvain: Peeters 1990, 44

63. Michel de Certeau, *La Faiblesse de Croire*, Paris: Edition du Seuil, 1987, 112, as quoted by Claude Geffré, 'The Christological Paradox as a Hermeneutical Key to Inter-Religious Dialogue', *Who Do You Say That I Am: Confessing the Mystery of Christ*, John C. Cavadini and Laura Holt (eds), Indiana: University of Notre Dame Press, 2004, 167

64. *NA*, a.4; see also *NA*, a.2

65. John Haughey, 'Ecumenism in the Pneumatology of Lonergan', *The Holy Spirit, The Church and Christian Unity: Proceedings of the Consultation held at the Monastery of Bose*, Italy (14–20 October 2002), Doris Donnelly, Adelbert Denaux and Joseph Famerée (eds), Louvain: Louvain University Press, 2005, 401

66. Raimon Panikkar 'Nine Ways Not to Talk about God', *Cross Currents*, 47, Summer, 1997, 150 and 153

67. Duffy, 'Mission and Dialogue in a Pluralistic Global City', 59

68. Thomas Aquinas, *In Sententiae* III d.25, q.1, a.1 and *Summa Theologica* II a-II ae, q.1 a.6

69. David Tracy, *The Analogical Imagination: Christian Theology and the Culture of Pluralism*, New York: Crossroad, 1981, 198

70. Tracy, *Dialogue with the Other*, 43

71. Paul Tillich, *Theology of Culture*, New York: Oxford University Press, 1959, 47–9

72. Stephen J. Duffy, 'The Galilean Christ: Particularity and Universlity', *Journal of Ecumenical Studies*, 26, Winter 1989, 154–174 at 158

73. See Dermot A. Lane, *Challenges Facing Religious Education in Contemporary Ireland*, Dublin: Veritas, 2008, 50–4

IV. KARL RAHNER'S CONTRIBUTION TO INTER-RELIGIOUS DIALOGUE

Given the centrality of Christology to Christian faith, the focus on Christology in *Dominus Iesus* and other documents of the Catholic Church, and the increasing necessity to connect Christology to inter-religious dialogue as seen in Chapter Two, it is now necessary to look at the person of Christ in relation to other religions. Very few Christologists have developed their Christologies in dialogue with other religions. This is a theological task in search of an author. There are some exceptions, such as Jacques Dupuis, Roger Haight and Peter Phan – but some of their work has provoked critical reaction from the Congregation for the Doctrine of the Faith in Rome.

One theologian who did interface Christology with other religions has been Karl Rahner, though it would be misleading to give the impression that this was a central theme in Rahner. It is possible to detect an evolution in Rahner's Christology over his lifetime. The later Rahner does connect Christology with other religions in a few scattered essays. The purpose of this chapter is not to review Rahner's Christology in itself but rather to examine how Rahner relates Christ to the religious other.

There can be little doubt about Rahner's influence on the Council's Declaration on *The Relation of the Church to Non-Christian Religions* (*Nostra Aetate*, 1965). Some have described Rahner as 'the chief contributor' to *Nostra Aetate*,[1] while others see him as one of the major voices prompting the positive outlook of the Catholic Church towards other religions as expressed at the Council, not only in *Nostra Aetate* but also in *Lumen Gentium*, *Gaudium et Spes* and *Ad Gentes*.

There are five parts to this chapter. In the first instance we will introduce Rahner's preoccupation with the experience of God as background to his Christology. Second, we will summarise what Rahner says about Christ in relation to other religions. Third, we will review some of his explicit writings, not all, on other religions. Fourth, we will engage in a critical evaluation of Rahner's contribution to dialogue with other religions and the place of Christ within that dialogue. Finally, we will examine what a Christian theology of inter-religious dialogue might look like standing on the shoulders of Rahner.

1. RAHNER ON CHRIST AND OTHER RELIGIONS

There is general agreement that the person of Christ is at the centre of Rahner's theology, and the chapter on Christ in *Foundations of Christian Faith* is tellingly the longest chapter of the book. Essays on Christology in the *Theological Investigations* are quite frequent. Our treatment of Christ in Rahner here will be limited to the way Rahner links Christ to other religions. To look at Christ and other religions, it is necessary to start not with Christ but with a broader theme that permeates the whole of Rahner's theology, namely the experience of the mystery of God. Rahner's whole life was preoccupied with a multi-layered analysis of what was involved in what he called 'the experience of God'. This theme of 'the experience of God' is of course of vital significance to dialogue with other religions. Most religions in one way or another are concerned about putting people in touch with what Rahner calls 'the experience of God' or what others call the ultimately Real or the Sacred Presence at the centre of life. To begin with the experience of God, therefore, fulfils two purposes. It is to start with what might be called 'common ground' that exists across many religions, namely the search for God in experience, time and memory. Second, the universal experience of God is the context in which Rahner relates Christ to other religions.

a. The Experience of God

The experience of God is a key theme within Rahner's theology. Towards the end of his life he said in an interview: 'My ultimate purpose, in all that I have written, is but to say this one simple thing to my readers: whether they know it or not, whether they reflect on it or not, human beings are always and everywhere, in all times and places, oriented and directed to that ineffable mystery we call God'.[2] Whether we are talking about Rahner's philosophy as expounded in *Spirit in the World* (1939) or *Hearers of the Word* (1941), or whether we are referring to his early spiritual writings on Gregory of Nyssa, Evagrius, Bonaventure, or his 1956 article on Ignatian spirituality, or his 1978 Ignatian testimony (where Rahner imagines Ignatius talking to Jesuits in the twentieth century), or whether we are discussing his explicitly theological writings in the *Theological Investigations* and the *Foundations of Christian Faith*, or whether we are dealing with his pastoral and homiletical writings, he is always explicitly, formally and passionately seeking to articulate what is involved in what he calls 'the experience of God'.

What is distinctive about Rahner's theology of experience is his claim that everybody experiences God, even though they may deny this or may not be consciously aware of it, or may choose to interpret it non-theologically.[3] Examples of the experience of God include experiences of freedom and responsibility, the acceptance of death, the exercise of duty without reward, and expressions of selfless love.

Rahner seeks to rescue the experience of God from being something peculiar to saints, the preserve of mystics, or the privilege of the few; instead, he claims that every experience of God takes place in the ordinary everyday experiences of life that everybody undergoes. He talks about the omnipresence of God in human experience in order to highlight that the experience of God, in the normal course of events, is a mediated experience. At times he talks about 'the mediated immediacy of God' that takes place in human experience.[4]

The experience of God is something that can never be adequately expressed in language; there is always more to human experience than we are able to articulate. And yet we are compelled all the time to name, articulate, objectify, conceptualise and thematise this unobjective, unthematic and transcendental experience of God. Thus, when it comes to describing the experience of God, he consistently uses terms like 'ineffable', 'inexhaustible' and 'incomprehensible' to overcome any suggestion that the experience of God is just another experience. He also argues that the experience of God is an experience which is most intimate and for that reason most taken for granted, and yet often remains silent. To make sure that nobody reduces the experience of God to the level of an object alongside other objects, he talks about God as 'the whither of experience and human transcendence'.[5] In addition, to communicate the richness of what is involved in an experience of God, he talks about 'religious experience', at other times of 'mystical experience', and sometimes 'spiritual experience' but perhaps most frequently 'transcendental experience'.

Whichever description is used, the experience of God is always a co-experience of something else at the same time and therefore in the normal course is a mediated experience. There is throughout Rahner's theology an underlying tension between what he calls the universal transcendental experience and the categorical expression of that experience, a theme we will take up in Chapter Six. This tension between transcendental experience and the categorical expression of that experience is a feature of many religions and, according to Rahner, is given definitive, final and personal resolution in the Christ-event.

b. Relocating the Christ-Event within the History of the World

For Rahner, the Christ-event appears as that unique, unsurpassable, unrepeatable and irreversible moment within the history of the transcendental experience of God and categorical revelation. The person of Christ is the absolute break-through of God's gracious self-communication to humanity and humanity's free response to God's invitation. These divine-human and the human-divine thresholds have been crossed in Jesus. Rahner's theology of Grace and Revelation reach fulfilment and finality in Jesus, the crucified and risen one.

The doctrine of the Incarnation is the irreversible coming together of God and humanity and of humanity and of God in Jesus, and this coming together stands out as the radiating centre of the whole of Rahner's theology.

One of the many significant moves in Rahner's Christology is the relocation of the Christ-event within the larger history of humanity and other religions. Instead of seeing the Christ event as an external intervention in history, Rahner insists on presenting the person of Christ as the decisive moment internal to the unfolding of God's universal saving will within the whole history of the world. It is not so much that God in Christ comes into a profane world to change the course of history; rather it is that the saving grace of God is present at the centre of creation and in the heart of humanity, and it is this grace that breaks out in the life, death and resurrection of Jesus.

Rahner emphasises that the Christ-event is not the cause of God's universal will to save the humanity; instead the Christ-event is the consequence of God's universal saving will and is, therefore, 'brought about by the prior divine will to save humankind'.[6] Further, Rahner is anxious to show that the cross of Christ should not be presented as that which transforms the mind of God or that which changes an angry God into a loving, merciful God. Such images of Christ, though quite popular, are a distortion of the meaning of the theology of the history of salvation.

The question that most occupies the mind of Rahner in the context of relocating the Christ-event within the history of the world is this: how can we make a connection between the death of Jesus and the salvation of the world? The issue here concerns the link that exists between Jesus and the possible universal salvation of others. More specifically, the question is: what soteriological value can be attributed to the pre-Easter Jesus in the context of his death on the cross?

Rahner proposes a number of answers to this question. First of all there is a fundamental unity between Jesus and the rest of humanity. Here, he refers to an existential, ontological, historical and theological unity between Jesus and all other human beings without actually elaborating on these particular dimensions of the unity between Jesus and humanity. Equally important for Rahner is the patristic doctrine which emphasises the unity between the eternal *Logos* and humanity in Jesus. Thus the Incarnation is an important statement about the fundamental unity that exists between Jesus and the *Logos* and Jesus and humanity. A second answer focuses on the significance of the death of Jesus for the salvation of the world. It is the cross of Christ that mediates salvation to the world. But this begs a further question: how does the cross mediate salvation? To this Rahner responds by saying that the death of Jesus is the 'sacramental sign of salvation'[7] to the world. The cross is the tangible expression of the self-gift of God to the world.[8] The cross embodies in a definitive manner the double movement of the Incarnation, namely the gift of divine love and the free acceptance of this gift, which is sealed definitively in the death of Jesus.

As a sacramental sign, the cross is the cause of salvation. Christ is the primary sacrament of salvation (*ursakrament*) just as Vatican II describes the Church as the sacrament of the world's salvation.[9] Additional answers to the question about the soteriological significance of pre-Easter Jesus, says Rahner, would require reference to the solidarity of all human beings within the totality of human history, the connection between God's self-communication in Grace and the death of Jesus, and to the unity of the death and resurrection of Christ. Thus Rahner feels that by 'moving from Jesus to humanity as a whole ... a single historical event may be seen to possess universal meaning.'[10]

And yet in spite of this response a niggling question remains: how can salvation come through Christ for all those who lived before Christ and for those coming after Christ who believe that they are required by their conscience in some instances to refuse the Gospel of Christ? The only way out of this dilemma, says Rahner, is to attribute what he calls '"a Christology of quest" to all men and women of good will.'[11] A better translation of 'a Christology of quest' would be 'a searching Christology'.

c. The Presence of a Searching Christology within Other Religions

References in Rahner to the idea of a searching Christology are scarce enough, and yet this concept is of underlying importance because it has the potential to build a bridge between Christianity and other religions. According to Roman A. Siebenrock, Rahner's searching Christology has 'theological implications for Christianity's relations to other religions.'[12]

Rahner constructs the idea of a searching Christology as a way of answering the question: how are people related to Christ who have never heard of Christ? In response he suggests: 'If a person accepts his existence resolutely, he is really already living out in his existence something like "a searching Christology".'[13] This searching Christology may well be unreflexive or anonymous – but nonetheless people in this situation are grappling with questions and challenges that are at least implicitly, if not explicitly, Christological.

A searching Christology means 'that a person who is searching for something which is specific and yet unknown has a genuine existential connection ... with whatever he or she is seeking, even if he or she has not yet found it.'[14] Further, it should be remembered that this search in the first instance is 'brought about by Grace'[15] and since all grace is ultimately Christological, to be touched by grace is already to be given an orientation towards Christ. In addition, the non-Christian who accepts his or her humanity accepts implicitly Christ, because for Rahner: 'Anyone who accepts his own humanity in full ... has accepted the Son of God because God has accepted man in him.'[16] In this sense Rahner argues that those who came before and now come after the Christ-event have some existential, graced and anthropological connection with the person of Christ as the goal of salvation, even though they do not know Christ explicitly.[17] In effect, when people seek to live life to the full, they will perhaps unreflexively or even anonymously be living in a manner that is related to Christology.

Rahner provides three examples of what he has in mind in relation to a searching Christology. When someone loves their neighbour radically and unconditionally, they are implicitly affirming Christ in love and faith, because such a love 'is searching for a God-man'.[18] The second example he gives is about 'readiness for death'. If and when one faces death and acknowledges a certain powerlessness before death and yet accepts it in freedom and hope, then one is affirming at the same time something of the radical significance of the death of Jesus. The third example is 'an appeal to hope in the future'. When a person opens him or herself to the future and is prepared to seek out a goal of some kind or other, even though it may be outstanding or still in progress, then one is implicitly professing a faith in the meaning of the resurrection of Jesus.

In these three examples, or 'appeals' as he calls them, Rahner holds that 'man is searching for an absolute saviour' and 'affirming, at least unthematically, his past and future coming'.[19] In other words, by loving the neighbour absolutely, by being ready to accept death in freedom, and by hoping in the future, one is living out or engaging with or searching for a Christology – a Christology that finds historical expression in the life, death and Resurrection of Jesus of Nazareth. What Rahner says about a searching Christology presupposes and builds on what he says in his theology of transcendental anthropology and the universality of God's grace in the Spirit.

Here we need to recall the explicit link that exists for Rahner between anthropology and Christology: 'Christology may be studied as self-transcending anthropology, and anthropology as deficient Christology.'[20] This transcending anthropology is one of a radical questioning about the meaning of existence and the orientation of the person as subject towards mystery. This particular orientation of the person under the universality of grace finds its unique and irreversible and unrepeatable finality in the Christ-event. When Rahner, therefore, talks about a searching Christology in relation to other religions, he is referring to the existence of transcendental anthropology in other religions which is seeking something like Christological expression.

Another way of summing up Rahner's idea of 'a searching Christology' is as follows: there is within the heart of humanity, and especially among members of other religions, a searching anthropology taking place which amounts to a searching Christology, that is, a search for a messiah or saviour figure in history of one form or another. At the centre of this searching Christology is the presence of a 'hope and expectation of an advent kind'.[21] For Christians that search has been given historical shape and form and embodiment in Jesus of Nazareth, the crucified and Risen Christ, the Saviour of humanity. Within these perspectives, Rahner's idea of a searching Christology opens up a shared anthropological, and by implication soteriological, line of dialogue between Christianity and other religions.

2. THE EXPLICIT TREATMENT OF OTHER RELIGIONS

It should be noted that relative to the four thousand books and articles Rahner wrote during his life, there are very few articles dealing directly with other religions. Indeed it would be wrong to give the impression that inter-religious dialogue was at the centre of Rahner's theological enterprise. Perhaps it would be more accurate to say that Rahner was passionate about dialogue, dialogue between Christianity and the world, dialogue with atheism, Marxism, unbelievers, scientists, and it is within this context that dialogue with non-Christian religions arises. What Rahner has to say about dialogue between Christians and the world, about the intrinsically dialogical character of Christianity itself, about the critical correlation that can and should take place between the Church and the world, was immensely important and original and does have a direct bearing on inter-religious dialogue. It is this larger theology of dialogue that constitutes the context for understanding what he had to say about inter-religious dialogue. His articles on dialogue with the non-Christian religions are few enough but are no less important in their significance. What is striking about these few articles is that they entail the application of his Christology, directly or indirectly, to the particular question of the relationship that exists between Christianity and other religions. Exposition of some of these articles according to their chronological appearance will be made here. The articles chosen are selective and do not claim to be a comprehensive account of everything that Rahner had to say about the relationship between Christianity and the other religions.

a. The 1961 Lecture

The first and by far the most important and original article on other religions was a lecture given in 1961. In that lecture, unchanged in its published version in 1962, entitled 'Christianity and the Non-Christian Religions', he puts forward four theses with an introduction and a conclusion. He introduces the lecture with comments on an 'open Catholicism' which requires the Church to understand what is outside itself. He notes the existence of religious pluralism and sees it as both a threat and a challenge for the Church. He observes that the West is no longer shut up within itself and therefore no longer the centre of history and of culture.

In Thesis 1, he says that Christianity understands itself as an absolute religion, which is true and lawful, intended for all and therefore cannot recognise any other religion beside itself as of equal right. Christianity is 'the religion which binds humanity to God'[22] and has a history behind it.

Thesis 2 is the longest and the most important part of the article. Here he affirms that non-Christian religions 'have supernatural elements arising out of the Grace ... given as a gift on account of Christ.'[23]

As Christians we believe in the universal saving will of God directed towards all human beings. Consequently everybody comes under the influence of divine, supernatural grace which offers the possibility of an interior union with God, regardless of whether the individual accepts it or refuses it. This will only make sense, however, if and when we realise that nature and Grace are not two historical phases in time but rather one single reality. It is 'impossible to think that this offer of supernatural grace made to all on account of the salvific purposes of God should ... remain ineffective.'[24] Further, given that the Word was made flesh in Christ for the salvation of the world, we cannot view the world as if Christ had not come.[25] Lastly, we must remember that the transcendence of the individual, elevated by Grace, can be exercised in 'many different ways and under varied labels.'[26] In the light of God's universal saving will and the Christ-event, we must recognise that Grace is at work everywhere in the personal lives of people 'no matter how primitive, unenlightened, apathetic and earthbound such a life may appear to be.'[27]

The second half of Thesis 2 holds that the pre-Christian religions have 'a positive significance' in history and, therefore, they must be regarded as 'lawful'[28] provided they have some form of public and institutional existence. A lawful religion is one that is socially institutionalised and can be regarded as a positive means of gaining a right relationship to God and the attainment of salvation. Such lawful religions may be also regarded as 'positively included in God's plan of salvation'.[29] While Rahner makes the case for lawful religions principally by reference to the Old Testament, it is clear that he also has the other religions in mind.

If every human being is graced by God and if one of the effects of this grace is a change in consciousness, then we must acknowledge that other religions are the outcome of God's grace in the world. Traces of grace in other religions may be difficult to discern, says Rahner, but 'they must be there':[30] if we fail to see these traces of grace we may have only looked superficially for them and then with too little love.[31] Thus religions other than the Christian religion and Judaic religion do contain elements of supernatural grace. While this may seem obvious today, it was far from obvious within Catholic theology prior to the Vatican II.

In Thesis 3, Rahner points out in the light of Thesis 2 that Christians must not regard members of other religions as non-Christian but rather as anonymous Christians.[32] It would be wrong to regard the pagan as someone who has not been touched by God's grace and truth. To the contrary, when someone has been touched by God's grace and accepts this in freedom, they have already been given some form of revelation. When this person hears the proclamation of the Gospel, they are not hearing something that is absolutely unknown like a child being told about the existence of Bavaria; instead they are being given in objective concepts an expression of something they have already attained in the depths of their personal existence.[33]

In Thesis 4, Rahner says that religious pluralism is not going to disappear in the foreseeable future. Consequently, it is permissible for the Christian to interpret this non-Christianity as Christianity of an anonymous kind. The role of the missionary within this situation is to bring 'to consciousness that which belongs as a divine offer or to spell out what has already been accepted unreflectively and implicitly'.[34] If we can look at non-Christians in these terms, that is as people already touched by grace and in possession of some supernatural elements, 'then the Church will not regard itself as the exclusive community of those who have a claim on salvation, but rather as the historically tangible vanguard and historically and socially constituted expression of what is present as a hidden reality outside the visible Church.'[35]

Rahner acknowledges that non-Christians may think it is presumptuous for Christians to think that everything that is of value is the result of the grace of Christ and can therefore be interpreted as anonymous Christianity. However, the Christian cannot abandon this presumption; instead the Christian should approach this state of affairs with humility by recognising that God is greater than the individual and the Church. Rahner concludes by quoting the well known verse of St Paul: 'What you do not know and yet worship, that I proclaim to you.'[36]

While some of this material may sound obvious today in the second decade of the twenty-first century, we must remember that this vision of other religions was articulated by Rahner over fifty years ago, just before the Second Vatican Council. If anything, this article highlights the influence of Rahner at Vatican II, especially in regard to other religions.

b. Christ in Non-Christian Religions

In 1974 Rahner published a paper on 'Jesus Christ in Non-Christian Religions', which appeared in *Investigations,* Volume XXVII (1981) and subsequently was incorporated without much change into

Foundations. The purpose of this article was to explain how and in what sense it is possible to speak of Christ as present and active in other religions, especially in view of the particularity of the Christ-event. To this question, Rahner responds that Christ is present through the Spirit and that this Spirit is the Spirit of Christ, the Spirit that proceeds from the Father and the Son and which therefore can be called the Spirit of Christ. In addition, the Spirit that is present and active in other religions is the same Spirit poured out on the whole of humanity as a result of the universal saving will of God.

Rahner warns again against saying that Christ is the cause of the gift of the Spirit given to all because the source of the Spirit is God's universal saving will and is not as already seen the Christ-event strictly speaking. Here Rahner emphasises that it is important to recognise the sovereignty of God's saving will which cannot be moved or altered by external factors. However, we can say, using the terminology of the scholastics, that the Christ-event is 'the final cause' of the action of the Spirit in other religions in so far as Christ is the goal of all Grace.

Rahner explains the connection between the Spirit of God offered to all in virtue of God's universal saving will and the Spirit of Jesus Christ by reference to what he calls the 'entelechy' of the Spirit. The technical term 'entelechy' (which has Aristotelian roots) means an inner ordering or ordination of an entity towards its natural completion or towards a particular goal. When Rahner talks about the 'entelechy' of the universal Spirit of God, he is referring to the ordination of the Spirit of God towards its completion or realisation in God's final, historical self-communication in Christ as the Word made flesh.[37] This proposal of Rahner's concerning the relationship between the universal action of the Spirit of God in the world and the particular action of the Spirit in Christ is potentially another significant bridge between Christianity and the other religions.[38]

A second way in which we can talk about Christ being present in other religions is in and through what Rahner calls 'the searching memory of all faith'.[39] By this he means that within faith there is a searching dynamic going on which is looking for the existence of an absolute saviour figure. There is 'a prior principle of expectation, of searching, of hoping'[40] within memory. Rahner says he is using memory here in the way that Plato uses *anamnesis* and Augustine talks of *memoria*. This concept of a searching memory echoes to some extent Rahner's views on a searching Christology already touched upon in Section one above. For Rahner, human memory searches history in hope and expectation and anticipation of finding that event in which salvation has become historically concrete and tangible. Any search through memory for a saviour figure is a search ultimately for the person of Christ and in this particular sense we can say that Christ is present implicitly in the other world religions. This searching memory of faith anticipates the hope which Christians find realised in the person of Christ.

c. The Importance of Other Religions for Salvation

A third article entitled 'The Importance of Non-Christian Religions for Salvation' was given as a lecture in 1975 to an international congress on missiology in Rome. Interestingly this article was not incorporated into *Foundations*. Rahner notes that Vatican II, in *Nostra Aetate*, left open and undefined the question of the properly theological quality and soteriological character of non-Christian religions. Are other religions just constructs created by human beings, or can they act as sources of salvation for people? In raising these questions, Rahner notes the shift that has taken place from over a millennium of Augustinian pessimism to a new optimism at Vatican II concerning salvation, which teaches that salvation is available to all those who do not freely reject it.[41]

Can this optimism about salvation be applied to non-Christian religions today? In answering this question Rahner begins by affirming the existence of supernatural grace as 'always and everywhere present' in the world, offering the possibility of a salvific relationship with God. Further, because this gracious orientation of humanity towards transcendence is itself a form of revelation, the history of humanity, revelation and salvation are interrelated. This supernatural relationship of every individual to God, however, must be mediated through historical objectifications. These objectifications can in some instances be non-religious, for example in the case of an atheist who, following his or her conscience, can nonetheless be saved. If this is the case with atheists, then surely we must acknowledge that the 'institutions and theoretical objectifications of the non-Christian religions can be categorical mediations of a genuine salvific act.'[42] Rahner states that 'non-Christian religions, even though incomplete, rudimentary, partially debased, can be realities with a positive history of salvation and revelation.'[43] Such religions can, therefore, have a positive salvific function and become 'ways of salvation' through which people approach God and Christ.[44]

One further point in this article which is worth mentioning is what Rahner says about mysticism: 'It is not *a priori* forbidden to discover genuine supernatural mysticism in the mysticism of religions of higher cultures, even when this extra Christian mysticism is not itself by any means thematised in an explicit religious form.'[45] This brings us to the theme of the Holy Spirit in relation to other religious traditions.

d. The Universal Presence of the Spirit in the World

It is possible to discern an underlying preoccupation with the Spirit of God within the corpus of Rahner's writings. The theme of Spirit is present throughout Rahner's life. It is implicit in his early, foundational writings on *Spirit in the World* and *Hearers of the Word*, explicit in his spiritual writings, some of which are gathered in volume VII of *Investigations*, in his extensive ecclesiology, and also in his transcendental theology of grace and revelation. A theology of Spirit, therefore, has been present throughout his lifetime, so much so that it has been said that 'no-one in our century has contributed to the renewal of Systematic Theology through Pneumatology in such a fundamental way' as Rahner has done.[46]

Rahner's contribution to Pneumatology is singular and outstanding, especially his theology of the universal presence of the Spirit.[47] His treatment of the universality of the grace of God in the world is underpinned by his theology of the universal presence of the Spirit poured out on the world from the very beginning of time. For example, he points out: 'God ... has already communicated himself in His Holy Spirit, always and everywhere and to every person as the innermost centre of his existence, whether he wants it or not, whether he reflects on it or not, whether he accepts it or not.'[48] We have already seen how this universality of the Spirit of God is directed as entelechy towards the particularity of the Spirit of Christ.

Towards the end of his life he gave a series of interviews in which he picks up again on the theme of the Spirit of God and points out that the gift of the Spirit is the foundation on which Christianity is best understood. He states the 'the divinization of the world through the Spirit of God is humanly and speculatively the basic conception for Christianity, out of which the Incarnation and soteriology arise as an inner moment.'[49] In a very significant article on 'Aspects of European Theology'[50] published in 1983, just one year before his death, he links this emphasis on the universality of the Spirit with other religions. In that article he makes a number of points that are explicitly connected to the theme of inter-religious dialogue which are worth summarising. Four particular proposals are put forward in the context of other religions.

He suggests that Pneumatology might come before Christology, whereas up to now Christology has been 'accorded a place prior to Pneumatology'.[51] Second, he suggests that Pneumatology could become 'the fundamental point of departure' for the whole of theology. He gives two reasons for this: because 'of the universal salvific will of God and in legitimate respect for all the major world religions outside of Christianity.'[52] Third, if this can be done, then it might be possible 'to gain a real and radical understanding of Christology.'[53] Rahner acknowledges this could only happen with considerable effort because one would have to go beyond the statement of John 7:23 (there was no Spirit as yet because Jesus had not yet been glorified), a text which exists in contrast to other scriptural passages which extol the universal saving will of the Spirit of God. The fourth point is that if this shift were to happen, then this new Pneumatology would have to recognise the Spirit speaking 'through all prophets and know that the Spirit has been poured out on all flesh.'[54] Rahner, in characteristic style, simply makes these statements without much elaboration, thus leaving a new direction for the next generation of theologians.

3. A CRITICAL REVIEW OF RAHNER

It is now time to review Rahner's contribution to a theology of other religions. It would not be true to the spirit of Rahner's theology simply to parrot what he has said without engagement. Our review must be limited by our interest in the relationship between Christ and other religions and how this relationship influences inter-religious dialogue. This evaluation, therefore, is not a critique of Rahner's theology *per se* but rather an assessment of its contribution to and connection with inter-religious dialogue.

a. A Pioneer of Dialogue and Inclusivism

In general terms one can only admire the openness of Rahner's theology to dialogue with other religions and how, historically speaking, he anticipated in many respects developments that were to take place in the late 1980s and throughout the 1990s and into the new millennium. Rahner's theological approach to other religions enabled Catholic theology to make a number of significant shifts which we now take for granted. Foremost among these has been the shift from an exclusivist theology to an inclusivist Catholic theology.[55] Further, the move encouraged by Rahner from Augustinian pessimism about salvation which reigned for some fifteen hundred years to the optimism of the Second Vatican Council is highly significant. Thirdly, the adoption of a positive approach to other religions in contrast to what had been largely a hostile approach prior to Vatican II was facilitated on the one hand by Rahner's universalist, transcendental vision and on the other hand by his particular emphasis on the experience of God.

While we take these shifts for granted, it is not at all certain they would have gained ground without the weight of Rahner behind them, and indeed we know that even now not everybody is comfortable with them. Further, we must admire the coherence of the interlocking parts of Rahner's theology and their application to the question of other religions. What is said for example about the universality of the grace of the Spirit in the world and the particularity of the person of Christ is applied with consistency to the other religions.

Informing this positive theology of dialogue and inclusivity is Rahner's emphasis throughout his life on the experience of God as something available to all. His theology of the experience of God is rich and suggestive for all who are interested in religion. His ability to connect the most ordinary experiences of life with the omnipresence of the Sacred is surely striking as a possible point of departure for dialogue with other religions. His insistence that the experience of God is an experience of that which is ineffable, inexhaustible and incomprehensible is an attractive point of entry into dialogue with other religions.

b. A Critical Examination of Rahner on Christ in Relation to Other Religions

The person of Christ is at the centre of Rahner's theology and his approach to other religions. His presentation of the Incarnation as the unique point of contact and unity between God and humanity captures in a very credible manner an important part of what is distinctive about Christianity.

However, this view of the Incarnation needs to be filled out in terms of the drama that took place within the historical unfolding of the Incarnation. To be sure, Rahner gives particular attention to the historical death of Jesus on the cross and highlights this as the sacramental sign of salvation in the world. Yet, even though Rahner, especially the later Rahner, emphasises the importance of history, he fails to give much material content to the life of the historical Jesus. It is noticeable that in the 145 pages given over to Christology in *Foundations*, only one and a half pages deal with particular aspects of the historical life of Jesus.[56] In spite of protestations to the contrary by many of Rahner's commentators such as Leo O'Donovan, Declan

Marmion and Philip Endean on this point, there are others who argue that Rahner's transcendental Christology needs to be informed by a more rigorous historical Christology.[57] This would require that account be taken to some degree of the ongoing quest for the historical Jesus without, however, buying into the enlightenment presupposition that has dogged the search for the historical Jesus. Instead of supposing that some kind of hard historical core of data exists back there if only we could dig deep enough, a more moderate case can be made for constructing a narrative approach to the life of Jesus and in particular for outlining a historical narrative of the Gospels.

If this could be done then it would be easier to answer the very question that Rahner himself raises about the soteriological links that exist between the life of Jesus, the death of Jesus and the resurrection. This means making a historical connection between historical moments in the life of Jesus and the death of Jesus on the Cross. If the Cross of Jesus is the sacramental sign of salvation as Rahner argues, then a more explicit soteriological link must be established between the Cross and the life of Jesus. For example, the historical and prophetic actions of Jesus – such as the healings, exorcisms, forgiveness, table fellowship, the cleansing of the temple, the last supper, and the washing of the feet as signs of the coming reign of God – have soteriological connections with the Cross of Christ as the sacramental sign of salvation in the world. If these historical and soteriological links can be established, then it might be possible to indicate that certain aspects of the saving life, death and resurrection of Jesus in their particularity are of universal significance. For example, could it not be said in the light of the Christ-event that the shape of salvation is cruciform, that the structure of salvation is paschal, and that the colour of salvation is one of a 'bright darkness'?

In spite of these reservations, Rahner's relocation of Christology within historical perspectives that are larger than Judaism and therefore connected to other religions is surely important for inter-religious dialogue in the future. Further, his complex view of the presence of a searching Christology in other religions has important anthropological potential for dialogue between Christianity and other faiths.

c. Rahner's Treatment of Other Religions

We now turn to his treatment of the relationship between Christianity and other religions. His 1961 paper was by any standards an original, creative and influential contribution at that time. In that paper, Rahner called for an open Catholicism and suggests that the Church should look outwards; he recognised the reality of religious pluralism, both as a threat and an opportunity; he talked about the existence of the supernatural elements within other religions; he referred to the 'positive significance' other religions can have as 'a means of salvation';[58] he described other religions as 'legitimate, and a means which is therefore positively included in God's plan of salvation.'[59]

To fully appreciate the significance of his 1961 lecture, we need to remember it was given over fifty years ago, just before Vatican II, at a time when the Church saw itself as an entity over and against the world. Here was a Catholic theologian talking about the positive significance of other religions within God's plan of salvation at a time when the Church was struggling to admit that the Protestant Churches were channels of grace. This article was firmly grounded in Rahner's transcendental theology of the grace of the Spirit and Christ, and only makes sense within that wider context. The vision of this article was, as some saw it, a 'giant leap forward'[60] within Catholic theology at that time: it enabled the Church at Vatican II to take a positive view of other religions, without however spelling out the details. The footprints of Rahner are quite evident on the pages of *Nostra Aetate*, *Lumen Gentium*, *Ad Gentes* and *Gaudium et Spes*. Indeed, not only the footprints of Rahner but also some of his language, such as 'grace and truth', 'self-communication', and 'dialogue' is peppered throughout those documents. Further, the 1961 article enabled Catholic theologians to adopt and work out an inclusive view of other religions which is now taken for granted. Inclusivism could be described as the current Catholic approach to interfaith dialogue and Rahner's influence in making this possible is widely recognised.[61] Thirdly, this 1961 article has paved the way for the development of what is now known by some as 'inclusive pluralism' and by others as 'open inclusivism' within the current state of debate about inter-religious dialogue.

In making these judgements about Rahner's contribution, it should be noted that he argues not for the reality of salvation among other religions but for the possibility of salvation since no-one can be certain about the gift of salvation. Furthermore, Rahner also points out that he is talking as a dogmatic theologian from an *a priori* point of view and that therefore this theological perspective on other religions needs to be informed by *a posteriori* findings of the history of religions and phenomenology of religion.

The second article, entitled 'Jesus Christ in the Non-Christian Religions', was written in 1964 and subsequently incorporated unchanged into *Foundations*. The issue at stake in this article as we have seen is: how can Christ be present in other religions? Rahner replies that Christ is present through the Spirit and that this Spirit as entelechy is the Spirit of Christ. In the context of the mid-1970s, Rahner was asking a new question and proposing a new answer. His response, which focuses on the Spirit, especially the Spirit of Christ, was breaking new ground. By suggesting that the Spirit active in other religions is the Spirit of Christ in virtue of the Christ-event, Rahner was opening up pneumatological perspectives that can be found in writings among theologians and John Paul II.

A major theme today in inter-religious dialogue is the action of the Spirit within other religions prior to the Christ-event and subsequent to the Christ event, a theme taken up by John Paul II, especially in his encyclical on the Spirit entitled *Dominum et Vivificantem: On the Holy Spirit in the Life of the Church and the World* (1986).[62] Here John Paul talks about the action of the Spirit before the Christian dispensation and after the Christ event, 'both inside and outside the visible boundaries of the Church'. Before the Christian dispensation the Spirit was ordered to the Christ-event and after the Christ-event the Spirit is active in the Church, in other religions and in the world in virtue of the Christ-event. While this is now accepted teaching of the Church, it may be surmised it was the innovative thinking of Rahner in this and other articles, as well as the theology of other theologians like Yves Congar, Walter Kasper and Hans Urs von Balthasar, that made possible these new Pneumatological perspectives on other religions.

A question Rahner does not touch upon in this particular article is the need for criteria to discern the Spirit in other religions and in Christianity. Surely there must be some traces of continuity, some shared pattern, as well as differences and transformation between the stirrings of the Spirit in other religions and the action of the Spirit in the Christ-event. What might these elements of identity and difference between other religions and Christianity look like?

A second question that Rahner does not address in this article is the action of the Word of God in other religions prior to the Incarnation and subsequent to the Incarnation. What Rahner has to say about the Spirit could be said equally of the Word, especially in the light of the Patristic teachings on the relationship between the scattered word (*logos spermatikos*) and the Word made flesh in Jesus. A close parallel exists between the universal actions of the *Logos* and the Spirit and the particular expressions of *Logos* and Spirit in Jesus as the Christ. A further instance of Rahner's influence coming from this article is the current interest in Spirit-Christologies that begin with Jesus as a person of the Spirit in common with the founding figures of other religions, and then develop this in terms of what is specific to the action of the Spirit in Jesus.[63]

The other way Rahner sees Christ as present in other religions is through what he calls the searching memory of faith and a searching Christology. Both of these concepts, namely that of the searching memory of faith and a searching Christology, have a curious resonance, with some post-modern deconstructionists such as Jacques Derrida, which we will discuss in Section 4 of this chapter.

In the third article, 'On the Importance of Non Christian Religions for Salvation', written in 1975, there is some repetition of themes, more confidence and less qualifications. The statements are clearer about other religions as possible mediations of salvation, having a positive role in the history of salvation, and being 'ways of the salvation', even though Rahner is careful to point out that this salvific role of the non-Christian religions is incomplete and rudimentary and significantly different to the salvation offered in Christ.

A difficulty with this article on non-Christian religions concerns the nature and character of the salvation in question. It would help if Rahner had given some indication of the structure of salvation in question. He does, of course, talk about the importance of following one's own conscience, the exercise of freedom and responsibility and the acceptance of death. Is there any sense in which we can talk about salvation as a movement, a paschal and liberating movement from the self to the other, and from the other to the absolute Other? Perhaps these are issues for the current phase of inter-religious dialogue, whereas Rahner in the 1970s was establishing primarily the possibility of salvation, and not the shape and structure of salvation which are more questions for today.

4. STANDING ON THE SHOULDERS OF RAHNER IN THE CONTEXT OF INTER-RELIGIOUS DIALOGUE

In this concluding section I want to outline, briefly, how it is possible to see further by standing on the shoulders of Rahner in the context of inter-religious dialogue for the twenty-first century.

a. Rahner and Post-Modernism

The first area in which we can move forward in the company of Rahner concerns the context within which interfaith dialogue takes place. For those of us who live in the so-called developed world, that context is inescapably pluralist and post-modern as noted in the opening chapter. Rahner recognised the reality of pluralism years ahead of most Catholic theologians. Less obvious is Rahner's relationship with post-modern culture. And yet Declan Marmion suggests Rahner 'anticipated some of the characteristics' of post-modernity.[64] Allowing for the enormous ambiguity and fluidity attaching to the term 'post-modern', one of the agreed features of post-modern culture is its programme of deconstruction, especially in the work of Jacques Derrida.

In an odd and fascinating and unexpected way, one finds certain echoes of Derridian deconstruction in the work of Rahner.[65] Of course there are obvious, radical differences between Rahner and Derrida. In spite of these very substantial differences, there are some curious parallels which are worth noting because of their significance for inter-religious dialogue.

I have no doubt that Rahner, were he alive today, would be deeply involved in the important dialogue taking place at present between theology and post-modernity. Restricting ourselves to the specific issue of the relationship between Christianity and the religions, it is worth noting some of resonances between Rahner and Derrida.

The first point is that Derrida's deconstruction of philosophy and religion does not end up hammering the final nail in the coffin of religion. To the contrary there is as much unease among secularists as there is among believers with Derrida since he ends up affirming what he calls 'religion without religion, that is, religion without content, without dogma, without institution'. Derrida wants to affirm religion without talking about it, because once you talk about religion you end up asserting the superiority of one religion over another and it is precisely this that gives rise to violence and war. Further, according to Derrida there is a messianic structure attaching to experience, a certain expectation built into experience about the possibility of the impossible. Once you affirm the advent of the impossible then you find yourself in trouble with the existence of rival claims among the religions of the book, namely Judaism, Christianity and Islam.

Another way of saying this is to state that everyone is messianic in outlook, everyone is expectant in desire, everyone is hopeful towards the future. The role of deconstructionism is to keep open a messianic space within human experience by refusing to accept the advent of any of the messiahs. Thus Derrida seeks to be messianic without succumbing to messianisms, refusing to recognise the messianic claims of any of the Abrahamic religions. In this sense, Derrida affirms religion without religion, acknowledges the messianic structure of religion but declines to identify the advent of any messiah. For Derrida, the orientation of this messianic structure of experience is one of transcendence, hope and hospitality, expectation and justice. What Derrida sees himself doing here is excavating the sites of the various religions of all content while continuing to affirm the reality of religion without religion. In doing this, Derrida has shown a curious interest in faith, negative theology and the apophatic tradition, while at the same time declaring himself to be a special kind of atheist.[66]

Turning to Rahner, it must be acknowledged that he engaged in a considerable amount of deconstruction in order to modernise Catholic theology. What is of interest here is the parallel that exists between Rahner's emphasis on what he sometimes calls 'the searching memory of faith' and at other times refers to as 'a searching Christology'. Both of these concepts have an affinity with Derrida's emphasis on the messianic character of human experience. As seen, Rahner also uses the language of expectation, promise and hope to describe what is going on among non-Christians searching for salvation who do not know Christ or who have rejected Christ. In other words, there seems to be some common ground opening up here between Rahner and Derrida. Both emphasise the dynamism of human experience, both refer to a sense of expectation and hope within human experience, both speak out of a recognition of the underlying drive towards self transcendence. In brief, both acknowledge that there is deep within human experience an irrepressible and restless searching going on for what Derrida calls the messiah and Rahner refers to as the Saviour-figure.

A second echo between Rahner and Derrida can be found in Rahner's appreciation of apophatic theology and Derrida's radical programme of deconstruction which included what might be called a passing flirtation with negative theology. While Derrida did discern a certain 'family resemblance'[67] between the negations of apophatic theology and deconstruction, he ended up confessing, 'I would hesitate to inscribe what I put forward under the familiar heading of negative theology.'[68] In brief, Derrida gave up on the possibility and viability of a negative theology largely because of his suspicion of the presence of a latent 'hyperessentialism'. In the end, Derrida admits, 'nothing remains'.[69] The trouble with this, however, is that it is difficult to embrace only negations, or as Denys Turner puts it, paraphrasing Scotus within a post-modern context, you cannot go on loving a mere postponement.[70]

In contrast, Rahner's early studies of Gregory of Nyssa and Evagrius as well as his familiarity with Pseudo Dionysius and Meister Eckhart enabled him to affirm and negate the incomprehensibility of God in such a way that he could talk about 'knowing through unknowing'.[71]

In spite of these faint echoes, which contain suggestive openings for inter-religious dialogue, it must be pointed out that there is a very substantial difference between Rahner and Derrida. This fundamental difference comes down to Rahner's clear and explicit and unambiguous recognition of Jesus of Nazareth as the Christ and Saviour of the world.

On the other hand, Derrida refuses to identify the Messiah with any religious figure of history. This particular refusal by Derrida clearly challenges the Christian to give a better account of what it means to say the Messiah has come in Jesus and what that confession might mean today. If Christians declare that Jesus is the Messiah, and this is surely one of the early Christian creeds, then they have to ensure that this confession of faith, contrary to everything Derrida has to say, generates healing and not violence, gives rise to peace and not war, effects reconciliation and not division.

A further fundamental difference between Rahner and Derrida is Rahner's insistence that transcendence must be thematised, that grace is always mediated, and that faith exists in some form of creedal expression. The question that Derrida must answer more clearly is this: what is it that drives the process of deconstruction and is it possible to talk about a chemically pure transcendence, a historically pure faith, a culturally pure religion? The nearest Derrida comes to answering this question is as follows:

> ... what remains irreducible to any deconstruction, what remains as undeconstructible as the possibility itself of

deconstruction is, perhaps, a certain experience of the
emancipatory promised; it is perhaps even the formality of
a structural messianism, a messianism without religion, even
a messianic without messianism, an idea of justice ... and an
idea of democracy.[72]

Clearly, Derrida does admit there is something implicitly affirmed
in every act of deconstruction. His reluctance, however, to go any
further in terms of naming that something, of giving it some content,
and of making it explicit is ultimately unsatisfactory and frustrating
for his theological and religious interlocutors.

b. Inclusive Pluralism

Another area in which we can go forward in the company of Rahner
is in the development and ownership of what has now become
known as 'Inclusive Pluralism' or a 'pluralistic inclusivism',[73] not to
be confused with the radical pluralism of Alan Race and John Hick.
Rahner's promotion of an open inclusivism paved the way for the
development of this new perspective on a theology of religions.

In general terms, Rahner's strong emphasis on the universal
saving will of God and his relocation of the Christ-event as a
decisive moment within history has opened up a new way of
understanding Christianity in the world. More specifically, Rahner
has fleshed out this new vision in a variety of ways: the possibility
of the experience of God for all, the universality of God's grace
in the world, the existence of a transcendental revelation for all,
and the universal presence of the Spirit in the world. On the other
hand, his theology of the Incarnation as the concrete and categorical
and historical expression of these universal and transcendental
perspectives is of critical importance as well as his presentation of
the Incarnation as the definitive point of contact between God and
humanity and humanity and God – all of which point towards what
is unique, distinctive and final about Christianity. The common
thread running through these themes is one of inclusivity, an open,
Christian inclusivism.

By applying these themes to the non-Christian religions, he was able to recognise other religions as lawful, as possible ways of salvation for their followers, and most significantly as 'positively included in God's plan of salvation'.[74] In this way, Rahner, especially the later Rahner, recognised the growing reality of religious pluralism as challenge and opportunity for Christianity.

It was within this context that Jacques Dupuis came along and synthesised these two distinct and separate strands within Rahner's theology, coming up with what he called 'inclusive pluralism'. The category of 'inclusive pluralism' in Dupuis seeks to bring together inclusivism and pluralism in a way that avoids the relativism of radical pluralism and the absolutism of exclusivism. Further, inclusive pluralism overcomes the false antithesis put forward by some between a Christocentric and a theocentric approach to other religions, recognising instead the legitimacy of theocentric Christology within the context of dialogue with other religions.[75] Thirdly, inclusive pluralism safeguards the uniqueness of the Christ-event for the salvation of the world while at the same time recognising the possibility of salvation in other religions for their followers. The purpose of inclusive pluralism therefore in the words of Dupuis himself is 'to combine two fundamental affirmations which, though apparently contradictory, must be seen as complimentary',[76] namely 'the universal constitutive character of the Christ-event in the order of salvation' on the one hand, and 'the saving significance of ... religious traditions ... within the one manifold plan of God for humanity' on the other.[77]

Inclusive pluralism as put forward by Dupuis is an advance and development of Rahner's theology: it brings together the two strands of inclusivism and pluralism found within Rahner into a new and higher synthesis. This new synthesis was made possible by Rahner's recognition of the other religions as part of God's plan for the world. This insight enabled Dupuis to propose a pluralism not only *de facto* for all to see but also a pluralism of *de jure*, that is a pluralism in principle as somehow a part of God's providential plan for the world. This new theology of inclusive pluralism will only make sense in the larger context of Rahner's singular contribution to the positive appreciation of non-Christian religions. Indeed if inclusive pluralism is removed from its roots in Rahner's theology, it will surely be misunderstood and misrepresented, and one suspects that this was part at least of the controversy that surrounded Dupuis's earlier book *Towards a Christian Theology of Religious Pluralism* (1997).

c. Christianity as an Open and Unfinished Narrative

A final area in which we can go forward in the company of Rahner relates to the unfinished and incomplete character of revelation. It should be remembered that in Rahner's discussion about the relationship between the transcendental and categorical aspects of revelation, he points out as a matter of principle that the objectification of revelation 'is only partially successful' and 'always exists within a still unfinished history'.[78] This general principle applies to all forms of categorical revelation including objectifications of the Christ-event. To be sure, the revelation of God in Christ is unique, unsurpassable and unrepeatable, but there is also an important sense in which the Christ-event remains incomplete and unfinished from an eschatological point of view.

Inflated Christological and ecclesial claims have in the past inhibited authentic dialogue between Christianity and other religions. It is only when we have grasped the unfinished and incomplete character of revelation that we will begin to appreciate the real urgency of inter-religious dialogue in a global world, divided by political conflicts which are all too often related to the major religions.

One of the most striking features of the self-understanding of the first Christian community of Jews was the acute awareness that there was something still outstanding in their experience of the life, death and resurrection of Jesus. The unfinished work and incomplete character of the Christ-event, expressed in a variety of different but consistent ways, is a feature found in the earliest Christologies of the New Testament. One of the clearest expressions of this incompleteness of the Christ-event is given, as mentioned in Chapter Three, in the early prayer *Maranatha, come, Lord Jesus* (1 Cor 16:22). The early

Church expected the imminent return of Christ to complete what Jesus as the Christ had inaugurated and we know that this caused practical problems within the community of the Thessalonians.

Another expression of the unfinished nature of the Christ-event is found in some of the Pauline Christologies. There is an underlying tension in Paul's theology between what already exists in Christ and what is yet to come, a tension between being 'in Christ' and 'becoming in Christ', between the present and the future. The sense that there is something still outstanding about the Christ-event is also captured by Paul in the language which describes Christ as 'the first fruits' (1 Cor 15:20), 'the beginning of the end' and 'the first born among many', (Rom 8:29; Col 1:18). These perspectives of Paul of course must be balanced by an equally strong emphasis on Christ as 'the fullness of time' (Gal 4; Eph 1:10), 'the new Creation' (2 Cor 5:17), and 'the revelation of the mystery ... kept secret ... for ... ages but now disclosed' (Rom 16:25, 16:26; see also 1 Col 1:26; Eph 1:9-10, Eph 3:4-5; 1 Cor 2:7). While the language of Revelation in the New Testament recognises that a breakthrough occurred in Christ, it also looks forward to the future (1 Cor 13:12; 1 Jn 3:2).

A similar tension can be found in the Johannine Christology which balances a strong realised eschatology alongside a futurist eschatology.[79] One further expression of this sense of the unfinished character of the Christ-event can be found in the doctrine of the second coming of Christ/*Parousia* which not only pervades the New Testament but also the early creeds and liturgical celebrations.

For too long, elements of the already, of newness, and of the break-through associated with the Christ-event have been allowed to dominate the self-understanding of Christianity in theory and in praxis to the detriment of the relationship between Christianity and other living faiths. There is now a new awareness that this imbalance must be redressed without in any way diminishing the uniqueness and the universal significance of the Christ-event. David Tracy, for instance, points out that when 'the second coming of Christ ... becomes a symbol as important as the symbols of the incarnation, cross and resurrection', then 'the work of Christology will open into a ... theological interpretation of Christianity in relationship to other religions.'[80] In a similar vein, Claude Geffré notes that it is only a Christianity aware of its own lack that will be able to encounter fruitfully other religions; it is absence and not presence that makes things happen; actions occur more often than not because of what is lacking.[81]

In all of this it is important to stress, as the tradition does, that the God revealed in the Christ-event always remains the God who is hidden, that the God made manifest in Christ is also the God who continues to be concealed, that the God understood in the incarnation is the God who is incomprehensible. The corollary to this awareness of the unfinished character of the Christ-event is that Christianity was never intended to be a closed, introverted and self-sufficient, all-embracing meta-narrative. When the narrative closes in upon itself and encloses God within itself, then openness disappears, contact with the world is lost, the essential relationship between Christianity and other religions is eclipsed, and ultimately God seems to withdraw.[82]

In contrast to this, we must affirm that Christianity is an open narrative and the history of Christianity has been one of adjustment, accommodation and enculturation of God's enduring presence in creation and history. Christianity today faces a new challenge as it seeks to relate to other religions. Rahner telescopes the history of Christianity into three great eras: the Jewish Christian moment, followed by the long Christian-Hellenistic period, and now the current era whereby Christianity seeks to become a world church. It will only be able to make this adjustment to being a world-church if it operates out of an open, unfinished and incomplete narrative. Only an open narrative will be able to take seriously the narratives of other religions in the shared search for God in human experience and the historical memory of the world. Within this new context Christianity will be able to bring something specific and particular to the table of dialogue, but equally important it will be able to receive something from the other religions within dialogue.

It is surely instructive to note that when Rahner came to answer the question: 'Why am I a Christian today?' he could say, 'My Christianity

... is anything but an explanation of the world and my existence', and 'much more an instruction not to regard any experience, any understanding as final.'[83] It is this recovery of the unfinished character of the Christ-event that gives a new impetus and urgency to dialogue with other religions. If something is unfinished, it is better able to give and to receive within dialogue.

To sum up, a unique part of Rahner's legacy to theology has been his distinctive but somewhat neglected contribution to inter-religious dialogue. In the first instance he was influential in stimulating the Second Vatican Council to adopt a positive attitude towards other religions. In the second instance, the later Rahner did outline perspectives conducive to inter-religious dialogue. These perspectives include what he calls the searching memory of faith, the existence of a searching Christology in other religions, the universal presence of the grace of the Holy Spirit, and a call to give priority to pneumatology as a point of departure for theology in dialogue with other religions. It is perhaps his emphasis on Pneumatology, and its potential as a point of departure for dialogue with other religions, that may be his enduring legacy. It is, therefore, his focus on the Spirit, on the universal presence of the gift of the Spirit, that we must now explore in the next chapter.

NOTES

1. Joseph H. Wong, 'Anonymous Christians: Karl Rahner's Pneuma-Christocentrism and an East-West Dialogue', *Theological Studies*, December 1994, 609–37 at 610

2. *Karl Rahner Im Gespräch*, Band 1, 301

3. Karl Rahner, 'The Experience of God Today', *Theological Investigations* (hereafter *TI*), Vol. XI, London: Darton, Longman and Todd, 149–65 at 150

4. Karl Rahner, *Foundations of Christian Faith: An Introduction to the Ideas of Christianity*, New York, Crossroad, 1978, 83

5. *Karl Rahner in Dialogue: Conversations and Interviews, 1965–1982*, Paul Imhof and Hubert Biallowons (eds), New York: Crossroad, 1986, 76

6. 'The One Christ and the Universality of Salvation', *TI*, Vol. XVI, 214

7. Ibid., 212

8. Ibid., 213 and 214 respectively

9. Ibid., 214

10. Ibid., 216

11. Karl Rahner deals with a searching Christology in 'The One Christ and the Universality of Salvation', *TI*, Vol. XVI, 221, and later on in *Foundations of Christian Faith*, 295–8

12. Roman A. Siebenrock, 'Christology', *The Cambridge Companion to Karl Rahner*, Declan Marmion and Mary Hines (eds), Cambridge: Cambridge University Press, 2005, 112–27 at 121

13. Rahner, *Foundations of Christian Faith*, 295

14. Ibid.

15. Ibid., 221

16. Rahner, 'On the Theology of the Incarnation', *TI*, Vol. VI, 119

17. This concept of a searching Christology resonates to some degree with the work of Jacques Derrida who talks about the messianic character of human experience, though important difference exist between Derrida and Rahner when it comes to source and cause of a searching Christology. We will return to this particular echo between Rahner and Derrida in Part 4 of this chapter

18. Rahner, *Foundations of Christian Faith*, 296

19. Ibid.

20. Rahner, 'Current problems in Christology', *TI*, Vol. I, 164

21. Rahner, 'The One Christ and the Universality of Salvation', *TI*, Vol. XVI, 212

22. Rahner, 'Christianity and the Non-Christian Religions' *TI*, Vol. V, 118

23. Ibid., 121

24. Ibid., 123

25. Ibid., 124

26. Ibid.

27. Ibid., 125

28. Ibid.

29. Ibid.

30. Ibid., 130

31. Ibid.

32. For some this concept seemed to play down the need for explicit faith for salvation, for others it undermined the missionary trust of the Church, and for still others it seemed to water down the uniqueness of the Christian message. A few claimed it contained an imperial intent *vis-á-vis* other religions. Rahner took these criticisms very seriously and engaged with them throughout his writings. Because of the mixed reception that his theology of anonymous Christianity received, he did not use the terminology of anonymous Christianity in *Foundations*. On this debate, see Eamonn Conway, '"So as not to despise

God's Grace": Reassessing Rahner's Idea of the "Anonymous Christian"', *Louvain Studies*, Spring–Summer 2004, 107–30

33. Rahner, 'Christianity and the Non-Christian Religions', 131

34. Ibid., 133

35. Ibid., 133

36. Acts 17:23

37. See *Foundations of Christian Faith*, 316–18

38. A more detailed account of the concept of entelechy in Rahner and its suggestiveness can be found in David Coffey, 'The Spirit of Christ as Entelechy', in *Philosophy and Theology* (2001), Vol. 13, No. 2, 363–98, and Denis Edwards, 'Saving Grace and the Action of the Spirit outside the Church', *Sin and Salvation: Task of Theology Today*, Duncan Reid and Mark William Worthing (eds), Australia: Australian Theological Forum Press, 2003, 205–21 at 210–15

39. *Foundations of Christian Faith*, 318–20

40. Ibid., 319

41. Karl Rahner, 'On the Importance of the Non-Christian Religions for Salvation', *TI*, Vol. XVIII, 290–1

42. Ibid., 294

43. Ibid.

44. Ibid., 295

45. Ibid.

46. John R. Sachs, '"Do Not Stifle the Spirit", Karl Rahner, The Legacy of Vatican II, and its Urgency for Theology Today', *Proceedings of the Catholic Theological Society of America*, 1996, 15–38 at 20

47. See, for example, Rahner, 'Experience of the Spirit and Existential Commitment', *TI*, Vol. XVI; 'Experience of the Holy Spirit', *TI*, Vol. XVIII

48. *Foundations of Christian Faith*, 130

49. *Karl Rahner in Dialogue*, 126

50. Available in *TI*, Vol. XXI, 1988, 78–98

51. Rahner, 'Aspects of European Theology', *TI*, Vol. XXI, 97

52. Ibid., 97

53. Ibid., 98

54. Ibid., 98

55. Gavin d'Costa describes Rahner as 'probably the most influential inclusivist theologian of the twentieth century' in 'Theology of Religions', *The Modern Theologians: An Introduction to Christian Theology in the Twentieth Century*, David F. Ford (ed.), second edition, Oxford: Blackwell Publishing, 626–44 at 631

56. See *Foundations of Christian Faith*, 245–6
57. See J. B. Metz, *Faith in History and Society: Towards a Practical Fundamental Theology*, London: Burns and Oates, 1980, 159–62; Steven J. Duffy, *The Dynamics of Grace: Perspectives in Theological Anthropology*, Collegeville, MN: Michael M. Glazier Books/Liturgical Press, 1993, 311
58. Rahner, 'Christianity and the Non-Christian Religions', 125
59. Ibid.
60. Paul Knitter, *Introducing Theologies of Religions*, New York: Orbis Books, 2002, 68
61. Ibid., 68–75; Jacques Dupuis, *Christianity and the Religions: From Confrontation to Dialogue*, New York: Orbis Books, 2002, 52–5; James L. Fredericks, *Faith Among Faiths: Christian Theology and non-Christian Religions*, New York: Paulist Press, 1999, 22–33; Josephine Lombardi, *What Are They Saying about the Universal Saving Will of God*, New York: Paulist Press, 2008, 31–4; Terrence W. Tilley et al., *Religious Diversity and the America Experience: A Theological Approach*, New York: Continuum, 2007, 64–79
62. *DV*, a.53
63. The important work of the Australian theologian David Coffey is a good example of someone influenced by Rahner in the area of Spirit Theology and Spirit Christology. See for example his 'Spirit Christology and the Trinity', *Advents of the Spirit: An Introduction to the Current Study of Pneumatology*, Bradford E. Hinze and D. Lyle Dabney (eds), Marquette: Marquette University Press, 2001, 315–38. The contribution of David Coffey to the construction of a Trinitarian Spirit-Christology is the subject of original research by Declan O'Byrne in a PhD thesis that is now published as *Spirit Christology and Trinity in the Theology of David Coffey*, with a foreword by David Coffey, *Studies in Theology, Society and Culture* series, Vol. 4, Bern: Peter Lang, 2010
64. Declan Marmion, 'Theology, Spirituality, and the Role of Experience in Karl Rahner', *Louvain Studies*, Spring and Summer 2004, 49–76 at 76
65. One of the first to note this curious echo between Rahner and Derrida was Michael J. Scanlon in 'A Deconstruction of Religion: On Derrida and Rahner', *God, the Gift and Postmodernism*, John D. Caputo and Michael J. Scanlon (eds), Indiana: Indiana University Press, 1999, 223–8
66. See Jacques Derrida, 'Faith and Knowledge: The Two Sources of "Religion" at the Limits of Reason Alone', *Acts of Religion*, Gil Anidjar (ed.), London: Routledge, 42–101; John D. Caputo and Michael J. Scanlon, 'Introduction: Apology for the Impossible: Religion and Postmodernism', *God, the Gift and Postmodernism*, 1–19
67. Jacques Derrida, 'How to avoid speaking: Denials', in *Derrida and Negative Theology*, Harold Coward and Toby Foshay (eds), New York: State University of New York Press, 1992, 74

68. Ibid., 78

69. Jacques Derrida, *On the Name*, Thomas Dutoit (ed.), California: Stanford University Press, 1995, 51

70. Denys Turner, 'Apophaticism, Idolatry and the Claims of Reason', *Silence and the Word: Negative Theology and the Incarnation*, Oliver Davies and Denys Turner (eds), Cambridge: Cambridge University Press, 2002, 34

71. See Philip Endean, *Karl Rahner and Ignatian Spirituality*, Oxford: Oxford University Press, 2001, 22–3, who is quoting from Rahner's *Aszese und Mystik in der Väterzeit*, Freiburg: Herder, 1938

72. Jacques Derrida, *Spectres of Marx: The State of the Debt, the Work of Mourning, and the New International*, New York: Routledge, 1996, 59

73. This particular concept of inclusive pluralism has been put forward by Jacques Dupuis in *Christianity and the Religions* and has been defended by Dupuis in '"Christianity and the Religions" Revisited', *Louvain Studies*, 28 (2003), 363–83. This concept is also found in the writings of Claude Geffré. See, for example, C. Geffré, 'The Christological Paradox as a Hermeneutic Key to Inter-Religious Dialogue', *Who Do You Say I Am: Confessing the Mystery of Christ*, John C. Cavadini and Laura Holt (eds), Indiana: University of Notre Dame Press, 2004, 155–72

74. Rahner, 'Christianity and the Non-Christian Religions', *TI*, Vol. V, 125

75. On the concept of a theocentric Christology, see Dermot A. Lane, *The Reality of Jesus: An Essay in Christology*, Dublin/New York: Veritas/Paulist Press, 1976/2008, 142–6

76. Dupuis, '"Christianity and the Religions" Revisited', 369

77. Dupuis, *Christianity and the Religions*, 95

78. *Foundations of Christian Faith*, 173

79. See Dermot A. Lane, *Keeping Hope Alive: Stirrings in Christian Theology*, Dublin/New York: Gill & Macmillan/Paulist Press, 1996, 106–111

80. Scott Holland, 'This side of God: A Conversation with David Tracey', *Cross Currents*, Spring 2002, 58–9

81. Geffré, 'The Christological Paradox as a Hermeneutical Key to Inter-Religious Dialogue', 168 and 167. Geffré is drawing here on the work of Michel de Certeau

82. Lieven Boeve, *Interrupting Tradition: An Essay on Christian Faith in a Postmodern Context*, Louvain: Peeters, 2003, 175

83. Karl Rahner, 'Why I am a Christian Today', *The Practice of Faith: A Handbook of Contemporary Spirituality*, Karl Lehmann and Albert Raffelt (eds), New York: Crossroad, 1984, 3–17 at 6–7

V. THE TURN TO THE SPIRIT: ELEMENTS WITHIN A FUNDAMENTAL THEOLOGY OF THE HOLY SPIRIT

It is possible to discern distinct, but related, turns to the Spirit in the twentieth century. There was, on the one hand, the convening of the Second Vatican Council by John XXIII with the express intention that the Council would constitute a 'new Pentecost' in the life of the Church. This wish is reflected in the documents of the Council and in the theological developments after the Council in the 1970s. Further, there has been a renewed focus on the Holy Spirit in the late twentieth and early twenty-first centuries. In addition, there has been a turn to the Spirit in the post 9/11, multicultural, globalised, inter-faith era. It is this more radical turn to the Spirit that the substance of this chapter will address.

These developments call for a renewed fundamental theology of the Holy Spirit – a task that is beyond the scope of this chapter. It will be necessary, nonetheless, to point towards some of the elements that might go towards the construction of a new fundamental theology of the Spirit. This more radical turn to the Spirit belongs to the field of fundamental theology, rather than systematic theology which, strictly speaking, should be able to build on the principles established in fundamental theology. For example, David Tracy points out that 'the question of the other religions can no longer be left until the end of a Christian Systematic Theology but should enter at the very beginning.'[1] In a similar vein, Gerald O'Collins suggests that developments at Vatican II, especially the publication of *Nostra Aetate*, have far-reaching implications for the way we will do fundamental theology in the present and the future.[2]

In broad terms, the beginnings of a renewed theology of the Spirit took place at the Second Vatican Council and this was spearheaded by Karl Rahner, Yves Congar, Leon Joseph Suenens and others, and this in turn was given expression in the documents of the Council, especially *Lumen Gentium*, *Ad Gentes*, *Unitatis Redintegratio* and *Gaudium et Spes*.

More specifically, a renewed theology of the Spirit has been taking place since the mid-1990s through a variety of conferences and publications. In 1996, the annual meeting of the Catholic Theological Society of America had as its theme, 'Towards a Spirited Theology: The Holy Spirit's Challenge to the Theological Traditions'. In 1998, Marquette University held a symposium on Pneumatology and published the papers under the title *Advents of the Spirit: An Introduction to the Current Study of Pneumatology*. In October 2002, scholars gathered at the ecumenical monastery at Bose in Italy to discuss 'The Holy Spirit and Ecumenism' and the papers were published later by Peeters in 2005. The annual convention of the College Theology Society in the US in 2003 was devoted to 'Spirit, Church and World', and the Society published a selection of the papers later in 2004. Monographs on the Holy Spirit in the last ten years are quite numerous and include such notable names as Gary Badcock, Kilian McDonnell, Bernard Cooke, Denis Edwards, Veli-Matti Kärkkäinen, Kirsteen Kim, Eugene Rogers Jr., Michael Welker, David Coffey and Declan O'Byrne.[3] Alongside this theological renewal, there has been a phenomenal growth in the Pentecostal and Charismatic movements in the twentieth century, estimated to be the fastest growing branch of Christianity, numbering somewhere in the region of six hundred million followers.

In this chapter, we will first of all discuss what might be the appropriate point of departure for a Christian theology of other religions. We will then outline the contributions of Bernard Lonergan and Frederick Crowe to the adoption of Pneumatology as a starting point for theology. This will be followed by an outline of some obstacles to Spirit-talk, and an indication of how these might be addressed. The chapter will conclude with the proposal of principles to guide discourse about the Spirit of God.

1. A STARTING POINT FOR DIALOGUE WITH THE RELIGIONS: PNEUMATOLOGY AND/OR TRINITY?

A valuable debate has been taking place about the proper point of departure within theology for dialogue with other religions. Two distinct proposals are usually put forward: the one Trinitarian and the other Pneumatological.

a. Taking a Trinitarian Approach

Many suggest the Trinity as an appropriate point of departure. These include Jacques Dupuis, David Coffey, Gavin D'Costa, Veli-Matti Kärkkäinen, Darren Dias and Mark Heim. These authors opt for the Trinity because they see in the doctrine of the Trinity an expression of plurality within the unity of God and suggest that this may help to understand the existence and meaning of pluralism among religions today. It is pointed out that the Trinity is a theological statement about God that embraces diversity as something intrinsic to the life of God. It is also noted that the doctrine of the Trinity structures the story of salvation and therefore should organise all Christian discourse in relation to other religions. Furthermore, it should be acknowledged that among those who propose a Trinitarian approach to other religions, there is also a recognition of the importance of the Spirit within this approach. Many, for example, speak of the Trinitarian presence of the Spirit in other religions and insist that the presence of the Spirit within other religions is intrinsically Trinitarian. The only way to talk about the Spirit is Trinitarian. Further, those who wish to take a Trinitarian approach to inter-religious dialogue are concerned that a Pneumatological approach runs the risk of becoming separated from Christ and that this disconnection can lead to a separation of the Spirit from the Church and the Kingdom of God.[4] This of course is a legitimate concern and is one of the main challenges facing those who prefer a Pneumatological point of departure. The fact that some who take the turn to the Spirit as their point of departure run the risk of establishing two economies of salvation have and often end up disconnecting Christ and the Church is an alarm-bell for those who wish to take a Pneumatological approach to other religions. To opt for the Spirit, however, does not automatically necessitate a neglect of Christ, Church and Kingdom, as we will see in Chapter Seven.

b. Adopting Pneumatology

In contrast to a Trinitarian approach, there is a growing body of theologians recommending a pneumatological approach to other religions. These include Karl Rahner whom we saw in Chapter Four recommended Pneumatology as a point of departure for the whole of theology. In addition Bernard Lonergan, whom we will discuss presently, also favours an emphasis on the gift of the Spirit poured out on all as the basic starting point for theology. Paul Tillich, towards the end of his life, saw other religions as 'spiritual communities' and wanted to revise his systematic theology in the light of this new awareness of the Spirit in other religions, even though Volume 3 of his *Systematics* had been given over to the Spirit.[5] Amos Yong proposes Pneumatology as a way beyond the impasse within inter-religious dialogue.[6] D. Lyle Dabney calls for a theology of the last person of the Trinity to be first in theology.[7] Others like Michael Barnes and Kirsteen Kim also emphasise Pneumatology in approaching other religions.

Those favouring Pneumatology point out that within the history of Revelation the Spirit precedes the Trinity, noting the presence of the Spirit in the prophets of Israel and in the life of Jesus which opens up the mystery of the Trinity as a point of arrival within God's self-communication in history. Further, they point out that to begin with the Trinity is to begin with a doctrine that has assumptions which in the past have excluded other religions. It is also noted that discourse about the Trinity often slips too easily into a discourse about the immanent Trinity which would be difficult for other religions to follow, especially if introduced too early in the dialogue. Moreover, in beginning with the economic Trinity, one is invoking a doctrine that has often side-lined the importance of the Spirit over centuries with unhappy consequences for both theology *ad intra* and theology *ad extra* in its relationship with the religions. Successive Trinitarian revivals have done little to rehabilitate the role of the Spirit in theology, with some notable exceptions such as David Coffey and Walter Kasper. Moreover, it is pointed out that the doctrine of the Trinity has developed over the centuries in the western tradition without much contact with human experience and history – points of reference that are essential within any dialogue with other religions.

To start with Pneumatology does not exclude the Trinity, but rather sees the Trinity as a point of arrival, that is a culminating point in the historical unfolding of a movement from the gift of the Spirit poured out on the whole of humanity at the dawn of time. This same Spirit is uniquely present with the people of Israel, especially among the prophets, and is perceived by Jewish faith to be a part of the Creator-Spirit active in creation. It is this Spirit that leads some in Israel to Jesus as the one who is personally and eschatologicaly filled with the Spirit and thus gives rise to a Spirit-Christology in Paul and the Synoptics and eventually arrives via the *Logos* Christology of John's Gospel at an understanding of God as Trinitarian – a historical unfolding of the Mystery of God in the single economy of salvation.

c. Reasons for starting with Pneumatology

Within this chapter, therefore, I am proposing the adoption of Pneumatology as a point of departure for Christian dialogue with other religions. In making this suggestion, I do not wish to create an either-or position between Pneumatology and Trinity. Instead, I propose Pneumatology as a more inclusive point of departure for dialogue, especially in relation to other religions. Further, starting with Pneumatology has the potential to lead to the Trinity in the course of dialogue, and in that journey towards the Trinity, there is the possibility of opening up neglected aspects of the Trinity as a result of starting with the Spirit. Moreover, 'threesomeness' is not something exclusive to the Christian God and therefore a Pneumatological encounter with other forms of 'threesomeness' may enrich our understanding of the Pneumatological revelation of the Trinity in scripture. By focussing on the Spirit as a starting point in dialogue with other religions, one is also beginning with a recognition of the centrality of spiritualities and spiritual values within most religions.

Alongside these reasons in favour of Pneumatology, we would add that the Spirit as gift is universally present in the world and in the religions from the dawn of history. It is the gift of the Spirit in the creation of the human that marks out the dignity of every human being and constitutes each person as made in the image of God/*imago Dei*.

And yet, the adoption of Pneumatology as a point of departure begs the question: why this strong emphasis on the Holy Spirit? The principle reason is that it is through the Spirit that we get to know who God is and it is through the Spirit that God enters into our lives. Congar, for example, suggests that the Spirit is the way in which God can 'exist, as it were, out of Himself' and so the Spirit 'is the bond of unity not only in God, but also between God and creation, a unity of love.'[8] Kilian McDonnell describes the Spirit as 'the contact point' between God and humanity and 'the point of departure of our journey to God.'[9] Robert Doran goes so far as to suggest that the Spirit should become the centrepiece of systematic theology so that 'we can affirm that the Holy Spirit is poured out on all people and can be found in religions other than Christianity as well as in the Christian churches.'[10]

Further, it should be acknowledged that Pneumatology is not something that began at Pentecost. To suggest that a theology of the Spirit began only at Pentecost would imply that the life of Jesus, the history of Israel and the story of Creation were somehow 'Spirit-less'. Such a denial of the Spirit in the life of Jesus, within the history of Israel and the story of creation goes against the evidence of the Bible. Instead, we must begin theology by acknowledging that the Spirit of God is active from the dawn of time, 'hovering' over creation, active in the lives of all human beings, in the history of other religions, in the unique history of Israel, in the life of Jesus crucified and risen, and in the Christian community. In other words, historical evidence exists for giving not only centrality but a primacy and priority within fundamental theology to the Spirit.

The issue of an appropriate starting point for dialogue with other religions was not discussed at the Second Vatican Council. There are, however, passing references at the Council that would support the priority of Pneumatology. For example, the Council emphasises that the universal saving will of God and the offer of salvation to all are connected with the universal presence of the Spirit in the world. For instance, in the *Pastoral Constitution on the Church in the Modern World*, the Council says: 'Since the ultimate vocation of man is in fact one, and divine, we ought to believe that the Holy Spirit in a manner known only to God, offers to every human being the possibility of being associated with the Paschal Mystery' of Christ.[11] In the *Decree on the Church's Missionary Activity*, the Council states that 'The Holy Spirit was already at work in the world before Christ was glorified' and then goes on to point out, in a rarely noticed but fascinating footnote quoting St Leo the Great, that the Spirit precedes the Christ-event:

> When on the day of Pentecost the Holy Spirit filled the disciples of the Lord, it was not so much the beginning of a gift as it was the completion of one already bountifully possessed: because the patriarchs, the prophets, the priests, and all the holy men who preceded them were already quickened by the life of the same Spirit ... although they did not possess His gifts to the same degree.[12]

This reference to 'a gift already bountifully possessed' that had 'quickened' the lives of others is a recognition that the gift of the Holy Spirit had been given to all from the dawn of time and this, it might be argued, is one further reason for proposing Pneumatology as a point of departure for dialogue with other religions.

2. BERNARD LONERGAN AND FREDERICK CROWE ON THE PRIORITY OF PNEUMATOLOGY

Bernard Lonergan, especially towards the end of his life, became increasingly aware of the challenge other religious traditions posed for Christian theology. Lonergan left a number of principles peppered throughout *Method in Theology* and scattered in various articles, especially 'Prologomena to the Study of the Emerging Religious Consciousness of our Time'.[13] These principles have been gathered up and developed by Frederick Crowe in a few articles, especially in 'Son of God, Holy Spirit and the World Religions', an outstanding lecture that Crowe delivered coincidentally on the day Lonergan died, 26 November 1984.[14]

a. Lonergan's Principles

Among the principles that Lonergan articulated about other religions, the following stand out:

1. 'I am inclined to interpret the religions of mankind, in their positive moment, as the fruit of the gift of the Spirit, though diversified by many degrees of social and cultural development, and distorted by man's infidelity to self-transcendence to which he aspires.'[15] This recognition of religions as 'the fruit of the gift of the Spirit' is a highly significant step forward in understanding and appreciating other religions.

2. For Lonergan, the gift of the Holy Spirit has been given to all from the beginning of time, and is expressed in the love of God that has been poured out into our hearts through the Spirit – based on Romans 5:5, a text which played a pivotal role in Lonergan's theology.[16]

3. Lonergan talks about the unique relationship that exists between the inner word of the gift of the Spirit given to all and the outer word of the *Logos* given in the Incarnation of God in Jesus. Without the outer word, the inner word of the gift of the Spirit remains an orientation to mystery without a proper object, unless the outer word is uttered.[17] On the other hand, Lonergan affirms

that, 'without the invisible mission of the Spirit, the word enters into his own, but his own receives him not.'[18]

4. While emphasising the gift of the Spirit given to all, Lonergan insists: 'One needs the word, the word of tradition that has accumulated religious wisdom, the word of fellowship that unites those that share the gift of the Spirit of God's love, the word of the Gospel that announces that God has loved us first and, in the fullness of time, has revealed that love in Christ crucified, dead and risen.'[19]

5. To help explain the relationship between the inner word of the Spirit of God and the outer word of the Son, Lonergan invokes the image of the love between a man and a woman as an analogy for understanding the two divine missions:

'When a man and a woman love each other but do not avow their love, they are not yet in love. Their very silence means that their love has not reached the point of self-surrender and self-donation. It is the love that each freely and fully reveals to the other that brings about the radically new situation of being in love and that begins the unfolding of its lifelong implications.'[20]

It is only when the word of the *Logos* is made flesh, that the full meaning of the inner word of the gift of the Spirit becomes fully apparent.

6. Lonergan also talks about the relationship between the inner word of the Spirit in the secret of our hearts and the outer Word of the Son in terms of the bond that exists between the Spirit-generated infra-structure of being in love without an object and the super-structure of interpretation and knowledge on the other hand.[21] It should

be noted in passing here that this distinction between the Spirit-generated infra-structure of being in love and the super-structure of interpretation echoes in many respects Rahner's distinction between transcendental Revelation and categorical revelation.

b. Crowe's Development of Lonergan

It is against the background of these principles that Frederick Crowe develops what he calls 'the tacit supposition permeating all of Lonergan's later work on the Son and the Spirit.'[22] Crowe seeks to provide a coherent account of where Lonergan was heading, and since then others have been building on Crowe's work.[23] Crowe gets to the point quickly in his article on 'Son of God, Holy Spirit and the World Religions' about this tacit supposition:

> Here, then, is the basic thesis. We have simply to reverse the order in which we commonly think of the Son and the Spirit in the world. Commonly we think of God first sending the Son, and of the Spirit being sent in that context, to bring to completion the work of the Son.

Instead of this familiar outlook we must now reverse the order of the missions in the light of Lonergan's principles:

> God first sent the Spirit, and then sent the Son in the context of the Spirit's mission, to bring to completion – perhaps not precisely the work of the Spirit, but the work which God had conceived as one work to be executed in two steps of the two-fold mission of first the Spirit and then the Son.[24]

Conscious that he is suggesting something here which may appear contrary to the foundations of Christianity, he says he is proposing 'not so much a new doctrine as a rearranging of doctrines already widely held.'[25] In defence of this thesis, Crowe argues he is following a principle that is widely held, namely 'that what is first in our eyes is not first in itself; on the contrary what is first in our eyes is last in itself, and what is last in our eyes is first in itself.'[26] He applies this principle to the visible mission of the Son and the invisible mission of the Spirit, noting that what is visible will be first in the cognitional order of discovery (i.e., first for us) and what is invisible will be last for us. But 'is it not to be expected, that the real order (that is the ontological order) is the exact opposite to the cognitional order',[27] namely that the invisible mission of the Spirit is first and the visible mission of the Son is second.

Crowe goes on to say that Lonergan did not invent the idea of the Spirit as God's first gift; instead he says Lonergan found it in Augustine and in Aquinas. However, what Lonergan does imply and Crowe spells out is that the first gift of the Spirit is 'universally applicable throughout the world' and so we can 'come to a theology of the Spirit's widespread presence among us, a presence from the beginning of human time to the ends of space.'[28]

For Crowe, the outer Word represents an objectification of the inner word of the Spirit and these two words, namely the Spirit and the Son, must be kept together. In asking us to reverse our account of the order of Trinitarian persons, Crowe is not in any sense denying the traditional order of the Father, Son and Holy Spirit. Instead he is applying that ancient Aristotelian principle, that what is first for us, namely the appearance of the *Logos* incarnate in Jesus, is last in the ultimate or ontological order of things. Further, it should be remembered that some of the early fathers reversed the order of the Son and the Spirit to the Spirit and the Son.[29] David Coffey, for example, also acknowledges that the order of the Son and the Spirit should be reversed from a historical point of view – but there can be no re-ordering of the immanent Trinity. The real value in re-ordering the economic Trinity is the recovery of the Spirit and the Spirit's relationship to the Son.[30]

Crowe talks about 'our new relationship to the world religions' in the light of the inner word of the gift of the Spirit given to all. He spells out that new relationship in the following way: 'We do not, therefore, go to the world religions as to strangers, as to heathens, pagans, or enemies of God.' Instead, 'we are one with them in the Spirit.'[31] Further, Crowe says we should 'expect to find in them (that is the other religions) the fruits of the Spirit'[32] and if we find the fruits of the Spirit are lacking in the other religions, we should remember that they are far too often also lacking among ourselves, even though we have been given the outer Word.[33] In the light of this new relationship with the other religions, we need to come up with a new, shared language to spell out what this new relationship might mean. This new language should seek to express the shared experience of the inner word that Christians and other religions enjoy, and that this new language, while informed by particular narratives, should seek to be inclusive in its outreach to others.

c. Consequences and Challenges

A number of important consequences flow from this vision of Lonergan and Crowe:

1. It changes the relationship between Christianity and other religions, moving beyond any suggestion that other religions are simply a pale reflection of Christianity.

2. It requires a new attitude and outlook from Christians towards other religions, approaching them no longer as enemies, but as friends, experiencing and enjoying one and the same inner gift of the Spirit.

3. It now becomes apparent that what distinguishes Christians from the members of other religions is not God's grace which is given to all through the gift of the Spirit — but rather the unique expression of that gift of grace through the person of Jesus Christ, crucified, risen and present in the Spirit.[34]

In the light of these consequences, new challenges present themselves. More attention needs to be given to the relationship between the inner word of the Spirit and the outer Word of the Son, especially the unfolding within Judaism of the outer Word of God and its completion in the Christ-event through the life, death and resurrection of the Word Incarnate. Further, the relationship between the inner and outer Word, not only in Christianity but also in other religions, needs to be amplified. What is the relationship between the outer Word of Christianity and the outer W/word of other religions? Most importantly, how in Christianity, and how in the other religions, working together, might it be possible to express and articulate the impulses and movements and promptings of the gift of the Spirit poured out on all? What is the inner word of the Spirit that stirs the human spirit today in the twenty-first century saying to humanity? And, equally, what is it of the gift of the Spirit that holds Christianity and Islam and Judaism together in some loose association as children of Abraham and yet compels them to remain as separate religions? In other words, the proposal to give priority to Pneumatology must surely serve to expand, enrich and deepen our awareness of the invisible guest of the Spirit residing in the members of all religions. This Spirit seeks to be the midwife of a new mutual regard and respect for each other in a world that is so broken and dangerously divided.

Clearly, the preferred starting-point for inter-faith dialogue is the micro-structure of the experiences of transcendence and of being in love, generated by the gift of the Holy Spirit, rather than the supra-structure of interpretation and knowledge. What is it about the micro-structure that fails to communicate the experience of the gift of the Holy Spirit? John C. Haughey suggests that the main enemy of discovering the deeper dimensions of faith 'is a stolid classicism and dogmatic conceptualism'.[35] Our understanding of the outer Word is all too content to stay with previously achieved concepts and expressions which over time become archaic and oblivious to the fact that all, in virtue of the gift of the Spirit, 'are vectored towards a not-yet'.[36]

One other challenge is worth noting at this stage. If there is a new relationship between the religions, and if, therefore, the religions are no longer to be seen as over and against each other in view of the gift of the Spirit, then we must begin to realise that what is good for one religion should be in principle good for all religions. Thus, when one religion is ridiculed or diminished for whatever reason, there is a sense in which all religions are ridiculed or diminished, and this should introduce a new sense of shared responsibility and mutual support among the religions of the world.

One cannot help noting the parallels that exist between Lonergan's principles as developed by Crowe and Rahner's views on the Spirit as outlined in Chapter Four. At the risk of repetition, it may be helpful to note that Rahner, echoing Lonergan, points out that the Spirit is already there, ahead of us, given as gift, and it is this basic truth that enables Rahner to talk about the gift of a transcendental revelation offered to all. From that point of departure, Rahner goes on to stress the importance of categorical revelation which expresses and communicates the content of transcendental revelation in history, thus paralleling Lonergan on the inner and outer Word, the micro structure of the experience of the Spirit and on the supra-structure of knowledge.

It is against this background that we should understand Rahner's passionate plea on the eve of the Second Vatican Council to take the Spirit more seriously in an address entitled 'Do Not Stifle the Spirit', a title taken from the First Letter of Paul to the Thessalonians 5:19. Of course, the context was different, and Rahner would have been thinking primarily of the upcoming Second Vatican Council. Nonetheless, in a strange and disturbing way, what Rahner had to say in that talk is as applicable today as it was in 1962:

> We must face the possibility, with fear and trembling, that we could be the ones who stifle the Spirit – stifle him through that pride in 'knowing better', that inertia of the heart, that cowardice, that unteachableness with which we react to fresh impulses and new pressures in the Church.[37]

Rahner is clear that the stirring of the Spirit 'is not ... confined to official pronouncements by the Church'[38] and that a creative interplay should take place between the charismatic and the hierarchical elements of the Church.[39]

Some twenty years later Rahner observed, as we saw in Chapter Four, that European theology, by and large, had treated Christology before developing a theology of the Spirit. He goes on to say: 'Perhaps an Eastern theology will one day reverse this perspective' by putting Pneumatology before Christology. Why? He gives two reasons. First of all because of God's universal salvific will, and secondly 'in ... respect for all major world religions'.[40]

3. PHILOSOPHICAL PROBLEMS WITH SPIRIT-TALK

It is one thing to talk about adopting Pneumatology as a starting point for theology and quite another to put that proposal into practice. Many, such as Harvey Cox, Mark Wallace, and Philip Clayton, claim that we in the twenty-first century are living in 'the age of the Spirit'. Nearly all agree on the neglect of the Spirit and the need to recover new Pneumatological perspectives – but thereafter agreement ends. John Paul II talks about the presence of the Spirit among the religions of the world, in culture, the arts and the achievement of modern science.[41]

The danger with this new-found enthusiasm for the Spirit is that it will end up, to borrow a phrase from another context, a matter of simply 'add Spirit and stir' and this, as we know, will not work. If this renaissance in the theology of the Spirit is to succeed, we need to do a couple of things. First of all, we should acknowledge that difficulties attach to discourse about the Holy Spirit. There are serious problems surrounding 'Spirit-talk' in the modern era. It is necessary, as it were, to understand the prejudice against this move in theology, and to know some of the challenges it entails if there is to be a genuine recovery of Pneumatology within theology. Further, Spirit-talk needs to be more philosophically and theologically robust.

a. A Cultural Awkwardness with Spirit-Talk

It should be acknowledged that there is deep suspicion within modern culture, and especially in the academy, about references to spirit. People do not talk about the Spirit, either with a small 's' or with a capital 'S' at social gatherings, or in the public square, or in university lecture halls. There is an academic awkwardness around the language of Spirit.

For many, the language of the Spirit is too vague, too subjective, too elusive, too disembodied, and too removed from experience to be taken seriously, or indeed to hold people's attention for any length of time.

b. Summary of Prejudices against a Discourse about the Spirit

According to Charles Taylor, 'we tend in our [modern] culture to stifle the Spirit': we seem to have suffered something of 'a spiritual lobotomy' in our enlightenment culture, partly because of the damage done by religions in history, especially the religious wars after the Reformation, and partly because of the rise of modern naturalism.[42] Philip Rossi talks about the existence of 'Spirit-stifling practices' which are 'part of a global, post-industrial and market-driven capitalism'.[43] Mark Wallace discusses the 'conventional assumptions' about the spirit in philosophy and theology. He points to the deep-seated separation of spirit and matter, and suggests that talk about the spirit remains saddled with ethereal and perjorative connotations: 'Conjuring up images of ghosts, phantoms and other incorporeal forces; [images] of vaporous clouds and gaseous substance; images of whatever is airy, immaterial, invisible, non-substantial, bloodless, bodiless, passionless and unearthly.'[44] Others, like David H. Jensen, point to the popular perception that the spirit is opposed to the flesh and bodies and that the spirit shuns the body out of holiness.[45] Kathryn Tanner says that some see the activity of the spirit as something that happens 'instantaneously' in an 'unmediated' manner and this is present in some forms of the Pentecostal movement.[46] Denis Edwards cautions that what is often claimed as an experience of the Spirit may be simply the projection of imagination or just delusion. In particular, there is need for some critical stance when people claim to experience the Spirit and have a message for others to follow.[47]

This is a formidable list of problems against Spirit-talk, and these need to be recognised if we are to construct a credible theology of the Holy Spirit. Many of these prejudices against Spirit-discourse are philosophical and therefore we must look at what philosophical resources are available to help in the reconstruction of a credible Pneumatology for the twenty-first century.

4. PHILOSOPHICAL RESOURCES FOR SPIRIT-TALK

Within the modern era, there have been a number of developments in philosophy that can help to address some of the linguistic deficits and philosophical difficulties surrounding Spirit-talk. In modern philosophy, there has been a shift from a substance philosophy (metaphysics) towards a subject-centred philosophy. This turn to the subject is sometimes known as the 'transcendental turn', giving rise to the transcendental method present in theologians like Maréchal, Lonergan and Rahner. Attention to, and analysis of human subjectivity is at the heart of knowing and understanding. It is the self-conscious subject who knows and acts and endures throughout history. Within this emphasis on the subject, there has developed a philosophy of interiority which places considerable emphasis on, in the first instance, human awareness, and then the dawning of self-consciousness. This reality of self-consciousness is held up as part of the data of sense experience, and should therefore qualify for inclusion within an empirical approach to life. Attention is focussed on the multilayered dynamism of self-consciousness, and this dynamism includes human affectivity, intentionality and irrepressible questioning.

a. The Shift from Substance to Subject

This breakthrough in the movement from substance to subject was enabled by three influential philosophers in the modern era. The first of these is Immanuel Kant, who highlights the centrality of the human subject in the process of knowing and understanding. He argues in the *Critique of Pure Reason* for the presence of an underlying ground that accompanies all human knowing. He identifies that ground in 'the abiding and unchanging "I"' that knows. The 'I' or the 'self' or 'subject' is conscious of itself as one and the same identical reality that receives representations of things, effects synthesis of these representations and moves towards intuition. For Kant, knowing and understanding resides in the enduring reality of the self-conscious subject.[48]

The second influential modern philosopher enabling the turn from a philosophy of substance to a philosophy of subject was Hegel. This shift is presented by Hegel in *The Phenomenology of Mind*, which in the German edition is *The Phenomenology of Spirit* (*Phänomenologie des Geistes*). In this text, Hegel argues for the primacy of spirit as the source and goal of all knowledge and that with a dialectical movement between spirit and world, one arrives at a heightened level of self-consciousness of the human spirit. As with Kant, the primacy and centrality of the human spirit as a point of departure and a point of arrival is firmly established. This turn to the spirit enabled Hegel to affirm and arrive at a dialectical unity of the human spirit and God as absolute Spirit.

The third philosopher is Emmanuel Levinas. He holds that the 'self' can be 'enclosed' and even 'implodes' until and unless it is engaged with an 'other' that breaks the boundaries of the self. To see this 'other' as 'other' is to open up the bounded self and emerge as a subject.[49]

In showing how the shift from substance to subject and spirit opens up ways for constructing a Pneumatology, it is important not to conflate the human spirit and divine Spirit. Philosophy and theology must emphasise not only the relationship between the human and the divine, but also the radical difference between the human and the divine. For some, the only way of maintaining this difference between the human and the divine is to stress the infinity of the divine over the finiteness of the human. There are two important challenges here that must be acknowledged.

On the one hand, if you over-emphasise the difference between the infinite Spirit and the finite spirit, you run the risk of offending, indeed negating, the image of God (*imago Dei*) within the human.

The doctrine of the human, made in the image of God, must moderate our understanding of the relationship between the human spirit and the divine Spirit. On the other hand, if you stress the infinity of God, you end up affirming what Hegel calls 'the bad infinite' and thereby neglecting the 'true infinite'. For Hegel, the 'true infinite' must include reference to the finite as part of the infinite, without however denying the distinction between the infinite and the finite. This close relationship between the infinite and the finite is borne out by the doctrines of creation and the incarnation of God in Jesus of Nazareth. The Incarnation is an illustration of what Hegel is saying, namely that the infinite contains reference to the finite, and the finite contains reference to the infinite. For Christianity, the ultimate claim is that the infinite God contains reference to the finiteness of humanity in virtue of what happened in the Christ-event. The core doctrine of the Incarnation must be allowed to influence the way Christians understand the relationship between the divine Spirit and human spirit.

In a similar way, though from a different theological point of view, Emanuel Levinas suggests that the finite is related to the infinite, since the infinite is thought by the finite. The finite spirit is able to think the unthinkable of the infinite Spirit and so the infinite is somehow a part of the finite. This rapport between the finite and the infinite, even when the finite is thinking about what is incomprehensible, suggests that a similar kind of relationship is possible between the human spirit and the divine Spirit.[50]

b. Engaging critically with the Turn to the Subject

One of the initial objections to, and arguments against, the turn to the subject is that it engenders subjectivism. That of course is always a possibility, but this objection ignores or fails to appreciate the dynamism and intentionality of the human subject. It was this awareness of the dynamic intentionality of the human subject that prompted theologians influenced by the transcendental method to point out that authentic subjectivity is the basis of genuine objectivity.[51] Further, in this regard, if the encounter between the divine Spirit and the human spirit does not take place within the depths of human subjectivity, in what Rahner refers to as 'the innermost centre of existence', it will leave the subject unaffected and unchanged, whereas one of the distinguishing features of the encounter of the human subject with the divine Spirit is the change and conversion it effects at a variety of levels: moral, intellectual and religious.[52] Thus, the turn to the subject does not necessarily end in subjectivism and there is nothing wrong about subjectivity as a point of departure in arriving at objective knowing and understanding.

A second difficulty surrounding the turn to the subject to be addressed is that in some instances, the modern turn to the subject has excluded reference to God as the divine Subject. It was suggested that affirmations of a divine Subject alongside the human subject somehow diminished the freedom of the human subject or detracted from the autonomy and self-sufficiency of the human subject. This perceived opposition or rivalry between the human subject and the divine Subject is a misplaced dichotomy, based on a misunderstanding of both the human subject and the divine Spirit. The human subject is never quite as autonomous as it would like to think; it is always inter-dependent, inter-related, and inter-connected from birth throughout life, but this radical relationality does not diminish its autonomy but rather enables that autonomy to develop in freedom. On the other hand, the divine Spirit is present as gift and not as rival, as invitation and not imposition, as summons and not command which, when freely accepted, awakens new possibility and enriches the life of the human spirit.

While the turn to the subject within modernity may be used to stifle Spirit-talk and to suppress reference to God, it can also at the same time be used to open up Spirit-talk and enable reference to God. Charles Taylor in *A Secular Age,* and others point out that unanswered questions persist around the turn to the subject, questions in regard to relationality, subjectivity and inter-subjectivity, and these questions can be used as much to open up the issue of the relationship between the human spirit and the divine Spirit, as to deny this relationship. In this regard, Taylor refers to 'un-quiet frontiers of modernity',[53] while others discuss irrepressible questions around the shaky self-sufficiency of the human subject, or what indeed some refer to as the vulnerable and fragile character of the human subject.

It would be disingenuous, perhaps a good example of having one's head in the sand, however, to ignore the critique of the subject within modernity that comes from post-modernity. Some postmodern theorists complain that there is nothing present in the subject beyond what we put there. At best, the human subject is merely a kind of crossroads, an artificial site that facilitates cultural and linguistic exchanges. After these exchanges, there is nothing. The value of this particular criticism is that it forces us to move from the modern question about *what* is the subject to the post-modern question of who is the subject. The full turn, therefore, is from substance to subject and from subject to agent. There is always someone *who* is acting, someone *who* is performing, including the post-modern person who asks not *what* is the subject, but *who* is the subject? The answer to this question is that the subject is the one who acts and who therefore leaves a trace, often more than a trace, in human exchanges and relationships. The subject as agent cannot be ignored, or denied, or suppressed. It is the subject as agent who acts, performs and interrupts the movement of human relationships. Access to the subject is available not as a construct, nor as a fixed or finished entity, but as one who acts and performs and interrupts as agent. The subject as agent comes into view within the mapping of a narrative. Every narrative contains an element of memory, memory about where the subject as agent in the past has come from, and where the subject as agent is going in the future through the power of imagination. It is imagination that is a spring-board for the *praxis* of the subject as agent moving into the future.[54] To this extent, the subject-as-agent is always a work in progress, an open and unfinished narrative.

In talking about the subject as agent in these particular terms, we are employing a model that could be used analogously to describe the action of the Spirit of God in creation and in history, in Israel and in Jesus, in the churches and in the religions of the world in the past and in the future.

c. New Analogies

This new emphasis in philosophy on the human subject, on the human spirit, on self-consciousness, on human interiority and on inter-subjectivity gives us a language that enables us to talk analogously about the divine Spirit. Terms like subject, self-consciousness and inter-subjectivity provide possible models of what and how the divine Spirit is and acts analogously speaking; they point towards the possibility of a relationship between the divine and human spirit, not unlike the relationship that exists between one human subject and another human subject. Terms like subject, inter-subjectivity and interiority provide resources for expanding the theological imagination in its reference to the divine Spirit. Secondly, discourse about the subject, about the human spirit, and human self-consciousness, provides us with a context and a location in which an encounter between the human spirit and the divine Spirit might be placed. Thirdly, we know that these terms of subject and spirit and human self-consciousness exist only as embodied, and are only available as incarnated in living human beings, and not as disembodied or excarnated realities. This suggests that when we talk about the divine Spirit, we can only talk about the Spirit as somehow embodied, incarnated and incorporated in other living realities.

Frederick Crowe sums up this turn to the subject, and its significance for a new discourse about the Spirit in the following way:

> It is only with the turn to the subject, with the emergence of a philosophy of interiority, with the replacement of causality by meaning as a basic category, that we have the conceptual system that we need for an integrated theology of the roles of the Son and the Spirit in the world.[55]

5. SIGNPOSTS TO SPIRIT-TALK

Arising out of this review of the philosophical resources, with its focus on the turn to the subject, the emergence of the self-conscious subject, the importance of the dynamic intentionality of the human subject, the place of interiority, and the significance of inter-subjectivity, are the following points:

- The human subject is only available as narrated and embodied;
- The human spirit is always mediated by the body;
- The self becomes a subject through encounter with the other
- Self-consciousness is activated by dialogue with others;
- Interiority emerges from engagement with exteriority.

What begins to emerge in the movement from the substance to subject is that we must put spirit back into matter and therefore we must begin to overcome the dualism between body and soul, the dichotomy between spirit and matter, and the divorce between flesh and the subject because subject and spirit and soul exist only as embodied and enfleshed and incarnated. In a word, we must begin to realise that matter matters, that bodies are spiritual and sacred, that the flesh is symbolic, and that the earth is alive with an inner dynamism. In other words, we need to know matter if we are to know and understand spirit; we need to experience the body if we are to encounter spirit, we need to engage the earth if we are to find spirit. This does not necessarily mean collapsing spirit into matter or inflating matter into spirit. Instead, we are saying that spirit and matter are inseparable and yet at the same time distinguishable.

A second perspective emerging from these philosophical resources for Spirit-talk is the recognition that a theology of the Spirit must be compatible with the philosophy of the human spirit. There can be no discourse about the divine Spirit that is not at the same time a discourse about the human spirit. It is a key theological principle that there can be no talk about God without talk at the same time about the 'humanum'. Likewise there can be no talk about the divine Spirit of God without talk about the human spirit. This does not mean reducing the divine Spirit into the human spirit; instead it demands that we must recognise the distinction and yet the close relationship that exists between God and the world, between the human and the divine, between nature and grace as revealed in the Incarnation of God in Jesus of Nazareth. Consequently, developments in understanding the human spirit will help towards the rehabilitation of a theology of the Holy Spirit. As is recognised in Catholic theology, a close relationship exists, and has always existed, between anthropology and theology, and this relationship should be mirrored in the unity that obtains between pneumatology and Pneumatology. In the light of these introductory remarks about signposts to the spirit, we will now outline some observations on the relationship between anthropology and pneumatology.

a. Anthropology and Pneumatology

Getting in touch with the human spirit or indeed with the human self is not easy. Western thought has been distorted by the turn to the subject within modernity, especially under the influence of René Descartes. His slogan 'I think, therefore, I am' has given rise to the creation of the self-sufficient subject, the subject of modernity which in turn gave birth to the emergence of a strong individualism. This strong self of modernity has been critiqued by feminism, contemporary cosmologies and ecology.[56] What emerges from these critiques is a relational, social and cosmic self. There is a sense in which the human is an embodied work of art in process.

When I look into myself, what do I find? I do not find a substance, or a fixed entity, or a settled self, but a set of relationships that constitute me as a subject: family, friends, community, work, relationships, the earth, and the cosmos which, when taken together, contribute to the identity of the human subject. The question is: how is the subject constituted? Is the subject alone or is the subject constituted by others and, if so, what others? When I look inside, I discover that I am sustained by a network of relationships such as family, friends and community who are all gifts in one way or another. When I dig a little deeper, when I drill deep down, I find I am sustained by something that transcends family, friends and community, and that something is variously described as a sacred

Spirit, an enduring companion, a 'divine guest resident in the hearts and lives of all',[57] a divinising gift of grace. It is this sacred Spirit, this Holy Spirit, this enduring co-presence, that enables humans to realise that the human is never simply alone, is never just a self, is never just an 'I' but also a 'we'. For this to happen, however, there must be stillness, there must be a journey inward, there must be an awareness of interiority, there must be a turn to the data of self-consciousness, there must be a getting-in-touch with what Merton called 'the inner self' in contrast to 'the outer self' decked out in all its splendid superficiality. In brief, there must be attention to the inner experience of the gift of the Spirit. A Carthusian monk, after fifty years of silence and prayer, when asked how to pray replied: 'When you pray, pray in and not up.' Of course the more we 'pray in', the more we will want to 'pray up'. It is the experience of immanence that puts us in touch with transcendence, or better that grounds transcendence, both an immanent transcendence as well as a Transcendent transcendence.

But the journey inwards is just one way of getting in touch with the Holy Spirit. There is also the movement outwards, the encounter with the other, that awakens something inside that stirs the silent Spirit within, that puts us in touch with something greater than simply the human spirit. This movement from the outside to the inside can take place through the experiences of others, through the Christian community's ritual celebration of Word and Sacrament, but also through our encounter with the creative arts such as music and visual creations. The experience of beauty stirs the human spirit to the interior presence of the divine Spirit as well as the transcendent presence of the Holy Spirit in creation, history and other human beings.

In this way we can suggest that there is a link and a relationship between anthropology and Pneumatology, a relationship between the self as spirit and the inner gift of the Holy Spirit. This can happen through the journey inwards which puts us in touch with the in-dwelling, resident guest of the Holy Spirit, or it can happen through an external experience that awakens something within the human spirit. What these reflections on the relationship between the Holy Spirit and the human spirit reveal is the need to put Spirit back into matter.

b. Putting Spirit Back into Matter

One philosopher-theologian among others who has helped to re-unite spirit and matter without confusing or conflating them is Karl Rahner. Rahner's second published work was *Spirit in the World* (1939), which dealt with epistemology in Aquinas and Heidegger. Since then, the gift of the Holy Spirit has been an underlying theme in Rahner, rooted in a few foundational articles such as 'The Unity of Spirit and Matter in Christian Faith'[58] and some reflections on Ascension.[59]

In his article on 'The Unity of Spirit and Matter in the Christian Understanding of Faith', Rahner observes that Christian faith recognises a unity of spirit and matter and he proposes three reasons for this unity. These reasons are: in virtue of the origin, the history and the goal of spirit and matter. Rahner does not develop these reasons in this particular article, but it is quite clear that in relation to the origin of spirit and matter, he is referring to the doctrine of creation; in relation to the history of spirit and matter, he has in mind the evolution of the world under the influence of Spirit; and in relation to the goal of spirit and matter, he is pointing towards the Christian doctrine of the New Creation through death and resurrection.

Rahner notes that all too often 'matter has been experienced as something dark and anti-divine, obscure or chaotic'.[60] For too many, matter is seen as something standing in contradiction and bitter combat against spirit. According to this outlook, it is Spirit that represents the image of God in the world, and this particular image is something that needs to be challenged by recovering the fundamental unity of spirit and matter.[61]

In contrast, Rahner wishes to affirm a fundamental unity of spirit and matter while, at the same time, recognising that there is a need to make a basic distinction between spirit and matter. Christianity, says Rahner, 'has always recognised this relationship and the mutual correlation of spirit and matter'.[62] Within the Christian vision, matter can be traced back to the creative act of the creator God who is called Spirit.[63] Matter 'is created by God ... for the sake of and in view of spirit' and so 'matter cannot rest incommensurable beside spirit'.[64] For Rahner, according to Christian philosophy and theology, 'matter is connected with and oriented towards spirit'; matter is endowed from the beginning with a dynamism towards spirit. It is against this background that Rahner makes the remarkable statement, that materiality within Christianity, can be seen as 'frozen spirit', that is, that matter is in a manner of speaking spirit-frozen-in time. In other words, materiality is about matter that has not yet become conscious of itself in its transcendence towards absolute being. In addition, materiality is spirit stopped short in its development and evolution under the impulse of the Creator-Spirit. Consequently, for Rahner, matter is oriented, in virtue of creation, towards 'becoming conscious of itself, *viz*. man'.[65] And so, matter is oriented towards spirit and the human spirit is, in a limited sense, the fulfilment of matter. In the light of these remarks, Rahner says, if you accept this fundamental unity of spirit and matter, then spirit must not be construed as something which must move away from matter in order to become perfect. Nor should it be said that spirit grows in proportion to its distance from matter. Instead, for Rahner, 'the finite spirit searches for, and finds itself, through fulfilment of the material itself.'[66]

Given this unity, this intrinsic relationship between spirit and matter, we must not see Spirit and matter as existing simply side by side, or as entities that are somehow alien to one another. Instead, spirit and matter are not disparate from one another, are not particular regions of reality: Spirit and matter 'are co-relative constitutive moments of one reality'.[67]

Another way of stating this unity of spirit and matter, found in the later Rahner, is that the whole of created reality, as uniquely embodied in the human, seeks to become more than it is in itself and this 'more' becomes manifested in the advent of the human within the evolution of creation. In the human being, the cosmos becomes conscious of itself: the human is able to recapitulate the whole of creation. A further development, or better transformation, of the human as embodied matter takes place in the death and resurrection of Jesus from the dead, as the culminating expression of the glorification of the whole of material creation. The death and resurrection of Jesus crystallises the unity of spirit and matter given in the creation of the world from the beginning. In brief, for Rahner, within the evolution of creation, matter becomes life, and life in matter becomes conscious of itself in the human, and the future of the human as embodied consciousness is prefigured in the bodily resurrection of Jesus from the dead.[68]

In a short reflection on the meaning of the Ascension, Rahner points out that 'we Christians ... are the most sublime of materialists', because we cannot conceive of the fullness of reality without thinking also of matter enduring in a state of perfection.[69] He goes on to say: 'As materialists, we are more crassly materialist than those who call themselves so.' To justify this statement, he points out that the inner dynamism of matter 'is the *Holy Pneuma* of God'.[70]

It will be difficult to follow Rahner on the unity of spirit and matter and the underlying materiality of Christian faith only for those who forget:

- That the Incarnation of God took place in the historical flesh of Jesus;
- That the Resurrection of the body of Jesus is an event in the history of creation;
- That the empty tomb symbolises the transformation of the materiality of the body of Jesus;
- That the Assumption of Mary is about the transformation of her body and soul into heaven.

Against this background of the unity of spirit and matter, we can begin to make sense of Mark Wallace's proposal, in the light of the ecological crisis, that what is now needed is a 'nature-based pneumatology' even though Wallace seems rather shy in moving from a creation-based pneumatology to a Spirit-based Christology and ecclesiology.[71] What is increasingly important and evident in the ecological movement is an awareness that there are delicate life-forms in nature, and in a certain sense we can say following Genesis Chapter 1 that the breath of God, the Spirit of God, inhabits the earth and that, therefore, the integrity of the earth must be respected and protected for Pneumatological reasons. Without this sense of the breath of God in the earth, humans will continue to treat nature as a machine, inert and lifeless, made up of empty matter, at the disposal of humans for insensitive exploitation.

Another way of stating this is to affirm that the Spirit of God inhabits the earth and suffuses the whole of creation without, however, reducing the divine presence simply to the totality of creation. Many theologians opt for not pantheism, but pan-en-theism, which sees the divine Spirit as part of creation but, at the same time, far more than creation. Pan-en-theism is one way of addressing the complex questions about the relationship that exists between God and the world and the world and God. Some find echoes of pan-en-theism in the biblical stories of creation in the book of Genesis and in the New Testament reference to the God *in* whom 'we live and move and have our being' (Acts 17:28)

In discussing the relationship between Spirit and matter, Rahner is aware that his view about matter as spiritual is not altogether new, and that it can be found in medieval ontology.[72] This is a reference, especially to Bonaventure, who saw matter as 'spiritualised', crying out for perfection.[73] Bonaventure saw matter as something dynamic, with an orientation towards a higher form, namely the human condition and therefore through the human, matter seeks the highest form which is union with God, which comes about in the Incarnation. Indeed, for Bonaventure, the Incarnation is possible in virtue of this spiritual orientation of matter.

Obviously, Bonaventure does not talk about what we call evolution, but what he says about the dynamism of matter is congenial to what we mean by evolution today. In an important sense, matter for Bonaventure is loaded with spiritual possibilities and these potentialities of matter derive from God's involvement with creation. This divine involvement with creation is described in terms of the Spirit of God drawing matter to perfection, not only through human embodiment, but ultimately through union with God, a prototype of which is given in the Incarnation.[74]

c. 'To Think Spirit … Think Materially'

A further principle to guide Spirit-talk is found in the work of Eugene Rogers: 'To think Spirit, you have to think materially.'[75] Rogers is pointing out a fundamental principle that should inform the reconstruction of Pneumatology, namely that the Spirit of God, in this life, exists primarily as embodied, as that which inhabits bodies, indwells in the human person and resides in the Christian community – and therefore not over and above creation, or outside of history, or beyond people, but within creation, as a part of history, and in the corporate lives of people and individuals. An overview of the activity of the Spirit in the Judaeo-Christian tradition bears this principle out.

The Spirit of God:

- Broods over the face of the waters at the beginning of time;
- Inhabits the earth;
- Enlivens the dust of the earth;
- Presides within the people of Israel;
- Prompts the Prophets of Israel;
- Overshadows the womb of Mary;
- Rests on Jesus in his baptism in the Jordan;
- Mends and heals broken bodies in the Gospels;
- Raises up the crucified body of Christ;
- Descends at Pentecost on the gathered assembly of disciples and apostles;
- Indwells in members of the body of Christ on earth.

David Jensen, echoing Rogers, points out that 'the Holy Spirit seeks bodies' and that the 'tendency to divorce Spirit from body ... runs counter to the Spirit's descent on bodies in Scripture'.[76]

To sum up, these reflections on the turn to the Spirit, we can say that Pneumatology as a point of departure for dialogue with other religions opens up new possibilities without excluding the Trinity, but rather seeing the Trinity, at least for Christians, as a point of arrival within dialogue. This turn to the Spirit requires an awareness of prejudices against Spirit-talk, and therefore some degree of philosophical refinement in Spirit-discourse if it is to succeed. Prominent within this philosophical rigour concerning discourse about the Spirit is the importance of putting spirit back into matter by recovering the unity of spirit in matter without collapsing them. Complementary to this is the importance of realising that the Spirit of God exists in this life primarily as embodied in creation, history, people and communities. The gift of the Spirit is the outcome of God's self-communication outside the divine. This self-bestowal of the Spirit of God happens gradually over millennia in the creation of matter, in the evolution of matter into life forms, in the development of nature-based life forms into human self-consciousness. Within matter, there is a dynamic drive towards transcendence and spiritual realisation in the human. Matter is thus oriented towards self-consciousness and the fulfilment of that self-consciousness is to be found in the Incarnation of the Word made flesh and the bodily Resurrection of Jesus from the dead. The developments in recognising Pneumatology as a point of departure for theology and inter-religious dialogue need to be applied to an understanding of revelation as also central to theology and inter-religious dialogue – a task to be addressed in the next chapter.

NOTES

1. David Tracy, 'Christianity in the Wider Context: Demands and Transformations', *Religion and Intellectual Life*, 4, 1987, 8

2. Gerald O'Collins, 'Vatican II and Fundamental Theology', *Irish Theological Quarterly*, 74, 2009, 379–88

adcock, *Light of Truth and Fire of Love: A Theology of the Holy Spirit*, /. B. Eerdmans, 1997; Veli-Matti Kärkkäinen, *Pneumatology: The Holy ... ecumenical, International and Contextual Perspective*, Michigan: Baker Academic, 2002; Kilian McDonnell, *The Other Hand of God: The Holy Spirit as the Universal Touch and Goal*, Collegeville, MN: Liturgical Press, 2003; Bernard Cooke, *Power and the Spirit of God: Towards on Experience-Based Pneumatology*, New York: Oxford University Press, 2004; David Coffey, *Did You Receive the Holy Spirit When You Believed?: Some Basic Questions for Pneumatology*, The Pear Marquette Lecture in Theology, Wisconsin: Marquette University Press, 2005; Michael Welker (ed.), *The Work of the Spirit: Pneumatology and Pentecostalism*, Michigan: W. B. Eerdmans, 2006; Kirsteen Kim, *The Holy Spirit in the World: A Global Conversation*, New York: Orbis Books, 2007; Declan O'Byrne, *Spirit Christology and Trinity in the Theology of David Coffey*, Bern: Peter Lang, 2010

4. See Veli-Matti Kärkkäinen, 'How to Speak of the Spirit among Religions: Trinitarian Prolegomena from a Pneumatological Theology of Religions', *The Work of the Spirit: Pneumatology and Pentecostalism*, 47–70 at 48

5. See Frederick J. Parrella, 'Tillich's Theology of the Concrete Spirit' and Marc Boss, 'Tillich in Dialogue with Japanese Buddhism: A Paradigmatic Illustration of His Approach to Inter-Religious Dialogue', *The Cambridge Companion to Paul Tillich*, Russell Re Manning (ed.), Cambridge: Cambridge University Press, 2009, 74–90 and 254–72 respectively

6. Amos Yong, *Beyond the Impasse: Towards a Pneumatological Theology of Religions*, Grand Rapids: Baker Academic, 2003

7. D. Lyle Dabney, 'Why Should the Last be First? The Priority of Pneumatology in Recent Theological Discussion', *Advents of the Spirit: An Introduction to the Current Study of Pneumatology*, Bradford E. Hinze and D. Lyle Dabney (eds), Marquette: Marquette University Press, 2001, 240–61

8. Yves Congar, *I Believe in the Holy Spirit*, Vol. 3, London: Chapman, 1983, 149

9. Kilian McDonnell, *The Other Hand of God*, 111 and 115 respectively

10. Robert Doran, 'The Starting Point of Systematic Theology', *Theological Studies*, December 2006, 771

11. *GS*, a.22

12. *AG*, a.4 n. 10. Translation in this instance taken from the Abbot edition of the Council Documents

13. Bernard Lonergan, 'Prolegomena to the Study of the Emerging Religious Consciousness of Our Time', *A Third Collection*, Frederick Crowe (ed.), New York: Paulist Press, 1985, 55–73

14. This lecture was subsequently published in the first instance by Regis Press in 1985 and is now available in *Appropriating the Lonergan Idea*, Michael Vertin (ed.), Washington, DC: Catholic University of America Press, 1989, 324–43

15. Bernard Lonergan, 'The Response of the Jesuit as Priest and Apostle in the Modern World', *A Second Collection*, William F. J. Ryan and Bernard J. Tyrrell (eds), Toronto: University of Toronto Press, 1996, 165–87 at 174

16. See, for example, *Method in Theology*, 105, 278, 282, 327, 340

17. *Method in Theology*, 112 and 119

18. Lonergan, 'Mission and Spirit', *A Third Collection*, 32

19. Ibid., 113

20. Ibid., 112–13. See also 'The Response of the Jesuit', *A Second Collection*, 173–4

21. Lonergan, 'Prolegomena to the Study of the Emerging Religious Consciousness of Our Time', 70–1

22. Frederick Crowe, 'Son of God, The Holy Spirit and World Religions', op. cit., 325, n.3

23. See Doran, 'The Starting Point of Systematic Theology', and papers presented to the Lonergan Colloquium at Marquette University on 29/30 October 2009 by Darren Dias and John Dadosky. Available at www.bernardlonergan.com (accessed on 25 October, 2010)

24. Frederick Crowe, 'Son of God, The Holy Spirit and World Religions', op. cit., 325

25. Ibid., 327

26. Ibid.

27. Ibid., 328

28. Ibid., 329

29. See references in Dermot A. Lane, 'Pneumatology in the Service of Ecumenism and Inter-Religious Dialogue: A Case of Neglect?', *Louvain Studies*, Spring–Summer 2008, 136–58 at 141

30. David Coffey, 'A Promising Development in Christology: An Address to the Sydney Heretics Club', *The Heretics Club (1916–2006): Ninetieth Anniversary Papers*, William W. Emilsen and Geoffrey R. Treloar (eds), Sydney: Origen Press, 2009, 31–46

31. Crowe, 'Son of God, the Holy Spirit and World Religions', op. cit., 335

32. Ibid.

33. Ibid.

34. See Lonergan, 'The Future of Christianity', *A Second Collection*, 156

35. John C. Haughey, 'The Wider Ecumenism in the Pneumatology of Bernard Lonergan', *The Holy Spirit, the Church and Christian Unity: Proceeding of the*

Consultation held at the Monastery of Bose, Italy (14–20 October, 2002), Doris Donnelly, Adelbert Denaux and Joseph Famerée (eds), Louvain: Louvain University Press, 2005, 383–403 at 401

36. Ibid.

37. Karl Rahner, 'Do Not Stifle the Spirit', *TI*, Vol. VII, 1971, 80

38. Ibid., 80

39. Ibid., 80–2

40. Karl Rahner, 'Aspects of European Theology', *TI*, Vol. XXI, 1988, 78–98 at 97

41. *RM*, a.28

42. Charles Taylor, *Sources of the Self: The Making of the Modern Identity*, Cambridge: Cambridge University Press, 1989, 520

43. Philip Rossi, 'The Idiom of the Spirit: Discourse, Human Nature and Otherness. A Response to Philip Clayton and Stephen G. Smith', *Advents of the Spirit*, 231–9 at 235

44. Mark Wallace, 'The Wounded Spirit as Basis for Hope in an Age of Radical Ecology', *Christianity and Ecology: Seeking the Well-Being of Earth and Humans*, Dieter T. Hessel and Rosemary Radford Ruether (eds), Cambridge, MA: Harvard University Press, 2000, 5–72 at 55

45. David H. Jensen, 'Discerning the Spirit: A Historical Introduction', *The Lord and Giver of Life: Perspectives on Constructive Pneumatology*, David H. Jensen (ed.), Kentucky: Westminster John Knox Press, 2008, 1–24 at 1

46. Kathryn Tanner, 'The Workings of the Spirit: Simplicity or Complexity?', *The Work of the Spirit*, Michael Welker (ed.), 87–105 at 87

47. Denis Edwards, 'Saving Grace and the Action of the Spirit outside the Church', *Sin and Salvation: Task of Theology Today III*, Duncan Reid and Mark William Worthing (eds), Australia: Australian Theological Forum Press, 2003, 205–21 at 207

48. See the discussion by Philip Clayton, 'From Substance to Subject: Rethinking Spirit in the Modern World', *Advents in the Spirit: God, World, Divine Action*, Philip Clayton, Minneapolis: Fortress Press, 2008, 133–56 with a quotation from Kant's *Critique of Pure Reason*

49. See, for example, Emmanuel Levinas, *God, Death, and Time*, Stanford, CA: Stanford University Press, 2000, 144–8 and 174–5. I am grateful to Terrence Tilley for bringing this perspective of Levinas to my attention

50. This point is discussed by Philip Clayton, art. cit., 151–2

51. See Lonergan, *Method in Theology*, 265 and 292, and Rahner, *Foundations of Christian Faith*, New York: Crossroad, 1978, 14–23

52. See Lonergan, *Method in Theology*, 243–4
53. See Taylor, *A Secular Age,* Cambridge: Harvard University Presds, 2007, 711ff.
54. On the relationship between memory and imagination, see Dermot A. Lane, 'Imagination and Theology: The *Status Quaestionis*', *Louvain Studies,* 34 (2009–2010), 123–49
55. Frederick Crowe, 'Son and Spirit: Tensions in the Divine Missions', *Appropriating the Lonergan Idea*, Washington, DC: The Catholic University of America Press, 1989, 304
56. See Dermot A. Lane, *Keeping Hope Alive: Stirrings in Christian Theology*, Dublin/ New York: Gill and Macmillan/Paulist Press, 1996, Chapter 3
57. Amos Jong, *Hospitality and the Other: Pentecost, Christian Practices, and the Neighbor,* New York: Orbis Book, 2008, 104
58. Rahner, 'The Unity of Spirit and Matter in the Christian Understanding of Faith', *TI*, Vol. VI, 153–77
59. Rahner, 'The Festival of the Future of the World', *TI*, Vol. VII, 181–5
60. Rahner, 'The Unity of Spirit and Matter in the Christian Understanding of Faith', 155
61. Ibid., 155
62. Ibid., 167
63. Ibid.
64. Ibid., 168
65. Ibid., 169
66. Ibid.
67. Ibid., 171
68. Rahner, 'Natural Science and Christian Faith', *TI*, Vol. XXI, 1988, 16–55
69. Rahner, 'The Festival of the Future of the World', *TI*, Vol. VII, 183
70. Rahner, ibid., 184
71. Wallace, 'The Wounded Spirit as Basis for Hope in an Age of Radical Ecology', 55
72. See Rahner, 'Natural Science and Reasonable Faith', *TI*, Vol. XXI, 16–55 at 29
73. See Ilia Delio, 'Revisiting the Franciscan Doctrine of Christ', *Theological Studies*, March 2003, 3–24 at 13
74. A helpful introduction to this aspect of Bonaventure's theology is given by Ilia Delio, *A Franciscan View of Creation: Learning to Live in a Sacramental World*, Ohio: Book Masters, 2003
75. Eugene Rogers, *After The Spirit: A Constructive Pneumatology from Resources Outside the Modern West,* Michigan: W. B. Eerdmans, 2005, 90
76. Jensen, 'Discerning the Spirit: A Historical Introduction'

VI. PNEUMATOLOGY AND REVELATION

It is one thing to recognise Pneumatology as a point of departure for theology and the emerging platform for dialogue between Christianity and other religious traditions, it is quite another task however to develop a Christian Pneumatology of Revelation that will serve theology and inter-religious dialogue. Revelation is a foundational category within Judaism and Christianity, and analogously to a greater or lesser degree among most religions. One's understanding of the revelation of God will inform faith and shape the conduct of theology and inter-faith dialogue. For that reason, the theology of revelation can be a contentious area and anyone who doubts this should consult the internal debates on revelation at the Second Vatican Council. The issue of revelation is now a key issue within Christian reflection on inter-religious dialogue: is there revelation in other religions and, if so, how does it relate to Christian revelation? Is Christian revelation separate and distinct from that of other religions or is it related to other religions? Can other religions enrich the Christian understanding of revelation?

The purpose of this chapter is not to answer these questions but to provide perspectives from which we might address these questions. We will begin with an outline of some of the reasons why a Pneumatology of revelation is necessary at this time. We will then review the teaching of Vatican II on revelation. In the light of that review, we will seek to build on the teaching of Vatican II on revelation by drawing out a link between revelation and imagination in the service of inter-religious dialogue. Finally, we will map out some of the ingredients that might help towards a development of Vatican II on revelation.

TERMS AND CONDITIONS

We accept no responsibility for loss
or damage to vehicle or contents.

We do not take custody of vehicle
but only rent space.

NON TRANSFERABLE

TERMS AND CONDITIONS

We accept no responsibility for loss
or damage to vehicle or contents.

We do not take custody of vehicle
but only rent space.

NON TRANSFERABLE

TERMS AND CONDITIONS

We accept no responsibility for loss
or damage to vehicle or contents.

We do not take custody of vehicle

PERMIT & RECEIPT
UCLA

Parking Structure 04
Do Not Park
In Reserved Spaces

Stall # 4464

Expiration Date/Time

06:59 AM

NOV 23, 2015

Purchase Date/Time: 11:53am Nov 22, 2015
Total Due: $12.00   Rate: All Day $12
Total Paid: $12.00   Payment Type: Card
Ticket #: 00078893
S/N #: 500012290681
Setting: Structure 04
Mach Name: 04-4

Card #****--4438, Visa

Auth #: 325220

1. REASONS PROMPTING A PNEUMATOLOGY OF REVELATION

As already noted in Chapter Two, the Second Vatican Council adopted a positive approach to other living faiths.

a. Vatican II and John Paul II

Part of the reason prompting this new approach to other religions was an awareness of the link between the Spirit and the existence of other religions as expressed by Vatican II. For example, *The Decree on the Missions* recognised that the Spirit of God was active in other religions before the Christ-event and by implication after the Christ-event also.[1] Further, the *Pastoral Constitution on the Church in the Modern World* talks about the Spirit offering to all in ways known only to God the possibility of being partners in the saving reality of the Paschal Mystery.[2] In addition, Vatican II links the history of revelation with the history of salvation and vice versa.[3] Several documents point towards the universality of God's offer of salvation to those outside the Judaeo-Christian tradition.[4]

This positive regard towards other religions and references to the connection between the Spirit and other religions has been well received in the Church since Vatican II. For example, as seen in Chapter Two, John Paul II wrote two encyclicals on the Spirit. In *On the Holy Spirit in the Life of the Church and the World: Dominum et Vivificantem*, 1986, he acknowledged the universal action of the Spirit in the world before Christ and pointed to the Spirit who influences the course of history and religions.[5] In response to criticisms from the Roman Curia for gathering the religions of the world in Assisi in 1986, he pointed out in his December address to the Curia that it is the Spirit who is the source of prayer in the lives of people.

In *The Permanent Validity of the Church's Missionary Mandate: Redemptoris Missio*, 1990, he wrote about the Spirit as the source of religious questioning and as active in the lives of individuals, society, history, peoples, cultures and religions.[6] He also talked about 'the universal action of the Spirit in the world', describing the Spirit as the one 'who sows the seeds of the Word ... and who holds all things together'.[7] These references to the Spirit at Vatican II and in the teaching of John Paul II are not only important resources, they also point us in the direction of a much-needed Pneumatology of revelation.

Among theologians, Yves Congar wrote three volumes on the Holy Spirit after the Council which highlighted the link between the experience of the Spirit and Revelation. Volume One was originally entitled 'The Holy Spirit in the Economy: Revelation and the Experience of God'.[8]

b. Pauline Literature Links the Spirit with Revelation

A second reason why a Pneumatology of revelation is necessary is that St Paul and the Deutero-Pauline letters makes an explicit connection between the action of the Holy Spirit and the Revelation of God in Christ. This is particularly evident in the first letter of Paul to the Corinthians where it is the Holy Spirit who helps us to know the depth of the mystery of God:

> But, as it is written, 'what no eye has seen, nor ear heard, nor human heart conceived, what God has prepared for those who love Him' – these things God has revealed to us through the Holy Spirit; for the Spirit searches everything, even the depths of God ... no-one comprehends what is truly God's except the Spirit of God.[9]

In the Deutero-Pauline letters, there is also an emphasis on the Spirit as the one who enlightens our understanding of the mystery of Christ, and though 'in former generations this mystery was not made known to humankind ... it has now been revealed to his apostles and prophets by the Spirit.'[10] Within the Pauline literature, the Spirit is the source and agent of revelation.

c. The Action of the Spirit in Judaism and Creation

A third reason why we need a Pneumatology of revelation is that the action of the Spirit in the world precedes the revelation of God in Christ as indicated in the previous chapter. It was only in virtue of that action of the Spirit in creation, in history and in Israel, that the

Revelation of God in Christ could assume decisive significance and finality. Without reference to the prior revelation of God at least in Judaism, and the possibility of revelations in different ways in other religions, the Christ-event loses its defining significance. Not only that, but the ongoing significance of the Christ-event for understanding God in the world, in history, in religions and in the Church today is in danger of being hidden and lost if it is not explicitly linked to the ongoing action of the Holy Spirit in the world. It is through the prior activities of the Spirit and the *Logos* in creation and history that the final revelation of God in Jesus Christ takes place. Without these impulses of the Spirit and the *Logos* in history, it is difficult to see how Christ could have been recognised as the Word made flesh. The ongoing action of the Spirit, past, present and future, is central to understanding the revelation of God in Christ in the past, present and future. Without attention to the dynamic presence of the Spirit in history, there is the danger that the Christian revelation of God becomes frozen in time. A Pneumatology of revelation will help to overcome this particular danger.

d. The Spirit as 'the Subjective Possibility of Revelation'
A final reason why a Pneumatology of revelation is required at this time is that the Bible makes it clear that it is in and through the Spirit, the universal gift of the Spirit, that we get to know who God is. It is not possible for the human spirit by its own powers to penetrate the depths of divinity; this only happens through the gift of the Spirit.[11] Likewise, it is only through the gift of the Spirit that it is possible to address God as Father.[12] Equally it is through the inner gift of the Spirit that we can recognise the love of God given to us in Christ Jesus. If this is the case, then the Spirit must be recognised, as both Barth and Kasper point out, as 'the subjective possibility of Revelation'.[13] Because the Spirit is given as a gift, as an inner subjective gift to every human being, then all have the possibility of recognising the revelation of the love of God made visible in creation, in history, in Judaism, in Jesus and in the Church. It is, in brief, the Spirit who reveals the love of God as the gift offered in creation and history.

207

Another way of saying this is to note that 'the Spirit ... expresses the innermost nature of God – God as self-communicating love – in such a way that this innermost reality proves at the same time to be the outermost ... reality of God's being outside of Himself. The Spirit is, as it were, the ecstasy of God.'[14] For both Congar and Kasper, the Spirit is the externality of God's inner self in the world in the first instance, and so the Spirit is the ecstasy of God, the expression of the love and grace of God in the world[15] – a point that is of major importance in distinguishing the difference between the Revelation of God in the monotheistic religions and the mystical revelations of God in the East. Thus, the Spirit, as subjective possibility and source of revelation, begins to emerge as the agent of God's self-revelation before, during and after the Christ-event.

2. REVIEW OF *DEI VERBUM*

Given that the Second Vatican Council produced a rich, full-blown theology of revelation, one might legitimately ask why do we need a Pneumatology of revelation? To answer this question adequately, we need to review in the first instance the contents of *Dei Verbum*.

a. A Shift in the Understanding of Revelation at Vatican II

There is general agreement that the *Dogmatic Constitution on Divine Revelation* is one of the outstanding achievements of the Second Vatican Council. According to George Schner:

> The document *Dei Verbum* is the most fundamental of the Council's documents. In asking for a reassessment of the basic rules of Christian discourse and action, involving a reappropriation of the place of scripture in the life of the Catholic Church, the Council fathers were indeed taking seriously Pope John's request for a Pastoral and Ecumenical Council.[16]

The internal history of *Dei Verbum* suggests that there was significant development at the Council around the nature of revelation. The initial draft on revelation was largely a reproduction of the manuals and did not receive the required number of votes to be passed at the Council. Thus John XXIII intervened, and this resulted in a different draft which was eventually accepted. For many, the drama surrounding the document on revelation at Vatican II marked a turning point, and opened the way for other developments, especially in ecclesiology, ecumenism and the relationship between the Church and the modern world in *Gaudium et Spes*.

Probably the most significant shift was the move from a propositional and cognitive view of revelation to a personal and affective account of revelation. Thus, Peter de Mey talks about 'a change of paradigm in understanding God's self-revelation' at the Council which he describes as 'a fundamental innovation'.[17] Given this shift, it is possible to discern within the final document various tensions, compromises and juxtapositions.[18] Donald Senior acknowledges that 'opposing world views rumble beneath this text.'[19] However, these tensions internal to the document should not detract from the breakthrough that did occur at Vatican II concerning the Church's understanding of revelation and it is that breakthrough which we must now sketch.

b. An Overview of *Dei Verbum*

This breakthrough at Vatican II on revelation may be summarised in the following way. *Dei Verbum*, in contrast for example to *Dei Filius* of Vatican I, adopted a personalist approach to revelation in contrast to the propositionalist view that had been dominant prior to the Council. Revelation is described as the personal self-communication of God to humanity in contrast to the existence of a series of divine statements about God which had been the view prior to Vatican II. Revelation, therefore, is not simply information about God, nor just another piece of knowledge to be added to the existing store of knowledge. To be sure, the personal revelation of God in history does issue in key propositional statements about the Mystery of God. It is important to note that there is an underlying distinction within *Dei Verbum* between the personal revelation of God in Christ and the expression of this in statements. Further, *Dei Verbum* notes that revelation takes place through the medium of human experience and that it was through experience that the people of Israel came to know God.[20] In addition, *Dei Verbum* transcended the Catholic and Protestant controversy about the sources of revelation in terms of giving priority to tradition or priority to scripture respectively. Instead, *Dei Verbum* locates the meaning of scripture and tradition in Christ, highlighting that there is one source of revelation, namely the person of Jesus Christ, the Son of God Incarnate, crucified and risen, who is available in tradition and scripture.

Dei Verbum is also noteworthy for its Christocentric understanding of God's revelation. Christ is 'in himself the mediator and fullness of all revelation' (a.2), the one who 'completed and perfected Revelation and confirmed it with divine guarantees' (a.4), and this took place through 'words and deeds, signs and miracles, but above all by his death and glorious resurrection from the dead, and finally by the sending of the Spirit of truth' (a.4). Since what happened in Christ is the new and definitive covenant, 'no new public Revelation is to be expected before the glorious manifestation of our Lord Jesus Christ' (a.4).

Other positive points about *Dei Verbum* include a recognition of the place of the historical critical method in the study of the Bible for a balanced understanding of revelation, the adoption of the language of self-communication for describing God's revelation, the inseparability of the history of revelation and salvation history, and the recognition that the response of faith to God's revelation is a response of the whole person, involving the intellect, but also 'the heart as moved by the Spirit' (a.5). This emphasis on the affective dimension of faith exists in contrast to those theologies that correlated revelation with reason alone.

c. Gaps in *Dei Verbum*

In spite of these new emphases on experience, the single source of revelation in Christ, and the Christocentric character of revelation, the promotion of the historical critical method and the emphasis on the affective, nonetheless there are certain deficits in *Dei Verbum* which are now more apparent nearly half a century later. These include the failure to deal with the actual dynamics of revelation, inattention to the human capacity from an anthropological point of view to receive revelation,[21] the neglect of the complexity of questions surrounding the interpretation of scripture.[22] A further difficulty with *Dei Verbum* is the presence of un-nuanced references to the revelation of God in Christ as the 'fulfilment' of the history of salvation. References about 'fulfilment' need to be qualified in the light of the teaching of *Nostra Aetate* about God's unrevoked Covenant with Israel. If references to fulfilment must be made, then they must be expressed in a way that does not support supersessionism in regard to Judaism, or indeed the equivalent of supersessionism regarding other religions. We now know painfully from history about the negative effects of supersessionism in regard to Judaism.[23]

The most serious gap, however, throughout *Dei Verbum* is the relative neglect of the role of the Spirit who is at the centre of the reception in faith of God's personal revelation. This may not be immediately apparent because *Dei Verbum* does contain some twenty-seven references to the Holy Spirit. However, as Gerald O'Collins points out, the Christocentric character of the document displays the Latin tendency to subordinate the Holy Spirit to the Son. O'Collins notes that if Vatican II had taken place in the 1990s, more emphasis would have been given to the Holy Spirit: 'the Holy Spirit would have bulked larger in *Dei Verbum*.'[24]

There are a number of issues here that need to be highlighted in reference to the role of the Spirit. I am not suggesting that we now simply move from a Christocentric understanding of revelation to a Pneumato-centric view of revelation. What is required in any theology of revelation is an awareness that the revelation of God takes place as gift through the Spirit and the Word working together in history, in Judaism, in Jesus of Nazareth, and in the Church. It is within that context that we recognise the Spirit as the One who inspires and enables the reception of God's revelation to take place in faith.

Ormond Rush notes that in the two sections dealing with revelation in creation and God's relationship with humanity and the chosen people (DV a.2 and DV a.14-16), there is not one reference to the Holy Spirit.[25] What needs to be highlighted in any theology of revelation is that it is the Spirit who prompts and enables the response of faith to receive God's revelation. This point, as Rush notes, is recognised elsewhere in *Dei Verbum*: 'The response and obedience of faith to God's revelation must have the interior helps of the Holy Spirit who moves the heart and converts it to God' (a.5). This role of the Spirit within the process of revelation applies to revelation in creation, history, other religions, Judaism, the life of Jesus, and the Christian churches. By attending to the role of the Spirit in the reception by faith of God's revelation in the past, we may learn how to focus on the role of the Spirit in the reception of God's on-going revelation in the present – one of the most neglected and yet urgent tasks facing Christianity today.[26]

d. Linking Pneumatology and Christology in the Service of Revelation

There is a need to develop a Pneumatology of revelation that can be integrated with the Christocentric emphasis on revelation in *Dei Verbum*. This will mean taking account, as Paul does in his Letter to the Romans (Rom 1:18-20), of universal revelation before the particular revelation that took place in Judaism and reached completion in Christ. In this way, one should be able to see some on-going continuum between the primordial, universal revelation of God in creation and history, and the particular revelation of God in Judaism and the finality of that revelation in the Christ-event. It is instructive and suggestive to note that when *Gaudium et Spes* talks about Christ as 'the key, the focal point, and the goal of history' (a.10 and a.45), it goes back to history before Judaism. This means that we must relocate the Christ-event within the wider frame of world history. Such relocation of the Christ-event will require a Pneumatology that is able to discern the universal action of the Spirit prior to the Judaeo-Christian dispensation as well as the particular action of the Spirit within Judaism and Christianity and the action of the Spirit in Israel and the Church today.

This means in effect that the theology of revelation in *Dei Verbum* needs to be brought together with the positive statements about other religious traditions contained in *Nostra Aetate* and the other documents of Vatican II as outlined in Chapter Two. The relationship between Christ as the fullness of God's revelation and the existence of 'seeds of the Word of God', 'elements of truth and grace', the presence of the Spirit, the universality of the grace of God, the ray of truth that enlightens all, and the presence of moral truths in other religions, all of which exist in varying degrees in other religions, needs to be developed. How can the Christocentric theology of revelation in *Dei Verbum* be expanded by a Pneumatology of revelation that embraces the different degrees of revelation in other religions? Is it possible to integrate Christology and Pneumatology in the service of a wider idea concept of revelation that includes other religions without dumbing down what is distinctive about the particular revelation in Judaism and the unique revelation of God in the Christ-event alongside some elements of revelation in Islam and the more mystical religions of the East? Can *Dei Verbum* and *Nostra Aetate* be brought together into a unified Pneumatology of revelation among the religions in a way that scripture and tradition were brought together into a single source in Christ creating a new relationship between Catholics and Protestants?

This integration of Pneumatology and Christology with a view to expanding our understanding of revelation can only happen if we can recover the forgotten connection between imagination and revelation in the first instance. Further, the unique relationship that exists between the Spirit and imagination must also be retrieved if we are to construct a Pneumatology of revelation that will serve inter-religious dialogue in the twenty-first century. This is the matter to which I now turn.

3. THE INGREDIENTS OF A PNEUMATOLOGY OF REVELATION

In recent years, there has been a renewed appreciation of the role of imagination in the performance of faith seeking understanding.[27] There is a growing awareness that reason needs the impulses of imagination, and that imagination needs the controlling influence of reason. Thus, William Dych suggests: 'There is a very necessary and intrinsic connection between theological reflection about God and the life of imagination.'[28]

a. Imagination and Theology

If one looks at the history of theology, one will find instances of the creative imagination at work in major moments of breakthrough. For example, the move from a Jewish-Christian self-understanding of the early Church to that of a Hellenistic self-understanding of Christian identity was an act of the imagination. Likewise, the contrasting perspectives concerning the identity of Jesus as truly human (*Vere Homo*) and truly divine (*Vere Deus*) united in one divine person (*hypostasis*) at the Council of Chalcedon in 451, was clearly an act of the creative imagination. Equally, the positive regard towards other religions as expressed at Vatican II in *Nostra Aetate* and other documents was an act of the creative imagination as suggested in Chapter Two.

This connection between theology and imagination is particularly pertinent in the area of revelation. A close relationship exists between the emergence of revelation and the human imagination. According to Richard Kearney, it is at the level of imagination, prior to and after the details of religion, that primordial revelation takes place in so far as 'the aboriginal signs of heart cave are first sounded and received in each religion'. Imagination facilitates 'the becoming visible and audible of the Divine' in images, sounds and liturgies – an originating experience found in many religions – that in turn over time become translated into sacred texts, rituals and art.[29] In this sense revelation is received in the imagination and continues to take place in the imagination. It is in the human imagination that the divine-human and human-divine exchange takes place. The threshold between God and humanity and humanity and God is traversed in and through the human imagination. It is this journey of the imagination that has been recognised by poets and theologians. For example, the poet Elizabeth Jennings speaks for many poets when she writes:

> May I set ajar
> The doors of closed minds. Words come and words go
> And poetry is pain as well as passion.
> But in the large flights of imagination
> I see, for one crammed second, order so
> Explicit that I need no more persuasion.[30]

Among theologians, Michael Scanlon describes imagination as: 'the seat of Revelation'.[31] Richard Cote refers to imagination as the 'natural inborn faculty for transcendence',[32] for going beyond what we call reality, that is beyond what seems initially to be the real. Ormond Rush describes imagination as the human capacity to make sense of revelation.[33] In other words it is in and through imagination that the offer, address and communication of God's self to the human person takes place, and it is in and through the human imagination that the person is able to receive this divine outreach into the heart of humanity in creation, history, religions, the person of Jesus and the Christian community. Michael Paul Gallagher expresses this better than most: 'it is through imagination that we cope with the difficult docking manoeuvre between a hidden God and a fallen humanity.'[34] One of the reasons why imagination is able to receive this divine human communication is that it is not just one faculty among others but is in truth 'the whole mind working in a certain way'.[35] Imagination, unlike reason alone, or the cold rationality of modernity, carries 'an emotional charge'[36] and is 'loaded with affect'.[37] Imagination has the capacity to enable the whole person to respond to the divine offer of Revelation, or as *Dei Verbum* puts it, to 'commit his/her entire self to God' (a.5), namely the intellect, the will and the heart 'assisted' by 'the grace of God' and 'the interior helps of the Holy Spirit' (a.5).

In highlighting the imagination as the point of contact between the communication of God's Spirit in love and humanity's reception in faith of this divine offer, we are invoking not just the visual imagination, sometimes referred to as the 'eye of the imagination' but also including the 'ears' of the imagination, as well as the other senses of touching, smelling and tasting. It is instructive to note the number of times that Jesus talks about those who have eyes but do not see, and those who have ears but do not hear (e.g., Mk 8:18). Similarly, Paul talks about revelation and faith as that which comes through hearing the Word (Rom 10:17). Likewise, the Psalmist invites us 'to taste and see the goodness of the Lord' (Ps 34:8). In associating imagination with the offer of God's self-communication in the history of humanity, we are invoking the play of all the senses as well as the dynamic capacity of the human spirit to receive what lies beyond the merely empirical view of life. This means that the activities of the imagination must not be restricted to just the visible or the audible or the tactile but must also include the mediating, representational and synthesising activities of imagination in making this link between imagination and divine revelation.

In this way, imagination provides an opening, perhaps a sacred space or what others call 'a God-shaped hole', within the human spirit for the reception of God's gracious self-communication in history. This reception of divine revelation provokes the use of images, metaphors and narratives to describe the encounter between God and humanity. It is for this reason that the language of revelation, and especially the language of the Bible and sacred texts in other religions, is largely the language of poetry, drama and story, and not the more exact language of reason, logic and analysis. In other words the language of revelation is 'more akin to poetry than prose because it is in the poetic mode that language finds its highest possibilities'.[38]

b. Imagination and the Holy Spirit

This close connection between imagination and revelation mirrors the unique relationship that obtains between imagination and the Spirit. Imagination is the place where the creative Spirit of God is most active. For example, Trevor Hart suggests that Imagination is 'a locus within our humanity where, we must suppose, God's Spirit is active in shaping and reshaping life.'[39] We must begin to think of the human imagination as that particular location within the human where the human spirit encounters the divine Spirit, or more correctly, where the Spirit of God addresses and invites and summons the human spirit. It is in the imagination of the human spirit that the otherness as well as the nearness of the divine Spirit is experienced. The divine Spirit comes in many guises, and these include the universal experiences of goodness, beauty and truth. Through the power of imagination, we can begin to see how the Holy Spirit energises the human spirit and how the divine creativity of the Spirit activates the creativity of the human spirit and how the power of the divine Spirit can enliven the life of the human spirit.

It is not surprising, therefore, to find theologians, especially biblical theologians, associating the action of the Spirit with imagination. Walter Brueggemann talks about the 'Spirit-led-imagination' within the biblical narrative and sees this influence of the divine Spirit played out in the creative actions of the prophets of Israel.[40] Bernard Cooke points out: 'Through imagination's role in the religious experience of the people [of Israel], the divine Spirit of prophecy worked to inject into Israel's understanding of its relationship to Yahweh the awareness of a personal bond of friendship.'[41] Amos Yong talks about 'the pneumatological imagination' as that aspect of the imagination that is open and vulnerable and attuned to the action of the Holy Spirit. Yong highlights three dimensions or root metaphors of the imagination as influenced and affected by the Spirit of God. The first is the primordial experience of the Spirit as the *dunamis* or power of creation and life. The second aspect of the imagination influenced by the Spirit is the pervasive presence of relationality throughout the whole of life, especially manifested in creation and community. The Spirit effects deep relationships with the presence of Yahweh in the Hebrew scriptures and the risen Christ in the Christian scriptures. The third foundational experience of the human imagination brought about by the Spirit is that of wind (*ruach* in Hebrew) or breath (*pneuma* in Greek) of God sustaining life. This experience of imagination is a reminder of the Revelation made explicit by Jesus that 'God is Spirit' (Jn 4:25).[42]

However, the most striking illustration of the power of the Spirit to enliven the imagination is found in the prophet Joel, which is taken up by Peter in Acts 2. Both the prophet Joel and the apostle Peter bring together and integrate the action of the Holy Spirit with the creativity of the human imagination. Invaded by the Spirit of God 'poured out on flesh' and now transformed by the Spirit of Christ at Pentecost inaugurating a new eschatological era, young and old, slaves and free, women and men are able, through the power of imagination, to 'prophesy ... see visions ... and dream dreams' (Acts 2:17). It is this intensified, eschatological outpouring of the gift of the Spirit of Christ that enabled the Christian imagination to talk about the dawning of a new creation, the inauguration of the reign of God and the beginning of the end time of salvation.

In making these claims for a creative link between imagination and the Spirit, we must recognise that there are deep ambiguities and dangers attached to this relationship. History testifies to the capacity of the human imagination to generate extraordinary evil. One has only to think how the human imagination was led astray in the construction of Nazi Germany and the destruction of six million Jews. It is for this reason that the action of the Spirit must always be tested, and the responses of the imagination subjected to close scrutiny. The action of the Spirit must be monitored by the equally important action of the Word (*Logos*) in creation and history. Once again, it becomes apparent that the work of the Spirit and presence of *Logos* must be kept together as one. As Henri de Lubac once pointed out in a discussion about the danger of pneumaticism in Joachim of Fiore: 'detached from Christ, the Spirit can become almost anything.'[43] Similarly, impulses of the human imagination must be held within the grasp of reason just as the life of reason must be enlivened by imagination. The balanced integration of Spirit and *Logos*, of imagination and reason, is called for in any theology of revelation.

In a well-known sketch by the nineteenth century artist Goya, there is a drawing of a figure, presumably of Goya himself, slouched over a table, tormented by monsters, symbolising what happens through the power of imagination when the sleep of reason takes place. Under the picture, the following lines capture the intention of Goya: 'Imagination abandoned by reason produces impossible monsters; united with her, she [imagination] is the mother of the Arts.' Imagination needs the controlling influence of reason. At the other end of the spectrum, reason alone can become just as destructive as imagination when left to its own devices, giving rise to a ruthless rationalism and authoritarianism which can be found scattered in the history of political and religious institutions. G. K. Chesterton, in 1908, captures this other possibility by pointing out: 'A madman is not the man who has lost reason. The madman is the man who has lost everything except his reason.'[44] Reason needs the creativity of imagination.

This bringing together of the gift of the Spirit, imagination and revelation provides some of the basic elements that would go into the construction of a Pneumatology of revelation. The point of departure is the gift of the Spirit poured out on all flesh, recognised and received in the imagination of the human spirit, and narrated in the many practices, creeds and rituals of different religions down through the centuries. It would be impossible here to track the history of revelation in the many religions. Instead, we will map out some of the many types of revelation that belong in varying degrees to the diversity of religions.

4. DIFFERENT TYPES OF REVELATION

There can be little doubt that there are different ways of categorising revelation, and the primary value of these different types is that they give us a way, a rather incomplete way, of discussing revelation among the religions. It will become apparent that the types selected here, largely as a guide, have their own limitations.

a. Rahner's Two-Fold Revelation: Transcendental and Categorical

We have already seen something of Rahner's theology of the experience of God in Chapter Four. It is worth returning to Rahner's discussion of experience in the context of the possibility of revelation in other religions, and the role that the Spirit plays in creating humanity's openness and readiness for revelation. Rahner's theology of revelation is developed in the context of his recurring claim that every human being experiences God, even though he or she may not know it. One of the roles of theology is to make people aware of that universal experience of God. The early Rahner grounded this generous claim in his theology of grace, especially his understanding of the primacy and priority of uncreated grace. The later Rahner identified the universal gift of God's grace with the gift of the Holy Spirit who is given to all. Rahner's commitment to the gift of the Spirit arises out of his understanding of the universal saving will of God. Because the gift of the Spirit has been offered to all, it affects, indeed alters, the innermost nature and depth of every human spirit. The human is born, turned and drawn towards God as a result of the gift of the Spirit of God poured out on all flesh, and this affects the very constitution of human interiority: open, dynamic, self-transcending. The gift of the Spirit, inhabiting the human spirit, orientates and ordains every human being towards the immediate experience of God, and this is what Rahner calls 'transcendental revelation'. This 'transcendental revelation' is one of orientation and ordination towards God in virtue of the gift of the Holy Spirit and is, for the most part, unobjective, unthematic and pre-reflective. Yet, transcendental revelation is a real experience which has an inner dynamism towards a realisation in history; it seeks objectification, thematisation and explicitation of that which is unobjective, unthematic and implicit, and this Rahner called 'categorical revelation'. 'Transcendental revelation' exists deep down within the realm of human consciousness: it is, as it were, 'conscious but not known'.[45]

'Categorical revelation' is about the historical mediation and thematisation of the gift of 'transcendental revelation'. This process of articulating 'transcendental revelation' has been taking place in history since the dawn of time and can be found to be present in various degrees in history, art, culture, science and the religions of the world. The religions, in particular, seek to mediate historically the inner gift of God's self-communication of the Spirit that is given to all in 'transcendental revelation'. An 'attempt is made in every religion ... to mediate the original unreflexive and non-objective revelation historically ... In all religions there are individual moments ... when God's self-communication becomes self-reflexive.'[46]

In this broad sense, it can be said that there is revelation of varying degrees in other religions. Rahner does note that success towards the historical realisation of transcendental revelation is, due to the human condition of sinfulness, intermingled with error and distortion, and therefore these objectifications of transcendental revelation are provisional and incomplete.[47]

It is against this background that Rahner states that the revelatory self-communication of God's Spirit to humanity reaches an unsurpassable climax in the person of Jesus Christ. Christ is the absolute breakthrough of God's gracious self-communication in the Spirit to humanity, and humanity's free response to God's Spirit-based invitation:

> In Jesus, God's communication to man in grace and at the same time its categorical self-interpretation in the corporeal, tangible and social dimension have reached their climax, have become Revelation in an absolute sense.[48]

In this way, Rahner situates the Christ-event not only within the history of Judaism, but also within the larger history of other religions and world history. Of course there is a unique relationship between Christianity and Judaism in the sense that Judaism is, as *Nostra Aetate* points out, the root of Christianity. It should be noted here that *Nostra Aetate* actually uses the term 'revelation' in reference to Judaism, specifically in reference to the Old Testament – but does not use the term 'revelation' in relation to the other religions.[49] Moreover, *Dei Verbum* talks explicitly about the 'Word of God' in the Old Testament.

After Judaism, there is a special relationship between Christianity and Islam because as *Nostra Aetate* points out, 'They worship God who is one, living and subsistent.'[50] The relationship of Christianity with the other religions is again significantly different and in that sense it does seem possible and necessary to talk about differentiated degrees of revelation or the existence of different modalities of revelation within the other religions of the world. This seems warranted in the first instance because all have been graced by the interior gift of the Spirit and responses to this gift and the objectifications of this transcendental revelation differ significantly across the many religions. Given that Vatican II talked, as we have seen in Chapter Two, about 'the seeds of the Word', the action of the Spirit, elements of 'truth and grace', the presence of spiritual and moral values within other religions, one can hardly deny varying degree of revelation within many of the other religious traditions of the world.

Rahner's distinction between transcendental and categorical revelation provides a framework for discussing the existence of revelation, especially transcendental revelation in other religions. Further, this map of Rahner on revelation offers a perspective within which one can make sense of the teaching of Vatican II about the elements of truth and grace, the presence of the Spirit, the existence of the 'seeds of the Word', the ray of truth that enlightens all, and the moral truths, all of which are found in differing degrees in other religions. Further, Rahner's categories of transcendental and categorical revelation shed some light on the historical particularity of most religions. As already seen, religions exist only as embodied in particular social and cultural forms, and not as free-floating universal forms above history or beyond culture or outside of society. There is no universal essence of religion available outside history, except for those who think they can step outside of history.

b. Monotheistic Revelation and Mystical Revelation

Another way of classifying the presence of revelation among other religions is to divide them into the following broad categories: the revelation of the monotheistic religions, and the revelation of the mystical religions of the East. This broad generalisation can be found in authors like Jacques Dupuis and Bede Griffiths.[51] The revelation of the monotheistic religions arises out of their appeal to the God of Abraham. The monotheistic religions emphasise the unity of God, recognising transcendence, focussing on an inter-personal encounter which is usually described in terms of some form of 'ecstasy', and these particular experiences are rooted in history. Thereafter, there are considerable theological differences among the monotheistic faiths concerning revelation which are expressed in a great variety of codes, creeds and cults.

On the other hand, the revelation found within the mystical faiths can be understood from a Christian point of view as taking place within a cosmic covenant. These religions emphasise immanence, union and absorption. The religious experience in this instance is one of 'intasy' which takes place 'in the cave of the heart' and often leads to absorption or 'extinction' (*nirvana*) or emptiness (*sunyata*) with a strong emphasis on the apophatic. Within this range of revelations within the mystical religions there are dazzling differences. This classification of revelations might be summarised, however schematically, in the following tendencies:

Monotheistic Revelation	Mystical Revelation
Historical	Cosmic
Ecstasy (without)	Intasy (within)
Personal encounter	Absorption
Kataphatic	Apophatic
Transcendence	Immanence
Exteriority	Interiority

The more one contrasts the differences between monotheistic revelation and mystical revelation, the more inadequate this classification appears. In fairness to Dupuis, he recognises that the polarity between monotheistic and mystical revelation breaks down and is unsatisfactory in many respects.[52] There are elements of the mystical tradition found explicitly within monotheistic revelations and faith. Indeed many would suggest that the shortcomings of a Christian theology of revelation are due to a neglect of those strands found in the mystical religions, such as the revelations that can be found in the cosmos, contemplative practices and the cultivation of a life of interiority and mindfulness. Equally, however, there are features of the monotheistic revelation found within the mystical traditions. Moreover, in suggesting there is some degree of continuity and complementarity between the monotheistic and mystical traditions of revelation, one must avoid the obvious temptations of syncretism, relativism and radical religious pluralism. Thus, it is equally important to emphasise that there are crucial points of difference and discontinuity between the monotheistic and mystical traditions of revelation.

c. Christ as the 'Completion' of the Revelation of God in History

For the Christian, the place and time where the monotheistic and the mystical come together in a new unity is in the life of Jesus, crucified and risen, present in and through the Spirit of Christ poured out at Pentecost. The life, death and resurrection of Jesus cross over the divine-human threshold of both monotheism and mysticism. Thus, many theologians like Paul Tillich and Claude Geffré recognise in the life of Jesus the personal-embodiment of 'the concrete universal' who is the personal Incarnation of the universal *logos* of creation and the action of the Spirit of God in the heart of humanity. The particularity of the life of Jesus has universal implications for the way we understand the mystery of God, the human condition, the cosmos, and their destiny. The articulation of these universal implications of the particularity of the Christ-event are strikingly spelled out in the early Christological hymns of the New Testament (Col 1:15-20; Eph 1:9-11; Jn 1:1-14; Phil 2:6-11).

It is because God's gracious self-communication through the Spirit reaches a historical climax and decisive culmination in the life of Jesus as the Word made flesh that *Dei Verbum,* and subsequently *Dominus Iesus,* talks about Christ as 'the unique mediator and the fullness of all Revelation',[53] and 'the completed and perfected Revelation';[54] in effect Christ is the completion, perfection and 'fulfilment' of revelation. Care, however, must be taken as already seen in how the language of 'fulfilment' is used, less it foster forms of supercessionism. D'Costa and others question the use of 'a one-sided conception of fulfilment theology'. He notes that 'Christianity is fulfilled in its reception and hearing and proclamation of the Word.' At the same time, he also notes that the Church is unfulfilled insofar as it fails to hear and proclaim the Word of God, and we might add here, insofar as it fails to listen and heed the Spirit of God.[55] Christianity is a religion of fulfilment, or better 'completion', since that is the word used by Jesus. That sense of completion takes place through the words and deeds, death and resurrection of Jesus and the outpouring of the Spirit. Even though God's plan of salvation reaches completion in the Paschal Mystery of Christ and the outpouring of the Spirit, there is still something outstanding and unfinished concerning the application of the Paschal Mystery to humanity and the world. This, as already noted in Chapter Four, was recognised in the experience of the early Church as formulated in the first known Christian prayer *Maranatha* and proclaimed in the Apostolic Creed when it declared: 'He will come again' summed up in the doctrine of the *Parousia.* Consequently, in any theology of fulfilment there must be an interplay between the centrality of the Incarnation and the place of the *Parousia,* between the importance of the First Coming alongside the significance of the Second Coming, between an emphasis found in Paul on being 'in Christ' in the present, and becoming 'in Christ' in the future, and lastly between the historical reality of the Christ-event and its eschatological realisation in relation to humanity and the world at the end of time. This tension between what has been revealed historically in Christ and what is yet to come in the *Eschaton* is essential to a balanced understanding of Revelation. It must be kept in mind that every revelation of God in this life contains moments of disclosure and concealment, of unveiling and hiddenness, and that this principle of revelation applies to the completed revelation that has taken place in Christ.

Running through these two different ways of looking at revelation is the underlying distinction made by Bernard Lonergan between the inner word and the outer word. As already mentioned, Lonergan talks about the inner word of the Spirit in the heart of every human being: 'the love of God has been poured out on all through the gift of the Holy Spirit who has been given to us' (Rom 5:5). This inner word of the Spirit in the heart seeks expression and articulation in the outer word and, for the Christian, that outer word has been revealed in the eternal *Logos* made flesh and personally manifested in Christ Jesus. However, the outer Word (the *Logos*) revealed in the historical life of Jesus only makes sense when people are in touch with the universality of the gift of the Spirit of God in the human heart and the universal *logos* scattered throughout creation and history. William Temple captured this essential truth in the following way:

> Only if God is revealed in the rising of the sun in the sky, can He be revealed in the rising of a Son of man from the dead; only if He is revealed in the history of the Syrians and Philistines can He be revealed in the history of Israel; only if He chooses all men for His own, can He choose any at all; only if nothing is profane can anything be sacred.[56]

d. The Universality of the Revelation of God among the Nations and the Religions

It is hard to deny the existence of some form of revelation among people not attached to any religion. What are we to say about people who seek to do good and to follow their consciences and to search for the truth? And what about the members of other religions? Once you acknowledge and affirm the universal saving will of God as both the Bible and the Christian tradition do (however unevenly), then theology must be careful not to deny the possibility of revelation beyond the visible horizons of the Judaeo-Christian tradition.

The saving will of God, as Rahner constantly emphasised, has a real effect on human nature. This effect he called the enduring presence of uncreated grace and the reality of what he called the 'supernatural existential': the underlying orientation of every human being towards God as discussed in Chapter Four. For Rahner, it is these realities that pre-dispose the individual to receive the gift of God's universal revelation in creation and in history. It is worth quoting Rahner once again on this fundamental orientation of every human being towards God since it has a direct bearing on the possibility of faith among the nations. The human 'is already subject to the universal salvific will of God' and 'is already redeemed and absolutely obliged to tend to his supernatural end'. This graced situation 'is not an external one; it is inclusively and inalienably precedent to man's free action, and determines that action.' This universality of God's grace 'does not only exist in God's thoughts and intentions, but is a real modification ... added to... nature by God's grace and therefore supernatural.'[57]

Other expressions of this universal saving will of God include the outpouring of the Spirit on the whole of humanity from the beginning of time (Gen 1:1-2), the existence of 'the seeds of the Word of God' scattered throughout creation, and the light of the *Logos* in the world. These theological realities, namely the universal saving will of God, the *semina verbi*, and the light of the *Logos* imply the existence and presence of universal Revelation throughout the history of the world, offered to every human being. The Bible talks about holy outsiders, priests and prophets outside of Judaism who are pleasing to God and who mediate God's presence.[58] Further, St Paul claims that 'ever since the creation of the world his eternal power and divine nature, invisible though they are, have been seen and understood through the things he has made.'[59] In the Areopagus, Paul could say:

Athenians, I see how extremely religious you are in every way. For as I went through the city and looked carefully at the objects you worship, I found among them an altar with the inscription 'To an Unknown God'. What, therefore, you worship as unknown, that I proclaim to you.[60]

The *Dogmatic Constitution on the Church* of Vatican II observes: 'Nor is God remote from those who in shadows and images seek the unknown God, since he gives to everyone life and breath and all things (see Acts 17:25-28) and since the Saviour wills everyone to be saved (see 1 Tim 2:4).'[61] The same document goes on to say: 'Those who, through no fault of their own, do not know the Gospel of Christ or his Church, but nevertheless seek God with a sincere heart, and moved by grace, try in their actions to do his will – these too may attain eternal salvation.'[62] In affirming the existence of this universal revelation of God it must also be pointed out that this revelation becomes effective in the life of the individual only insofar as there is a response of faith. There is no revelation, whether we are talking about universal, Jewish or Christian revelation, without the personal and free acceptance by the individual.

Whether universal revelation can elicit full theological faith or just belief is a matter of some debate. According to *Dominus Iesus,* 'the theological distinction between theological faith and belief in other religions must be firmly held.' It is necessary to make some further distinctions when applying this observation of *Dominus Iesus*. The first distinction relates to people of good will who seek justice and follow their consciences without any religious affiliation. Is it possible for the universal revelation of God in creation and through the gift of the Spirit to evoke theological faith within this category? Some would argue that the presence of God in creation and through the outpouring of the Spirit from the dawn of time is a somewhat impersonal presence and therefore unable to evoke theological faith. Others would suggest that the presence of God in creation, and especially the gift of the Spirit poured into the heart of every human being, is a personal presence found in the depths of self-consciousness and, therefore, able to evoke theological faith. In favour of this latter position, they would point to the *Letter to the Hebrews* which implies that all who please God, such as outsiders, do so in virtue of the gift of faith granted to them: 'And without faith it is impossible to please God, for whoever would approach him must believe that he exists and that he rewards those who seek him.'[63] Furthermore, the teaching of Vatican II in *Lumen Gentium* as just quoted above, seems to imply that such faith is possible. In addition, the *Decree on the Missionary Activity of the Church* says that: 'In ways known to God himself, God can lead those who, through no fault of their own, are ignorant of the Gospel, to that faith without which it is impossible to please God.'[64] This debate will continue to attract different schools of thought.

The second distinction that should be made relates to members of other religions. It seems harsh to hold that the 'distinction between theological faith and belief in other religions' must be applied to all other religions. It is particularly difficult to see this in the light of the positive regard of the Catholic Church towards Judaism in particular and other religions as outlined in *Nostra Aetate*, *Lumen Gentium*, *Ad Gentes* and *Gaudium et Spes*, and as summarised in Chapter Two. The application of this sharp distinction between faith and belief seems to go against the grain of *Dialogue and Proclamation* (1991), which says that:

> A sincere practice of what is good … in religious traditions and by following the dictates of their conscience … members of other religious traditions respond positively to God's invitation and receive salvation in Jesus Christ, even while they do not recognise or acknowledge him as their Saviour.[65]

Moreover, the application of this distinction between faith and belief is particularly problematic if and when it is applied to Judaism, since Vatican II explicitly affirms God's unrevoked covenant with Israel and describes the Jewish scriptures as part of the Word of God. It should be remembered that some months after the publication of *Dominus Iesus*, the Vatican issued a statement acknowledging that the position of Judaism is in fact quite different to other religions.

This review of the distinction between faith and belief in the context of God's universal revelation clearly challenges all to go beyond stereotypes of people of goodwill, other religions and Jews. One of the aims of inter-religious dialogue must be to protect the recognition of the generosity of the grace of God among the nations and in the religions, to safeguard a proper sense of the gift of the Spirit given to all as found in the Bible, and to defend the positive teaching of the Second Vatican Council concerning religions and the reception of that teaching in the post-conciliar period.

Thus we find Karl Rahner cautioning Christians against restricting God's Revelation in the following way: 'Because of God's universal salvific will, a Christian has no right to limit the actual event of salvation to the explicit history of salvation in the Old and New Testament, despite the theological axiom ... that outside the Church there is no salvation.'[66] What Rahner says here about salvation applies with equal force to the universal revelation of God. In a similar fashion we find the Catholic practitioner of comparative theology, Francis Clooney, making a like-minded point: 'The presence of holy others, saints outside Israel and outside the Church remind us that grace is indeed God's, not something we can limit or deny to the identifiable figures in other religions.'[67]

It also becomes apparent from this review of revelation that it is necessary to affirm the existence of the universal revelation of God in the world in order to recognise the particular mediation of this through the faith of other religions, through the faith of Judaism, and through the particular faith of Christians as centred in Christ as the definitive and decisive revelation of God. The actual dynamics, the interplay, between God's universal revelation and humanity is a task that theology must continually address in the light of the new context in which we live today, namely that of secularisation, globalisation and religious pluralism as seen in Chapter One.

Lastly, it should be clear from this discussion that it is possible to talk about different expressions of God's universal revelation, and that for Christians the expression of God's universal revelation is given definitively and decisively in Christ. Further, it should be recognised that this definitive and decisive revelation of God in Christ is precisely what sheds light on the revelation of God in other religions and among the nations. It is against the background of this theology of 'Pneumatology and revelation' that we can now attend to the possibility of working out a Christian theology of the Holy Spirit.

NOTES

1. *AG*, a.4; see also *GS*, a.41
2. *GS*, a.22
3. See *DV*, a.2 and a.4
4. For example, see *LG*, a.13 and a.16, *GS*, a.22, *AG*, a.4, a.9, a.11, *NA*, a.2
5. *DV*, a.53
6. *RM*, a.28
7. *RM*, a.29. Gerald O' Collins talks about a development of doctrine concerning the Holy Spirit in the teaching of John Paul II. See Gerald O'Collins, 'John Paul II and the Development of Doctrine', *The Legacy of John Paul II*, Gerald O' Collins and Michael Hayes (eds), London: Burns and Oates 2008, 1–16 at 11
8. See Yves Congar, *I Believe in the Holy Spirit*, 3 Volumes, London: Chapman, 1983
9. 1 Cor 2:9-10
10. Eph 3:5. This link between the Spirit and Revelation is emphasised by Ormond Rush in *The Eyes of Faith: The Sense of the Faithful and the Church's Reception of Revelation*, Washington, DC: The Catholic University of America Press, 2009, 18–19
11. See 1 Cor 2:10-11
12. Rom 8:15; Gal 4:6
13. Walter Kasper, *The God of Jesus Christ*, London: SCM Press, 1983, 2–5
14. Ibid., 226
15. Ibid.
16. George Schner, 'A Commentary on the Dogmatic Constitution on Divine Revelation – *Dei Verbum*', *Essays Catholic and Critical*, Philip G. Ziegler and Mark Husbands (eds), Vermont: Ashgate, 2003, 31–43 at 41
17. Peter de Mey, 'The Relationship between Revelation and Experience in *Dei Verbum*: An Evaluation in the Light of Post-Conciliar Theology', *Vatican II and its Legacy*, Mathijs Lamberigts and Leo Kenis (eds), Louvain: Louvain University Press, 2002, 95–105 at 95
18. See Ormond Rush, '*Dei Verbum* Forty Years On: Revelation, Inspiration and the Spirit', *Australian Catholic Record*, 83, 2006, 406–14 at 407

19. Donald Senior, 'Dogmatic Constitution on Divine Revelation: *Dei Verbum*, 18 November 1965', *Vatican II and its Documents: An American Reappraisal*, Timothy E. O'Connell (ed.), Delaware: M. Glazier, 1986, 122–140 at 129

20. *DV*, a.14 and a.8. This recognition of the place of experience was a significant step for a Church that only sixty years previously had condemned a particular understanding of experience during the Modernist crisis

21. This particular deficit has been supplemented *in nuce* in *The Catechism of the Catholic Church*, 1994, a.33–35, which points towards the human as *capax Dei*

22. This issue is addressed in part by the Pontifical Biblical Commission in *The Interpretation of the Bible in the Church*, 1993

23. A helpful document on this complex question has been issued by the Pontifical Biblical Commission entitled *The Jewish People and their Sacred Scriptures in the Christian Bible*, 2001

24. Gerald O'Collins, *Retrieving Fundamental Theology: Three Styles of Contemporary Theology*, London: Chapman, 1993, 56

25. Ormond Rush, '*Dei Verbum* Forty Years On: Revelation, Inspiration and the Spirit', 406–14 at 413

26. Ormond Rush deals in a comprehensive manner with the role of the Spirit in the reception of God's revelation in the past and in the present in his magisterial text, *The Eyes of Faith: The Sense of the Faithful and the Church's Reception of Revelation*

27. See Amos Wilder, *Theopoetic: Theology and the Religious Imagination*, Philadelphia: Fortress Press, 1972; Ray Hart, *Unfinished Man and the Imagination: Towards an Ontology and a Rhetoric of Revelation*, Atlanta, GA: Scholars Press, 1985; James P. Mackey (ed.), *The Religious Imagination*, Edinburgh: Edinburgh University Press, 1986; Richard Kearney, *Poetics of Imagining: Modern to Post-Modern*, new edition, Edinburgh: Edinburgh University Press, 1998; Dermot A. Lane, 'Imagination and Theology: The *Status Quaestionis*', *Louvain Studies*, 34 (2009–2010), 123–49; John Dyck, Paul Rowe and Jens Zimmermann (eds), *Politics and the Religious Imagination*, London: Routledge, 2010

28. William Dych, 'Theology and Imagination', *Thought*, 57, 1982, 116

29. Richard Kearney, 'Imagining the sacred stranger: hostility or hospitality', in *Politics and the Religious Imagination*, 15–30 at 29

30. Elizabeth Jennings, 'I Count the Moments', *Collected Poems: 1933–1985*, Manchester: Carcanet Press, 1986

31. Michael Scanlon, 'Christian Anthropology and Ethics', *Vision and Values: Ethical Viewpoints in the Catholic Tradition*, Judith A. Dwyer (ed.), 1999, 27–51 at 48

32. Richard G. Cote, 'Christology and the Paschal Imagination', *Concilium: Who Do You Say That I Am?*, Werner Jeanrond and Christoph Theobald (eds), London: SCM Press, 1997/1, 80–8 at 84

33. Ormond Rush, '*Sensus Fidei*: Faith "Making Sense" of Revelation', *Theological Studies*, June 2001, 231–261 at 240

34. Michael Paul Gallagher, 'Imagination and Faith', *The Way*, 1984, 122

35. John McIntyre, *Faith, Theology and Imagination,* Edinburgh: Handsel Press, 1987, 159

36. Trevor Hart, 'Transfiguring Reality: Imagination and the Reshaping of the Human', *Theology in Scotland*, 8, 2001, 5–22 at 14

37. Ormond Rush, art. cit., 247

38. Michael Scanlon, 'Revelation', *The Modern Catholic Encyclopaedia,* revised and expanded edition, Michael Glazier and Monika K. Hellwig (eds), Collegeville, MN: Liturgical Press, 2004, 74–9 at 78

39. Hart, art. cit., 17

40. Walter Brueggemann, 'Spirit-Led Imagination: Reality practised in a Sub-Version', *Mandate to Difference: An Invitation to the Contemporary Church*, Louisville: Westminster John Knox Press, 2007, 117–40

41. Bernard Cooke, *Power and the Spirit of God: Towards an Experience-Based Pneumatology*, New York: Oxford University Press, 2004, 117

42. See Amos Yong, *Spirit-Word-Community: Theological Hermeneutics in Trinitarian Perspective*, Burlington: Ashgate Publishing House, 2002, 133–41

43. Quotation is taken from Bradford E. Hinze, 'The Spirit in a Trinitarian Ecclesiology', *Advents of the Spirit: An Introduction to the Current Study of Pneumatology*, Bradford Hinze and D. Lyle Dabney (eds), Marquette: Marquette University Press, 2001, 347–81 at 364

44. G. K. Chesterton, 'The Maniac', *Orthodoxy*, London: John Lane, The Bodley Head, 1908, 30

45. Rahner, 'History of the World and Salvation', *TI*, Vol. V, 103

46. Rahner, *Foundations of Christian Faith: An Introduction to the Idea of Christianity*, New York: Crossroad, 1978, 173

47. Ibid., 172–3

48. Ibid., 174–5

49. Rahner suggests the Council had formulated premises for a conclusion it did not draw. See Rahner, 'On the Importance of the Non-Christian Religions for Salvation', *TI*, Vol. XVIII, 288–95 at 290–1

50. *NA*, a.3

51. Bede Griffiths, *The Marriage of East and West*, London: Collins, 1982, 17–180; Jacques Dupuis, *Christianity and the Religions: From Confrontation to Dialogue*, New York: Orbis, 2001, 120–2

52. Dupuis, *Christianity and the Religions*, 122–23

53. *DV*, a.2

54. *DV*, a.4

55. Gavin D'Costa, 'Revelation and Revelations: Discerning God in Other Religions, Beyond a Static Valuation', *Modern Theology*, April 1994, 165–83 at 178

56. William Temple, *Nature, Man and God*, Gifford Lectures, Edinburgh: T. and T. Clark, 1934, 306

57. Karl Rahner and Herbert Vorgrimler (eds), *Dictionary of Theology*, second edition, New York: Crossroad, 1981, 163–4

58. See Gerald O'Collins, *Salvation for All: God's Other Peoples*, New York: Oxford University Press, 2008

59. Rom 1:20

60. Acts 17:22-23

61. *LG*, a.16

62. *LG*, a.16, see also *AG*, a.7

63. Heb 11:6

64. *AG* a.7

65. *DP* a.29. Some have suggested that there is something of an internal tension within *Dominus Iesus* on this particular point when it insists on maintaining the sharp distinction between theological faith and belief in other religions. It is noted that there are some more generous statements within *Dominus Iesus* itself, such as the observation that 'Certainly, the various religious traditions contain and offer religious elements which come from God and which are part of what the Spirit brings about in human hearts and in the history of peoples; in cultures, and religions' (a.21)

66. Rahner, *Foundations of Christian Faith*, 147–8

67. Francis Clooney, 'Review Symposium on Gerald O'Collins' *Salvation for All: God's Other Peoples*', *Horizons*, Spring 2009, 126–30 at 127

VII. DEVELOPING A CHRISTIAN THEOLOGY OF THE HOLY SPIRIT

In the light of the principles outlined in Chapter Five that should inform Spirit-talk, and the place given to Pneumatology in a theology of revelation in Chapter Six, we are now in a position to develop a Christian theology of the Holy Spirit. This will entail an introduction to the theology of the Spirit within Judaism and early Christianity, an outline of the shape of a Spirit-Christology, a move towards a Spirit-centred ecclesiology, and concluding comments on criteria for discerning the gift of God's Spirit in the churches, religions and the world.

1. THE SPIRIT IN THE FIRST TESTAMENT[1]

The combination of the words 'Holy' and 'Spirit' rarely occurs in the Hebrew scriptures and, as such, belongs more to the New Testament, and even then with considerable constraint in comparison to the more general use of the word 'Spirit'. The bringing together of 'Spirit' and 'Holy' is more a post-New Testament development, especially after the definition of the divinity of the Spirit at the Council of Constantinople in 381.

The word 'spirit', *ruach* in Hebrew, occurs 378 times in the Hebrew scriptures. It usually means 'wind' or 'moving air' or 'breath'. *Ruach* can also refer to qualities of God or of human beings or animals or supernatural beings.

It is possible to discern at least two layers of usage: one in relation to the action of the Spirit of God in the history of Israel, and the other in relation to the action of the Spirit of God in the creation of the world, past and present, as well as the creation and sustaining of human beings in existence. It is not always easy to distinguish one layer from the other, but it seems safe to say that the action of the Spirit in the history of Israel precede the Hebrew understanding of the Spirit within creation.

a. Spirit in the History of Israel

In the first instance, the Spirit of God is manifested in the history of Israel through the prophets, leaders, judges and kings. The Spirit of God (*ruach Elohim*, *ruach Yahweh*) inspires people (known as prophets) to speak out on behalf of Yahweh and is also communicated to the leaders of Israel.[2] Hosea is described as a 'man of the Spirit',[3] Micah is 'filled with the Spirit of the Lord',[4] and Ezekiel talks about being lifted up by the Spirit.[5] On the other hand, Israel goes through different historical periods when the action of the Spirit is more prominent than at other times, and then there are periods when the action of the Spirit appears to be dormant. In time, the outpouring of the Spirit of God becomes associated with the promise of a messiah and the inauguration of a messianic era. For example, this messianic outlook can be found in the songs of the servant of Yahweh: 'A shoot shall come from the stump of Jesse, and a branch shall grow out of his roots. The spirit of the Lord shall rest on him, the spirit of wisdom and understanding, the spirit of counsel and might...'[6] In addition, the messianic figure is related to the servant of Yahweh: 'Here is my servant ... my chosen ... in whom my soul delights. I have put my spirit upon him; he will bring forth justice to the nations.'[7] This chosen one is given the Spirit of Yahweh to be the prophet who will bring justice to the oppressed: 'The spirit of the Lord God is upon me, because the Lord has anointed me to bring good news to the oppressed, to bind up the broken hearted, to proclaim liberty to captives ...'[8]

In the Exilic and post-Exilic period, it is expected that the Spirit of God will be 'poured out' on the House of Israel.[9] Ezekiel, in Chapter 37, declares over the valley of the dry bones, which represents 'the House of Israel', that the Spirit of God will effect a revivification and reanimation of the dead,[10] establish 'a covenant of peace with them',[11] and make a 'dwelling place ... with them'.[12] Further, the Spirit of God 'will cause you [the House of Israel] to walk in my statutes and be careful to observe my ordinances.'[13] This outpouring of the Spirit of God over time becomes associated with the eschatological 'Day of the Lord', the end-time when there will be judgement and cosmic upheaval, as well as rejoicing for Israel as intimated in the Book of Joel, Chapter 2.

Within Rabbinic theology, the Spirit of God is associated with the Spirit of prophecy. At the same time however, the Spirit of God 'is imparted primarily in the sanctuary, the place of God's presence',[14] and so, with the destruction of the first temple, there is a 'dormancy of the Spirit'.[15] Thus, later on, with 'the collapse of the second temple and the loss of this cultic centre as the locus of God's presence', there arises 'the notion of a prophet-less Spirit-less era' and this was the context in which the establishment of the Hebrew canon became important.[16]

b. Spirit in the Stories of Creation

A second, equally important, layer to the Jewish theology of Spirit can be found in stories about the creation of the world and human beings as contained in the book of Genesis and in parts of the Psalms. Genesis Chapter 1 must, however, be put into the context of the whole book of Genesis. Genesis is made up of fifty chapters and these contain two distinct stories of origins:

1. The origins of Israel contained in Chapters 12–50;
2. The origins of creation contained in Chapters 1–11.

In regard to 'God and Israel', we find God calling Abraham from whom Israel descends. Concerning 'God and the world', we have a confession of faith that links the God of Abraham to the creation of the world.

In a certain sense it can be said that Genesis 1:1–2:3 acts as a kind of prologue, or preface, not only to the other creation story (Gen 2:2–4:25), but also to the whole of the *Torah*. The story of the creation of heaven and earth in Chapter 1 should not be taken as a speculation about origins, or even worse, a statement about how the world came to be scientifically, or as a historical account about the beginnings of the world. Instead, Genesis 1:1ff. is a statement of faith that the One whom Israel follows, worships and serves (Chapters 12–50) is none other than the one who is also the creator and sustainer of the universe.[17]

Two different readings are possible for the first verse of Chapter 1 of Genesis. On the one hand it could be translated as: 'In the beginning God created the heavens and the earth'. On the other hand it could read: 'When God began to create heaven and earth ...' The first translation is the preferred reading because it corresponds more closely with a parallel statement later on which says: 'Thus the heavens and the earth were finished and all their multitude.'[18] In the light of these preliminary comments, we must now turn to some detail of the text of Genesis.

In the first creation story, Genesis 1:1 stands out as an introductory comment summarising the content of the passage. It should be noted that the story of creation begins with the breath of God (*ruach*) and not with the Word of God. The breath of God precedes the speaking of the Word of God and so, in an important sense, the presence of the Spirit is presupposed by the Word of God. It is in the context of the blowing of the breath of God that God's Word is spoken. Before we can say 'God said', we must recognise that the breath of God was breathing or hovering or hatching like a mother hen over the world. The first creation story closes with reference to 'everything that has the breath of life',[19] which comes from the breath of God which in the first instance 'swept over the face of waters'.[20]

Of course one cannot construct a theology on the basis of a single text and so we must look for other references to the breath of God. In the second story of creation, Genesis 2:2–4:25, often referred to as the Yahwist tradition, the breath of God also appears and is associated with the creation of the human. It is stated that God formed the human from the dust of the earth 'and breathed into his nostrils the breath of life and man became a living being.'[21] There are a number of points to be noted here.

First of all, it is the breath of God that gives rise to a living being. The human is created and sustained by the breath of God. Secondly, it must be noted that *Adam*, the human, comes from *Adama*, the earth, that is, the human comes out of the dust of the earth, and therefore a better translation, and perhaps a more accurate translation, of *Adam* would be 'an earthling' or 'a child of the earth' or perhaps 'a worldling'. In other words, there is no way in which we can say that human beings are separate or above the earth. Human beings are not passers-by, nor are they tourists from another planet, nor are they outsiders to the earth. Instead, the human, *homo*, comes from the *humus*, from the dust of the earth; the human is *Adam*, a child of the earth, born from *Adama*, the life-giving earth, all of which resonates with contemporary cosmologies which often talk about the human as cosmic dust in a state of consciousness or, to paraphrase Wilfred Owen, 'clay grown tall'.

The breath of God is found to be active therefore at the beginning of the creation-narrative of the heavens and the earth, and at the end of the creation-narrative of the human. It is this appearance of the breath of God at both ends of the creation story that prompts a reading of origins with an explicitly Pneumatological framework.

This reading of Genesis is further confirmed when we look briefly at the Creation-centred Psalms of the Psalter. For example, Psalm 33:6 observes:

> By the Word of the Lord the heavens were made,
> All their host by the breath of His mouth.

Or again, Psalm 104:29-30 reads:

> When you hide your face, they are dismayed;
> When you take away their breath, they die and return to their dust,
> When you send forth your Spirit, they are created and you renew the face of the ground.

Another example can be found in Psalm 139:7-15. There we find that God is present to the whole of creation through his Spirit, present in the heavens, in the farthest limits of the sea (v.9), in the darkness of life (v.11-12), and in the inner parts of one's being (v.13). An underlying unity appears between the Spirit in creation and the Spirit in the life of the human.

One further example can be found in the dry bones prophesy of Ezekiel. There the Lord says:

> I will cause breath to enter you and you shall live,[22]

and again the Lord says:

> Come from the four winds, o breath, and breathe upon these slain, that they may live...
> I will put my Spirit within you, and you shall live ...;
> then you shall know that I, the Lord, have spoken and will act.[23]

Note here, as in Genesis, the Spirit precedes the Word.

When the two creation stories of Genesis are read in conjunction with these other texts of the Hebrew scriptures, there is more than just the hint of a theology of the Spirit as the source of life poured out on the whole of creation and on all flesh at the dawn time. As one author puts it, the whole of creation is 'enspirited by God'[24] since the beginning. In the light of this summary overview of the Spirit of God in the Hebrew scriptures, we can begin to say that:

- The Spirit of God *ab initio* is connected to the story of creation and yet is different from creation;
- The Spirit of God is intimately involved in creation as divine possibility and promise, and yet remains distinct from creation;
- The Spirit of God suffuses the whole of creation and sustains humans, holding both together in a fundamental unity;

- The Spirit of God is, in a manner of speaking, the 'soul' or 'subject' or 'agent' of creation, and yet the Spirit is separate from creation;
- The Spirit of God is the source of life for all beings that breath.

What begins to emerge from this overview of the stories of creation in Genesis is a picture, not only of creation out of nothing (*creatio ex nihilo*) but also a story about the initiating and continuing presence of the Spirit of God in the world both as possibility and promise (*creatio continua*). This on-going activity of the Spirit in the world and in Judaism prompts people to refer to the Spirit as the Creator-Spirit.

Further, creation is neither identical with the creator, which would be a form of pantheism, nor is creation autonomous from the creator which would be a form of deism. Instead there is a fundamental difference between God and the world, a certain separateness of the Spirit from the world, and yet at the same time there is an underlying intimacy between the Spirit of God and the reality of creation and this is often referred to as a form of pan-en-theism.

In emphasising the primacy of the Spirit within these creation stories, we do not intend to subordinate the Word to the Spirit. Rather, we are attempting to take seriously the sequence of the story of creation as given in Genesis, which is one of the Spirit and Word working together in that order. Putting the Spirit first does not displace or diminish or replace the importance of the Word. If anything, it highlights the centrality of the Word as presupposed by the presence of the Spirit.

A somewhat similar sequence concerning the primacy of the Spirit can also be found in the New Testament account of the Christ-event. In the story of the Incarnation, it is first said to the woman: 'The Holy Spirit will come upon you and the power of the most high will overshadow you'[25] and, in the light of that promise, the Word is made flesh. So, just as in the creation story so now in the story of Incarnation, the Spirit is portrayed as primary and is presupposed by the Word in both instances.

This overview of the Spirit in the Hebrew scriptures clearly indicates that there was no single theology of the Spirit of God within Judaism. There are, however, enough references to the Spirit of God to suggest that there was a deep awareness among the people of Israel of different presences of the Spirit in their lives: a presence in the creation of the earth and the human, a presence in the prophets and leaders of Israel, a gift that would be given to the promised Messiah and poured out on the Messianic people. Thus the breath of God (*ruach*) initiates and holds creation together, specifically creating and sustaining the human in existence. It is this gift of the Spirit given to the people of Israel as well as the presence of the Spirit hovering/brooding/hatching over the creation of the world at the dawn of time and thereafter, that provides the background and context for understanding the presence and action of the Spirit of God in the New Testament era.

2. THE SPIRIT IN THE SECOND TESTAMENT

The word Spirit, *pneuma*, occurs 379 times in the New Testament. Two hundred and seventy-five of these references are to the Spirit of God, and of these, 149 refer to the 'Holy Spirit'. In forty-seven instances, *pneuma* refers to the human condition, and another thirty-eight instances are about evil spirits, or unclean spirits.[26]

Three important points come across clearly in the New Testament writings that serve as an introduction to a review of the Spirit. There is the continuous presence of the Spirit in the life of Jesus, an awareness that the early Christian community is 'a Spirit-endowed entity', and that the gift of the Spirit given at Pentecost is recognised 'as a present eschatological event'.[27]

a. The Gift of the Holy Spirit in the Life of Jesus
F. W. Horn in the *Anchor Bible Dictionary* discerns different levels in which the Spirit of God is given.[28] There is first of all the 'pre-Easter gift of the Spirit' to Jesus and this is manifested in the activities of the ministry of Jesus recorded in the Gospels. These activities would have been seen from a Jewish point of view as Spirit-inspired

activities: the baptism in the Jordan, the claim to be a prophet, preaching in the synagogue, the announcement of the coming Reign of God, the forgiveness of sins, healings, exorcisms, and the authoritative interpretation of the law. These activities suggest at least 'an implicit Pneumatic self-consciousness' in the life of Jesus[29] which the authors of the Gospels, especially the Synoptic Gospels, make explicit in their accounts of the life of Jesus, especially in the light of the Easter-event.

Second, there is the pre-Easter endowment of the disciples of Jesus with the Spirit, and again the different activities of the disciples would be perceived as Spirit-connected in the Hebrew mind: the preaching of repentance,[30] the performance of exorcisms,[31] acts of healing[32] and the proclamation of the Reign of God.

Third, there is 'the gift of the Spirit at Easter'. In the fourth Gospel, Easter and Pentecost come together.[33] The risen Jesus appears to the disciples and imparts his Spirit to them on the day of resurrection: 'He breathed on them'[34] – an expression that echoes what happened in the story of creation: 'God formed man out of the dust from the ground, and breathed into his nostrils the breath of life.'[35] Further, there is a linking of the gift of the Spirit with the forgiveness of sins.[36]

Fourth, there is the 'post-Easter gift' of the Spirit. This gift of the Spirit occurs on the first Pentecost after Easter and is recorded in Acts 2:1-4: 'And they were filled with the Holy Spirit and began to speak in other tongues as the Spirit gave them utterance.'[37] Peter interprets this phenomenon as an eschatological fulfilment of the Prophet Joel 1:1-5. In addition to Pentecost, the linking of the Resurrection and the gift of the Spirit has the vision of Ezekiel, 37:5, 9-10 in the background.

b. The Gift of the Spirit in the Early Christian Communities

There is a considerable evidence in the New Testament letters that the early Christian communities understood themselves as messianically endowed with the Spirit of God.

There are frequent Spirit-centred refrains describing this new awareness of the early Christian communities as Spirit-endowed. One such refrain is: 'God has given us the Spirit.'[38] A second refrain is 'You have received the Spirit.'[39] A third refrain is 'The Spirit of God dwells within you.'[40] While this explicit theology of the Spirit is present within early Christian communities, it must also be acknowledged that there is often tension between Palestinian Jewish Christians and Hellenistic Christians over the gift of the Spirit. This condensed overview of the gift of the Spirit in the life of Jesus and in the early Church paves the way for constructing a Spirit-Christology and a Spirit-centred ecclesiology.

3. CONSTRUCTING A SPIRIT CHRISTOLOGY

A number of theological reasons suggest the time is right for the construction of a Spirit-Christology in the service of a renewed understanding of the Trinity and the provision of a new platform for inter-religious dialogue. Perhaps the most important reason is that the person of Christ makes little sense without reference to the gift of the Spirit. It is through the Spirit that we recognise who Jesus is and through the action of the Spirit that we can hear the Word of God in Jesus.

a. Congar, Crowe and the Patristic Period

Yves Congar, more than most, had a deep theological awareness that the work of Christ and the Spirit are 'inseparable', and he articulates this conviction in a small book entitled *The Word and the Spirit*, in which he stresses the unity of the Word and Spirit.[41] Congar came up with a guiding principle on the relationship between Christ and the Spirit: 'No Christology without Pneumatology and no Pneumatology without Christology.'[42] This particular principle is found in other theologians who also emphasise the unique relationship between Christ and the Spirit, such as Hans von Balthasar,[43] Kilian McDonnell[44] and Walter Kasper.[45] Congar draws up this principle as a corrective to the presence of an excessive Christo-monism in Catholic and Protestant theology. Congar, however, is not alone in his criticism of Christo-monism and its diminishing impact on Pneumatology.

Frederick Crowe expresses a similar concern with Christo-monism: 'Neglect of the Spirit has been partly responsible for the distorted Christ-figures' in a lot of theology.[46] According to Crowe, 'The Spirit ... was brought into coincidence with the Son and so into a measure of oblivion.'[47] As a result of the presence of so much Christo-monism, Crowe asks: 'Have we demanded too much of the Son and by that very fact done irreverence to the Spirit the Father gave us?'[48] To remedy this situation, Crowe does not propose that we should simply replace Christ with the Spirit. Instead what is needed is a dual focus on the Son and the Spirit. To that end Crowe proposes the image of 'an ellipse with two foci in which the Son and the Spirit are distinct and complementary.'[49] Crowe is conscious that this is not an altogether satisfactory response to overcoming Christo-monism because 'Our God is triune and eventually we must find a place for the Father.'[50]

Another theologian, Eugene Rogers, is also concerned about the excesses of Christo-monism. Rogers notes that within the tradition there was nothing the Spirit could do that the Son could not do better.[51]

A significant number of commentators are agreed that the time has come not to replace Christo-monism with a new-fangled Pneumatocentricism, but to redress the neglect of the Spirit by recognising the inseparability of the Son and the Spirit without, however, collapsing the one into the other and ignoring their distinctiveness within the economy of salvation. To have a *Logos*-Christology without a *Pneuma*-Christology would be to miss the activity of the Spirit of God that makes the hearing of the Word of God possible.

Theologians are seeking to retrieve a tradition, lost in western theology, which is quite explicit in the Patristic period and can be found also in the New Testament concerning the underlying unity of Spirit and Word. It is pointed out, for example, that for Irenaeus (115–190 AD) the Spirit and the Word represent the two hands of God at work in the economy of creation and salvation. Athanasius (296–377 AD) insists on the inseparability of the Word and the Spirit, and suggests: 'Where the Word is, there is the Spirit also.'[52] In support of this, Athanasius quotes Psalm 32: 'By the Word of God the heavens were established, and by the Spirit of his mouth is all their power.' Similarly, Basil (330–379 AD), especially in his work *On the Holy Spirit,* insists that: 'In every operation, the Holy Spirit is invisibly united with the Father and the Son.' Basil sees the Spirit as the 'creative power at work in everything that exists.'[53] Lastly, Ambrose (339–397 AD) describes the Spirit as the source of Creation and 'the author of the Lord's Incarnation'.[54]

These patristic perspectives on the reciprocal relationship between Christ and the Spirit in turn are reflected in the New Testament, especially in the Synoptics and Paul, both of whom closely associate the activity of the Spirit with the work of Christ: in the historical life of Jesus, in the death and resurrection, and in the unity of the newly formed ecclesial communities. The New Testament not only emphasises the close relationship between Christ and the Spirit, but also makes it quite clear that it is only through the Spirit that we can recognise Jesus as Lord.[55] This emphasis on the role of the Spirit in understanding the identity of Jesus is as important today as it was in New Testament times. It is only in virtue of the invisible gift and action of the Spirit that we today can fully appreciate the centrality of Christ as the eternal Word of God Incarnate.

b. Reasons for a Spirit Christology

It is this unique inseparability, reciprocity and mutuality between the Word and the Spirit that provides a framework for the construction of a Spirit-Christology in the service of a theology of inter-religious dialogue. There are several reasons why the development of a Spirit-Christology is necessary at this time. For example, one of the failures within the renaissance of Christology in the second half of the twentieth century has been the inability of that renewed Christology to inform, correct and transform ecclesiology. It is remarkable how the advances of contemporary Christology have, practically speaking, left ecclesiology untouched and unchanged. One possible way of remedying this failure will be to develop a Spirit-Christology which, in turn, will lead more naturally and coherently and consistently to a much needed Spirit-based ecclesiology. The gap between Christology and ecclesiology is Pneumatology, and this gap can be bridged by the construction of a Spirit-Christology, which has the capacity to enable the Church to enter more fully into dialogue with other living faiths. A further reason why a Spirit-Christology is appropriate at this time is the recognition of the presence of the Spirit in other religions at Vatican II and in the writings of John Paul II, as already outlined in Chapter Two. Given this recognition of the Spirit in other religions, it seems that a Spirit-Christology is better suited to open up this new dialogue between Christianity and other religions. If the Spirit present in other religions is the same Spirit active in the life of Jesus, then an important point of contact is established between Christianity and many other religions. An additional reason favouring the adoption of a Spirit-Christology is that it has the capacity to open up neglected aspects of the theology of the Trinity. A Spirit-Christology, following the Synoptics and Paul, that recognises but also complements the existence of a *Logos* Christology gives a more comprehensive understanding of the Trinity than simply a *Logos* Christology on its own.[56] A renewed theology of the Trinity, rooted in the gift of the Spirit and the historical reality of Christ, would then be able to inform inter-faith dialogue.

One of the positive outcomes arising from the adoption of Pneumatology as a point of departure for theology is the development of a Spirit-Christology. This development of a Spirit-Christology has been gestating for some time and can be found with varying degrees of success in a variety of authors such as Piet Schoonenberg, James P. Mackey, Geoffrey Lampe, Roger Haight and Denis Edwards. David Coffey has made a distinctive contribution to the construction of a Spirit-Christology in his work on the Trinity. In a recent article, Coffey suggests that a Spirit-Christology 'holds out the greatest promise for the future development' of theology as a whole.[57] He argues persuasively that the *Logos* Christology of John's Gospel needs to be complemented by the Spirit-Christology of the Synoptics. In suggesting this, Coffey wants to construct a Spirit-Christology in which the Spirit is understood as 'the principle of Incarnation'.[58] It should be noted that Coffey's promotion of a Spirit-Christology is motivated by a desire to renew our understanding of the Trinity and in particular to recover what he calls 'the mutual love model' of the Trinity. The 'mutual love model' of the Trinity, or 'the bestowal model' of the Trinity, is a model in which the Spirit proceeds as the mutual love between the Father and the Son.[59]

c. A Plurality of Spirit Christologies

It is beyond the scope of this book to develop a fully-fledged Spirit-Christology. Suffice it to note that there is a variety of Spirit-Christologies in the New Testament. These include the Spirit Christologies of the Synoptics, of the Pauline literature, of the Acts of the Apostles, and of John's Gospel. In outlining these Spirit-Christologies of the New Testament, attention should be given to the unfolding historical awareness of the action of the Spirit in the life of Jesus and in the early Christian communities. This unfolding awareness will take account of the findings of the historical critical method as applied to the New Testament data. This historical and theological analysis of the Spirit in the New Testament would, in turn, be informed by developments in the Patristic period in relation to the Spirit in the second and third centuries, leading to the Council of Constantinople in 381 AD which defined the distinctive divine personhood of the Spirit and the equality of the Spirit with the Father and the Son.

It would be important that the development of a Spirit-Christology would follow the direction of a low-historical-ascending Christology without neglecting the content of a high Christology or indeed, in this instance, a high Pneumatology. Prior to the adoption of a historical methodology, Christology was dominated by the *Logos* Christology of John's Gospel. This pervasive presence of a *Logos* Christology needs to be balanced by a *Pneuma* Christology, and this can be done by attending to the historical and theological data of the Synoptics. Developments that have taken place in the search for the historical Jesus, and the fruits of those developments, should be allowed to influence the shape of a low-ascending-Spirit Christology. Further, it should be noted that the Christology of official Church documents across the denominations up to recently has been influenced largely by the *Logos* Christology of John's Gospel and this needs to be balanced by giving more attention to the Spirit-Christologies of the Synoptics, of Paul, and the early Church.

It is important in the development of a Spirit Christology that reference be made to the dynamics of the presence and action of the Spirit in the life of Jesus and the early Christian communities. If this can be done, it will inform the contemporary challenge of discerning what the Spirit might be saying to the churches today. Awareness of the action of the Spirit in the life of Jesus must surely inform the discernment of the agency of the Spirit in the churches today and among other religions.

A further guiding principle in the construction of a Spirit Christology is the need to attend to the role of the Spirit in the Synoptics as Coffey and others have emphasised, not in opposition to or in competition with the already existing *Logos* Christology of John, but rather as a complementary approach to and a way of retrieving the full meaning of Jesus as the Christ anointed by the Spirit.

Without pretending to present a full-blown Spirit Christology, we will offer a sketch of the shape that a Spirit Christology might take in the light of the above principles and that might enable Christianity to enter into dialogue with other religions. The point of departure must surely be the foundational Pneumatology already outlined, namely a recognition of the gift of the Spirit continuously hovering/brooding over creation and bestowed upon every human being from the dawn of time. That same Spirit, according to the Synoptics, surrounds the conception, the birth, the mission, the ministry, the death and resurrection of Jesus. If we look at the life of Jesus through the lens of Pneumatology, we will be struck by the number of references to the presence of the Spirit in the life of Jesus from the beginning to the end. A glance at the Synoptics reveals the historical life of Jesus as not only surrounded and empowered by the Spirit, but also a life lived in deep communion with the Spirit of God. A few examples of this omnipresence of the Spirit in the life of Jesus may give a sense of direction for the construction of a Spirit Christology.

Beginning with the Gospel of Mark, as the earliest Gospel, Jesus is announced as the one who will bring a baptism of water and the *Holy Spirit*. The ministry of Jesus is presented as mediating and bearing the eschatological Spirit of the end of time. At the baptism of Jesus in the Jordan, the Spirit descends on him, dove-like. This anointing of Jesus with the Spirit establishes his Messianic identity as God's Son. After his baptism, 'the Spirit immediately drove him out into the wilderness.'[60] The same Spirit sustains Jesus throughout his ministry.

In Matthew's Gospel, which probably builds on Mark, there is a somewhat different, but complementary, perspective. Matthew traces Jesus' link with the Spirit back to his conception and birth. Mary 'was found to be with the child from the Holy Spirit'[61] and Joseph is told, 'Do not be afraid to take Mary as your wife, for the child conceived in her is from the Holy Spirit.'[62] Like Mark, Matthew has John the Baptist announce that Jesus was baptised with the Holy Spirit and adds 'and with fire'.[63] Like Mark, the Spirit descends on Jesus and Jesus is 'led by the Spirit into the wilderness'.[64] Further, Jesus casts out demons 'by the Spirit of God'[65] and declares: 'Whoever speaks against the Holy Spirit will not be forgiven.'[66] Finally, the risen Christ commands the disciples 'to baptise in the name of the Father, and of the Son and of the Holy Spirit.'[67]

Luke, author of the Gospel of Luke and the Acts of the Apostles, has most to say about Jesus and the Spirit. In Luke's infancy narrative, the Spirit is found all over the place. John the Baptist is filled with the Holy Spirit; Elizabeth and Zachariah are 'filled with the Holy Spirit';[68] the Holy Spirit rested 'on Simeon'[69] and 'guided' Simeon,[70] and Simeon receives a revelation from the Holy Spirit.[71] Further, we are told that the Holy Spirit comes upon Mary and overshadows her and 'therefore the child to be born will be holy; he will be called Son of God'.[72]

John the Baptist announces Jesus will baptise 'with the Holy Spirit and fire'.[73] After his baptism in the Jordan, the Holy Spirit descends on Jesus, and then Jesus, full of the Holy Spirit, returned from the Jordan and was led by the Spirit into the wilderness for forty days. After the forty days, he returned to Galilee 'filled with the power of the Holy Spirit' and then reads in the synagogue the passage from Isaiah which says:

The Spirit of the Lord is upon me
Because he has anointed me to bring good news to the poor.[74]

Later, Luke has Jesus rejoicing in the Holy Spirit.[75] Jesus warns his disciples not to blaspheme against the Holy Spirit since this will not be forgiven and, at the same time, he says the Holy Spirit will teach the disciples what to say in difficult times.[76] Luke closes his Gospel with the risen Christ saying to the disciples: 'I am sending upon you what my Father promised',[77] namely the gift of the Holy Spirit.

In the Acts of the Apostles, sometimes called the Acts of the Holy Spirit, the Holy Spirit is presented as the Spirit of Jesus. For example, in Peter's speech to the House of Cornelius we are told that God anointed Jesus of Nazareth with the Holy Spirit and the power. There is some similarity as well as difference between the work of the Spirit in Jesus and the work of the Spirit in the disciples of Jesus. The Spirit poured out at Pentecost is the same Spirit who was active throughout Israel's history, the same Spirit who overshadowed Mary, that anointed Jesus, and led him in his ministry to his death and resurrection.[78]

In John's Gospel, Jesus is described as the one upon whom the Spirit descended and remains, and the one who baptises with the Holy Spirit.[79] Further, Jesus talks about being born of water and the Holy Spirit and that particular experience is described as being born 'from above'.[80] In his farewell discourse, Jesus talks in five places about sending the Paraclete.[81] The word 'paraclete' means advocate, or helper or witness, or comforter or 'the Spirit of truth who proceeds from the father'.[82] Finally, the risen Christ gives the Spirit to his disciples and apostles and so establishes a new ecclesial community empowered to forgive sins.

This review of the four gospels reveals a plurality of Spirit Christologies: Jesus is 'conceived' by the Spirit (Matthew), the one on whom the Spirit descends (Mark); the one who is 'filled' with the Spirit (Luke); the one in whom the Spirit 'abides' and who 'sends' the Spirit as Advocate (John).

d. Advantages of a Spirit Christology

This overview of the presence and action of the Spirit in the life of Jesus highlights Jesus as a man of the Spirit: one who is driven and energised by the Spirit, one who is in personal communion with the Spirit. It is clear that the Spirit plays a pivotal role in the historical unfolding of the Christ-event. It should also be clear that there are many advantages and insights to be gained by the adoption of a Spirit Christology.

On the one hand, a Spirit Christology provides a balance to the predominance of the *Logos* Christology and its impact on our understanding of the Trinity. A Spirit Christology nudges Trinitarian studies to move towards the adoption of a low-ascending historical approach to the Trinity as given in experience and salvation history. Secondly, a Spirit Christology offers another way of expressing the uniqueness and decisiveness of the Christ-event. The Jesus of history is uniquely endowed with the Spirit of God, and as such is the particular embodiment and personal revelation of the universal Spirit of God in the world. Moreover, a Spirit Christology helps to understand Rahner's complex theology of the Spirit of Christ as the entelechy of the universal Spirit of God given in the gift of creation, and even though Rahner does not himself use the term 'Spirit Christology', it is nonetheless implied in his article on 'Aspects of European Theology'[83] in which he talks about the possibility of giving priority to Pneumatology. Furthermore a Spirit Christology provides an important bridge to overcome the gap between Christology and ecclesiology as we will see presently. In addition, a Spirit Christology provides a perspective conducive to dialogue with other religions, given the claims of Lonergan that the other religions are 'the fruit of the Spirit' and of Michael Barnes who sees other religions are 'schools of the Spirit', and of John Paul II who holds that the other religions are 'effects of the Spirit'.[84] One further advantage of a Spirit

Christology that can only be mentioned is in passing is the capacity of a Spirit Christology to renew and deepen our understanding of the Trinity, a task clearly beyond the scope of this chapter.[85]

The Spirit now appears as the *sine qua non* of Christology. Within a Spirit Christology a significant transition takes place from the historical Jesus full of the Holy Spirit to Jesus as the crucified and risen Christ who breathes forth his Spirit upon his disciples. It is in virtue of this outpouring of the Spirit of the risen Christ that this community of disciples becomes a reform group within Judaism, a new community endowed with and constituted by the eschatological presence and agency of the Spirit. It is this new Spirit-filled community, the Church, held together invisibly by the Spirit of Christ at its centre that is sent to continue the mission and ministry of Jesus, crucified and risen as the Christ, in the world in dialogue with others and the religions.

4. TOWARDS A SPIRIT ECCLESIOLOGY

In proposing a move towards a Spirit-centred ecclesiology, we should remember how John XXIII, in convening the Second Vatican Council, expressed the hope that the Council would be a 'new Pentecost' for the Church. This image of a new Pentecost was a timely reminder that it is the Holy Spirit who guides and directs the Church, and that Pope and the bishops are called and designated to be discerners and servants of the Holy Spirit.

a. A New Pentecost at Vatican II?

It is hardly surprising, in the light of this orientation from John XXIII, that the Council did move towards the adoption of a Pneumatological ecclesiology. One of the most significant shifts at Vatican II in relation to the Holy Spirit is to be found in the *Decree on Ecumenism* (1964). This *Decree* declared that the Spirit 'is the principle of Church unity',[86] that the Holy Spirit is active in other churches and ecclesial communities as a means of salvation,[87] and that 'the grace of the Holy Spirit in the hearts of our separated brothers and sisters can contribute to our own edification' and 'bring a more perfect realisation of the very Mystery of Christ and the Church'.[88]

While these statements about the Spirit may seem unremarkable today, their appearance in the teaching of the Catholic Church in a *Decree on Ecumenism* was significant at the time. Their true significance lies in the way they pointed the Church for the first time since the Reformation in the explicit direction of a Spirit-driven ecclesiology and a Spirit-driven ecumenism. Equally valuable is the way other documents of the Council talk about the presence and action of the Spirit in the world and other religions. For example, *Gaudium et Spes* sees the Spirit of God directing the course of time and renewing the face of the earth,[89] being active in the hearts of people and strengthening the aspirations of humanity to make life more humane,[90] and assisting pastors and theologians to listen to the many voices of our times and to interpret them in the light of the Gospel.[91] Likewise, as already seen, the *Decree on the Missionary Activity of the Church* (1965) makes passing reference to the presence of the Spirit at work in the world before Christ was glorified.[92] A fascinating footnote is attached to that statement in the Decree which elaborates on its meaning: it points out that the advent of the Spirit at Pentecost 'was not the first exercise of his role but an extension of his bounty, because the patriarchs, the prophets and priests, and all holy people of previous ages were nourished by the same sanctifying Spirit ... although the measure of the gift was not the same.'[93] In a similar vein, the *Pastoral Constitution on the Church in the Modern World* (1965) says: 'We must hold that the Holy Spirit offers to all the possibility of being made partners, in a way known only to God, in the Paschal Mystery.'[94] While these references to the Spirit may appear rather obvious to us today, they were, however, pointing the Church in the direction of a wider and richer theology of the Spirit than had been the case prior to the Council. Clearly, the Council did not produce a worked out, systematic theology of the Holy Spirit. However, it can be said the Council sowed the seeds of a Pneumatological ecclesiology that currently awaits further development.

b. Calls for a Spirit-Centred Theology

In the first decade after the Council, there was a growing awareness of the need to develop a theology of the Holy Spirit. For example, Karl Barth in 1968, who it should be remembered was an observer at the Council, wrote:

> I think we, in the various confessions and churches, are particularly in need of a more serious theology of the third person ... he [the Spirit] can be very briefly defined as the inextinguishable power of the work and Word of Jesus Christ and thus the work and Word of God for and in the creature.[95]

Some five years later, in 1973, Paul VI called for the development of a new study and cult of the Holy Spirit as a necessary complement to the teaching of Vatican II on Christology and ecclesiology.[96] These calls for a more elaborate theology of the Holy Spirit were taken up by a number of Catholic theologians such as Heribert Mühlen, Walter Kasper, and Yves Congar in Europe, Kilian McDonnell and others in the US, David Coffey and Denis Edwards in Australia.

Alongside these developments in theology, there also emerged in the first decade or so after the Council what was known as the Catholic Charismatic Movement, led by Cardinal Léon Joseph Suenens and others. The Charismatic Movement sought to carry forward the vision of Vatican II at a pastoral level. It evoked a large following in the US (for example in the University of Notre Dame) and some parts of Europe. More and more emphasis, however, began to be placed on extraordinary manifestations of the Spirit in phenomena such as baptism in the Spirit, speaking in tongues, prophecy and healing, to the neglect of the reflective and sacramental mediations of the Spirit. Furthermore, the Charismatic Movement of the 1970s and early 1980s seemed to bypass the importance of human rights, the work of social justice and the alleviation of poverty. In addition, the Catholic Charismatic Movement emphasised the existence of spiritual unity between Catholics and Protestants, without, it would appear, paying sufficient attention to the challenges of institutional reform and unity between the churches. The unity envisaged by the Charismatic Movement did not seem to correspond to the goals of unity as outlined in the *Decree on Ecumenism*.[97] These apparent excesses of the Charismatic Movement had the unintended effect of making Church leaders draw back from the development of a pastoral and systematic theology of the Holy Spirit in the life of the Christian community.

Other Church documents, after Vatican II, continue to emphasise the importance of the Holy Spirit and this can be seen for instance in the writings of John Paul II, who wrote an encyclical *On the Holy Spirit in the Life of the Church and the World: Dominum et Vivificantem* in 1986. Here, John Paul talks about the Spirit as that which influences the course of history, peoples, cultures and religions.[98] In this same encyclical, he also talks about the Spirit of God as active in the world before Christianity:

> We cannot limit ourselves to the two thousand years since the birth of Christ. We need to go further back, to embrace the whole action of the Spirit before Christ.[99]

This same idea is repeated again by John Paul II in a further encyclical *On the Permanent Validity of the Church's Missionary Mandate: Redemptoris Missio* in 1990. In that encyclical, John Paul II has an eye on the wider ecumenism of dialogue with other religions and the place of the Holy Spirit within that dialogue.[100]

Of course, this wider ecumenism has implications for ecumenism among the churches. What is now beginning to emerge is that the Spirit who is active within the Christian churches is the same Spirit who is active in varying degrees in the evolution of creation, the history of humanity, and other religions.

In looking back at Vatican II, some like Walter Kasper talk about 'a new departure' in relation to the Spirit and the Church at the Council.[101] Others talk about 'a breakthrough' and a 'new Pneumatological awareness' at the Council.[102] Other voices, however, are more cautious. Congar, for example, says the Council marked the beginning of a move from Christo-monism to Pneumatology but only a beginning that must continue.[103] Kilian McDonnell describes the relationship between the Church and the Spirit which developed at the Council as 'less than ideal' because the Spirit arrives 'too late', coming after Christology.[104] It is against this background of Vatican II and subsequent developments concerning the importance of the action of the Spirit within the Christian churches and communities that we can now move towards the reconstruction of a pneumatological ecclesiology that could engage in serious dialogue with other churches and in particular with other religions.

c. Recovering a Spirit-Centred Ecclesiology

The first step in moving towards a Pneumatological ecclesiology must be the adoption of a Spirit-Christology along the lines already outlined. If we can agree and accept the desirability and rightness of a Spirit Christology at this time, then we can move towards a Spirit ecclesiology. The bridge between a Spirit Christology and a Spirit ecclesiology is the event of Pentecost. The pentecostal experience was about an encounter with the Spirit of the risen Christ that had a unifying and transformative effect on disciples who were dispersed, dejected and despondent by the scandal of the cross. This particular encounter incorporated the disciples and apostles into a new, messianic, Spirit-filled community with an eschatological consciousness. What happened to Jesus at the Jordan in terms of being anointed by the Spirit happened again to the disciples at Pentecost in terms of being anointed by the Spirit of Christ. Both Jesus and the disciples were anointed by the Spirit and sent by the Spirit in the service of the reign of God. According to James D. G. Dunn, 'a big bang' that jump-started the early Church was Pentecost and, as such, there is strong evidence that the first generation of Christianity 'understood itself as quintessentially a movement of the Spirit of God'.[105] It is, therefore, the action of the Spirit that co-creates, with Christ, the Church, and it is the recovery of that order and emphasis, namely the Spirit 'co-instituting' with Christ the Church, that is important for the reconstruction of a Spirit ecclesiology. In other words, it is the action of God as Spirit as well as the action of God as Word who creates the Church and therefore points us towards a Spirit-inspired and Word-driven ecclesiology in dialogue with other religions.

Once we see that the Church was 'co-instituted' by Christ *and* the Spirit, then we can begin to talk about the Church as the sacrament of Christ and the Spirit. The Church is, and ought to be, a place where the people of God encounter the Spirit of the living Christ. The dialogue between the Church and other religions may well help the Church to recover a sense of itself as the sacrament of the Spirit. This means, in effect, that the Church is truly itself when it is driven by the Spirit of Christ in a manner analogous to the way Jesus was driven by the Spirit of God throughout his mission and ministry in the service of the Reign of God. As already seen, there was a shift towards a Spirit ecclesiology at Vatican II, especially in the *Decree on Ecumenism*. That shift needs to be completed today by a clearer recognition:

- That it is the Spirit, the Spirit of Christ, who inhabits the new, messianic community of disciples;
- That it is the Spirit of Christ who is the source of unity among that community of disciples and apostles;
- That it is the Spirit of Christ who is the bond of unity within the whole Christian community;
- That it is the Spirit of Christ who is the agent of communion within the Church and among the churches;
- That it is the Spirit of Christ who is the point of contact between the Church and other religions.

d. Ecclesiology in the Service of Pneumatology

All of the elements that go to make up the Church, such as institution and charism, order and ministry, word and sacrament, exist in serving the Spirit of Christ and manifesting the ongoing presence of the Spirit in the world. This means, in effect, realising that the institutional Church does not control the Spirit, but rather the Spirit, the fruits and gifts of the Spirit, create and shape the Church of Christ. In pre-Vatican II ecclesiologies, the impression was given that the Spirit was controlled by the institutional Church, thereby giving us a Church-centred theology and an ecclesio-centric Pneumatology. In contrast, in the light of the gift of the Spirit poured out on the whole of humanity at the dawn of time, and in the light of the Spirit Christologies of Paul, the Synoptics, the Acts of the Apostles, and John, and in the light of the teaching of Vatican II on the Church and the Spirit, we can now move explicitly towards a Spirit ecclesiology or what Congar calls a 'Pneumatological ecclesiology'. Walter Kasper observed, as far back as 1972, that ecclesiology must be worked out within the framework of Pneumatology: 'Ecclesiology is a function of Pneumatology' and not the other way around.[106]

For too long, the impression was given that Pneumatology was a function of ecclesiology; that particular impression must now be reversed in the light of the New Testament and Vatican II. All ecclesial life is 'life in the Spirit' and this new 'life in the Spirit' offered by Christ transforms individuals and institutions into a new messianic eschatological communion 'in Christ'. For Congar, 'the life and activity of the Church can be seen totally as an *epiclesis*.'[107] In other words, take away the agency of the Spirit, and the Church collapses. Without the Spirit, the Church is just another organisation; without the Spirit, the teaching of the Church becomes an ideology; without the Spirit, the liturgy is reduced to an empty ritual; without the Spirit, ministry becomes a form of social activity. It is perhaps Irenaeus who best captures this underlying awareness of the centrality of the Pneumatology to revelation and the life of the Church when he asserts:

> Thus, without the Spirit it is not [possible] to see the Word of God, and without the Son one is not able to approach the Father; for the knowledge of the Father [is] the Son, and knowledge of the Son of God is through the Holy Spirit.[108]

It is this relationship of inseparability between Pneumatology and ecclesiology as well as the order of this relationship that was at stake at the time of the Reformation and continues to be an issue in the relationship between Catholics and Protestants today in the ecumenical movement. The reformed churches, by and large, defined themselves by the presence and action of the Spirit, whereas the counter-Reformation Church saw the presence of the Spirit as conditioned by the institutional Church. What is now necessary in the ecumenical movement is a new synthesis that transforms these two opposing points of view. The only way of resolving this tension is in and through a critical dialogue between Pneumatology and Christology. Congar, who wrote so much about the Spirit, was fond of reminding his readers that the source and soundness of Pneumatology consists in its relationship to Christology.[109] In the end, it is the person of Christ crucified and risen, namely Christology, that must shape not only Pneumatology, but also ecclesiology and this is best brought about today through the adoption of a Spirit Christology.[110] In brief, we are proposing to put Pneumatology at the centre of theology, and move from there to a Spirit Christology, and from a Spirit Christology via Pentecost to the construction of a full-fledged Spirit ecclesiology. This will require a number of reversals in theology to bring about a new Spirit ecclesiology: namely, a reversal from theology to Pneumatology, from an emphasis on the Son and the Spirit to the Spirit and the Son, and from a focus on the Church and the Spirit to the Spirit and the Church in the service of ecumenism and inter-faith dialogue. If these reversals succeed, then they will issue in a renewed ecclesiology which is not only Pneumatological and Christocentric but ultimately Trinitarian in structure, worship and witness. The logic of a focus on Pneumatology and Christology is the revelation of God as Triune as found in the story of salvation in the New Testament, defined at the Council of Nicaea in 325, expanded at the Council of Constantinople in 381, and synthesised at the second Council of Constantinople in 553.[111]

5. DISCERNING THE SPIRIT IN THE CHURCHES, IN RELIGIONS AND IN THE WORLD

The major challenge facing any theology of the Spirit and in particular a Pneumatological ecclesiology is that of discerning the ongoing action of the Spirit in the churches, in the living religions and in the world. Of course there is no definitive way of doing this, and any answer to this question must involve the discerning responses of faith, hope and love working together. The advice of the early Church is instructive. The first Christians were challenged to: 'test the Spirits to see if they are from God.'[112] On the other hand, the same Christians were warned: 'Do not stifle the Spirit.'[113] The Catholic Church, in dialogue with other churches, with other religions and the world, must follow with equal seriousness this two-fold advice: 'Test the Spirits' and 'Do not stifle the Spirit'. To respond to this challenge, I want to propose three different criteria for discerning the action of the Spirit of Christ in the Church, in religions and in the world. These criteria are the historical narrative of the Spirit in the Bible, specific theological criteria, and the importance of attending to the gifts and fruits of the Spirit.

a. Historical Narratives of the Spirit in Judaism and Christianity

The historical narratives of the Spirit in the Bible are key criteria for the Judaeo-Christian tradition. We have seen an outline of that narrative in the Hebrew scriptures: the Spirit in the presence of the historical prophets and the leaders of Israel, in the corporate life of Israel, especially in its adherence to the Torah, and in the biblical accounts of creation in the book of Genesis. That historical narrative is intensified in the life of Jesus and the particular interaction between the Spirit and Jesus: conception, birth, baptism in the Jordan, transfiguration, and the journey up to Jerusalem. In looking at the life of Jesus, anointed and driven by the Spirit, it is possible to say that the centre of that particular narrative is the Cross. Indeed the pattern of the action of the Spirit in the life of Jesus seems to be one of a Paschal movement towards Calvary, terminating in the personal act of the self-surrender of the Spirit of Jesus into the hands of God. A distinctive characteristic of the action of the Spirit in the life, death and destiny of Jesus is the Paschal demand of de-centring the self and re-centring on God, of self-emptying and rebirth, of losing one's life to save one's life. The Paschal movement of self-emptying (*kenosis*) is a sign of the Spirit of Christ animating the Christian community in the service of the reign of God.

If there is to be progress in the ecumenical movement, and in inter-religious dialogue, then it will entail a moment of self-emptying by the Spirit-filled messianic community of Christians in order to discern the action of the Spirit outside itself. It is essential to keep the Cross and Pneumatology together in order to avoid on the one hand ecclesial triumphalism and, on the other hand, to critique certain expressions of the Pentecostal movement that have become removed from the realities of historical experience. To quote Rowan Williams: 'It is the Spirit which takes us out of infantile transcendentalism, uncriticised theism, into the faith of Jesus crucified.'[114]

It is significant in this regard that when Vatican II speaks about the activity of the Spirit outside the Church, it talks about the Spirit offering the possibility of being associated with the Paschal Mystery in a manner known only to God.[115] Whether inside or outside the Christian community, the action of the Spirit entails a Paschal moment, a letting-go of ego-centredness to other-centredness, a self-emptying into the otherness of God in creation, history and religions. This means that the gift of the presence of the Spirit becomes available through a double movement: a movement outwards towards the other as a symbol of the Spirit and/or a movement inwards towards the Spirit as already given. One way or the other, an experience of the Spirit effects a paschal movement towards the crucified Christ. Thus, the action of the Spirit is not something that takes place in parallel to or outside the action of Christ; instead there is only one economy of salvation which is realised in the unified actions of the Spirit and Christ.[116]

An equally important part of the historical narrative of the New Testament must be an understanding of the way the Spirit of Christ was poured out at Pentecost and how that experience of Pentecost effected the creation of a new Spirit-filled Messianic community of disciples in the early decades of Christianity which has continued down to the twenty-first century. At least two accounts of Pentecost exist in the New Testament: one in the Acts of the Apostles[117] and the other in the Gospel of John, sometimes called the 'Johannine

Pentecost'.[118] Pentecost marked the inauguration of a new era of the Spirit, the co-institution of the Church as the messianic community of the Spirit, and the introduction of a world-wide mission. Pentecost is also a symbol reminding us that unity-within-diversity existed at the very beginnings of Christianity and is a clear indication that differences can be enriching rather than conflictual.

b. Theological Criteria

The second set of criteria for discerning the Spirit of God in the churches, the religions and the world are explicitly theological: Christological, doxological and ecclesiological. A primary sign of the Spirit active in the Church and the world is the way in which the Spirit enables people to confess that 'Jesus is Lord'[119] and that 'Jesus Christ has come in the flesh',[120] thereby highlighting the inseparable link that exists between Pneumatology and Christology. The action of the Spirit, poured out on all in the world, bears an inner orientation and relationship to Christ.[121] An important criterion, therefore, for discerning the action of the Spirit in the world and the churches and religions is whether it directs people towards the person of Christ and enables them to remember and celebrate imaginatively and prophetically the reality of the crucified and risen Christ in the world today.

A second theological criterion for discerning the action of the Spirit in the churches and among the religions is whether the Spirit in question promotes the worship of the one true God, since it is through the Spirit that we are enabled to cry out: 'Father, *Abba*'.[122]

A third theological criterion, an ecclesiological criterion, for discerning the action of the Spirit is whether the Spirit in question is given in the service of others and contributes to the building up of the body of Christ. In the early church, the gifts of the Spirit were distributed in the service of others and the building up of Christian congregations.[123]

c. Attending to the Gifts and Fruits of the Holy Spirit

The third set of criteria for discerning the action of the Spirit in the world, the religions and the Church are about the sighting and celebration of the gifts and fruits of the Spirit. In the first letter to the Corinthians, we are informed that there are a variety of gifts given by the Spirit 'who inspires them in everyone' for the purpose of serving 'the common good'.[124] These gifts include wisdom, knowledge, faith, healing, miracles, prophecy, discernment and the interpretation of tongues. Wherever and whenever these gifts are present, acting in the service of 'the common good', there we have expressions of the presence and action of the Spirit.

In a similar way, attention should be given to the fruits of the Spirit outlined in the letter to the Galatians: love, joy, peace, patience, kindness, goodness, faithfulness, generosity, and self-control.[125] These fruits of the Spirit can be found as much outside the Christian Church in the world and other religions as inside the Church. This point is a clear indication that the work of the Spirit extends beyond the boundaries of the Christian community. If this is the case, and surely there is evidence to this effect, then there is an invitation to Christians to enter into dialogue and collaboration, as put forward by Vatican II in *Nostra Aetate*, with all those in the world and other religions who manifest and enjoy these fruits of the Spirit.

An additional Christological criterion for discerning the Spirit in the churches and among the religions must also come from the doctrine of the Incarnation of the Word made flesh in Jesus of Nazareth. For Christians, the gift of the Spirit is embodied and mediated in the flesh of Jesus. The Spirit, active and revealed in Christ, is a Spirit-mediated-in-matter through creation, enfleshed in Jesus of Nazareth, and sacramentally embodied in the Christian community. The discernment of the Spirit in the world is about discerning the power of the Spirit in the wonders of creation and through the medium of human beings in the light of the Word made flesh. This emphasis is in sharp contrast to those who would suggest that the Spirit of God somehow 'intervenes' in the affairs of the Church, over and above the mediation of the Spirit in matter and flesh. In brief, it has to be acknowledged that in the ordinary course of events nothing happens between heaven and earth, between the human and the divine, between the Holy Spirit and the human spirit without the mediation of human beings and their responsive cooperation in faith with this divine presence.

NOTES

1. This section is indebted to the entry on the 'Holy Spirit' by F. W. Horn in *The Anchor Bible Dictionary,* David N. Freedman et al. (eds), Vol. 3, New York: Doubleday, 1992, 260–80

2. For example, Num 24:2, 11:25 and 29

3. Hos 9:7

4. Mic 3:8

5. Ez 3:12, 8:3, 11:1

6. Is 11:1-2

7. Is 42:1

8. Is 61:1-2

9. Is 44:3, 32:15

10. Ez 37:5-14

11. Ez 37:26

12. Ez 37:27, 39:25-29

13. Ez 36:27

14. *Anchor Bible Dictionary,* 264

15. Ibid.

16. Ibid.

17. D. Lyle Dabney, 'The Nature of the Spirit: Creation as Premonition of God', *The Work of the Spirit: Pneumatology and Pentecostalism,* Michael Welker (ed.), Michigan: W. B. Eerdmans 2006, 71–86 at 74

18. Gen 2:1

19. Gen 1:30

20. Gen 1:2

21. Gen 2:7

22. Ez 37:5; see also Ez 37:9 and 14

23. Ez 37:9 and 14

24. Jay McDaniel, 'Where is the Holy Spirit Anyway? Response to a Sceptic Environmentalist', *Ecumenical Review,* 22, 1990, 162–74

25. Lk 1:35; Mt 1:18

26. *Anchor Bible Dictionary,* 265

27. Ibid., 266

28. F. W. Horn describes three levels of gift of the Spirit. I have developed his treatment of the gifts of the Spirit into four levels

29. *Anchor Bible Dictionary*, 267

30. Acts 2:38

31. Acts 19:11

32. Jn 5:14; Acts 5:16

33. Jn 20:19-23

34. Jn 20:22

35. Gen 2:7

36. Jn 20:22; 1 Cor 6:11; Tt 3:4-11

37. Acts 2:4

38. Acts 5:32, 38:18; Rom 5:5; 2 Cor 1:22, 1 Thess 4:8; 1 Jn 3:24, 4:13

39. Jn 20:22; Acts 2:33, 38, 8:15, 17, 19, 10:47; 19:2; Rom 8:15; Gal 3:2, 14

40. 1 Cor 3:16, 6:19; Rom 8:9, 11

41. Yves Congar, *The Word and the Spirit*, London: Chapman, 1984

42. Ibid., 1

43. Hans Urs von Balthasar, *Creator Spirit*, Vol. 3 of *Explorations in Theology*, San Francisco: Ignatius Press, 1993, 27

44. Kilian McDonnell, *The Other Hand of God: The Holy Spirit as the Universal Touch and Goal*, Collegeville, MN: Liturgical Press, 2003, Chapter 12

45. Walter Kasper, 'The Renewal of Pneumatology in Contemporary Catholic Life and Theology: Towards a Rapprochement between East and West', *The Holy Spirit, the Church and Christian Unity: Proceedings of the Consultation held at the Monastery of Bose*, Italy (14–20 October 2002), Doris Donnelly, Adelbert Deneux and Joseph Famerée (eds), Louvain: Louvain University Press, 2005, 9–33

46. Frederick Crowe, 'Son and Spirit: Tensions in the Divine Missions?', *Frederick Crowe, Appropriating the Lonergan Idea*, Michael Vertin (ed.), Washington, DC: The Catholic University of America Press, 1989, 297–314 at 298. See also Frederick Crowe, 'Son of God, Holy Spirit and World Religions', 339, n. 26

47. Crowe, 'Son and Spirit: Tensions in the Divine Missions?', op. cit., 304

48. Crowe, 'A Three-fold Kenosis of the Son of God', op. cit., 323

49. Crowe, 'Son and Spirit: Tensions in the Divine Missions?', op. cit., 304

50. Ibid.

51. Eugene Rogers, *After the Spirit: A Constructive Pneumatology from Resources outside the Modern West*, Michigan: W. B. Eerdmans, 2005, 19–32

52. Athanasius, *Letter to Serapion*, 3.5

53. Basil, *On the Holy Spirit*, 16.37

54. Ambrose, *On the Holy Spirit*, 2.5.41. A more detailed account of the Spirit in the patristic period can found in Denis Edwards, *Breath of Life: A Theology of the Creator Spirit*, New York: Orbis Books, 2004, 39–43 and in the Proceedings of the Seventh International Patristic Conference in Maynooth, 2008, published as *The Holy Spirit in the Fathers of the Church*, D. Vincent Twomey and Janet E. Rutherford (eds), Dublin: Four Courts Press, 2010

55. 1 Cor 12:3; 1 Jn 4:1-3

56. See David Coffey, 'Spirit Christology and the Trinity', *Advents of the Spirit: An Introduction to the Current Study of Pneumatology*, B. Hinze and D. Lyle Dabney (eds), Marquette: Marquette University Press, 2001, 315–38 at 315–19

57. Coffey, 'A Promising Development in Christology', 21

58. David Coffey, art. cit., 29

59. David Coffey, art. cit., 29. This overriding concern within Coffey's very substantial corpus of writing on the Trinity and Pneumatology is, however, not without its own internal tensions. These tensions are caused by the way Coffey seems to give priority to the immanent Trinity in his reading of the unfolding of the economic Trinity in the history of salvation. There is also some tension in the way he holds that a Spirit-Christology can provide new data for understanding the Trinity and yet this new data does not seem to deepen or alter or add in any way to his understanding of the Trinity, which remains substantially the same as it was before the application of a Spirit Christology. The nearest Coffey gets to a new understanding of the Trinity can be found in his remark about the order (taxonomy) of the Trinity in which he favours Father, Spirit and Son, which we have seen in Chapter 5 does not go far enough. A further point of tension can be found in his reluctance to recognise the possibility or legitimacy of what he calls 'the pre-Nicene Spirit Christologies'. These are complex questions that are beyond the scope of this work. These issues and many others in the work of David Coffey have been addressed in an original way by Declan O'Byrne, *Spirit Christology and Trinity in the Theology of David Coffey*, Bern: Peter Lang, 2010

60. Mk 1:12

61. Mt 1:18

62. Mt 1:20

63. Mt 3:11

64. Mt 4:1

65. Mt 12:28

66. Mt 12:32

67. Mt 28:19

68. Lk 1:41, 67

69. Lk 2:25

70. Lk 2:27

71. Lk 2:26

72. Lk 1:35

73. Lk 3:16

74. Lk 4:16

75. Lk 11:13

76. Lk 10:10-12

77. Lk 24:49

78. See Joseph Fitzmyer, 'The Gospel according to Luke, i–ix', *The Anchor Bible Dictionary*, 228

79. Jn 1:33

80. Jn 3:5-8

81. Jn 14:15-17, 26, 15:26-27, 16:7-11, 12-14

82. Jn 15:26

83. See Karl Rahner, 'Aspects of European Theology', *TI*, Vol. XXI. Rahner had already intimated this move in a series of interviews in which he pointed out that the 'divinisation of the world through the Spirit of God is humanly and speculatively the more fundamental basic conception for Christianity, out of which the Incarnation and soteriology arise as an inner moment.' See *Karl Rahner in Dialogue, Conversations and Interviews, 1965–1982*, Paul Imhof and Hubert Biallowons (eds), New York: Crossroad, 1986, 126

84. Bernard Lonergan, 'The Response of the Jesuit as Priest and Apostle in the Modern World', *A Second Collection*, William F. J. Ryan and Bernard J. Tyrrell (eds), Toronto: University of Toronto Press, 1996, 165–87 at 174; Michael Barnes, 'Theology of Religions', *The Blackwell Companion to Christian Spirituality*, Arthur Holder (ed.), Oxford: Blackwell Publishing, 2005, 401–16 at 409, *RM*, a.28

85. A Spirit Christology opens the way for balancing the 'Christ-history of the Spirit' with a 'Spirit-history of Christ'. In this way a taxonomy of the economic Trinity as Spirit, Son and Father could be presented in a manner that complements the classical taxonomy of Father, Son and Spirit, not as an alternative but as a way of capturing the simultaneity and reciprocity that are intrinsic to the Trinitarian life of the one God. In this way the procession model of the Trinity would be enriched by a return model (as proposed by David Coffey and others). This move would of course have to be guided by the foundational axiom that the economic Trinity is the revelation of the immanent Trinity. These are issues that cannot be

addressed in this chapter (or indeed in this book), the primary purpose of which is to recover the primacy of Pneumatology and not that of the working out a theology of the Trinity

86. *UR*, a.2

87. Ibid., a.3. See also *LG*, a.8

88. Ibid., a.4

89. *GS*, a.26

90. Ibid., a.38 and a.41

91. Ibid., a.44

92. *AG*, a.4

93. Ibid., a.4, n.5

94. *GS*, a.22

95. Karl Barth and Hans Urs von Balthasar, *Einheit und Erneuerung der Kirche*, Fribourg: Paulus-Verlag, 1968, 12

96. General Audience, 6 June 1973, *Documentation Catholique*, 1 July 1973, 601

97. For an overview of the Catholic Charismatic Movement, see Yves Congar, *I Believe in the Holy Spirit*, Vol. 2, London: Chapman, 1983, 161–88

98. *DeV* a.28

99. Ibid., a.53

100. See *RM*, a.28 and a.29

101. See Walter Kasper, 'The Renewal of Pneumatology in Contemporary Catholic Life and Theology: Towards a Rapprochement between East and West', *The Holy Spirit, the Church and Christian Unity,* 13

102. John R. Sachs, 'Do Not Stifle the Spirit': Karl Rahner, the Legacy of Vatican II, and its Urgency for Theology Today', *Proceedings of the Catholic Theological Society of America*, Vol. 51, J. A. Dwyer (ed.), New York: St John's University, 1996, 17

103. Yves Congar, *Le Concile de Vatican II: Son Église, Peuple de Dieu et Corps du Christ*, *Théologie Historique*, 71, Paris: Beauchesne, 1984, 169

104. Kilian McDonnell, 'Pneumatological Overview', *Proceedings of the Catholic Theological Society of America*, 1996, 189

105. James D. G. Dunn, *Christianity in the Making*, Vol. 2: *Beginning from Jerusalem*, Michigan: W. B. Eerdmans, 2009, 168 and 171 respectively

106. Walter Kasper, *An Introduction to Christian Faith*, London: Burns and Oates, 1980, 138–9 (original German edition 1972)

107. Yves Congar, *I Believe in the Holy Spirit*, Vol. 3, 271

108. Irenaeus of Lyons, *On the Apostolic Preaching*, translation and introduction by John Behr, New York: St Vladimir's Seminary Press, 1997, 46, section 7

109. Yves Congar, *I Believe in the Holy Spirit*, Vol. 2, 152 and 210
110. On the relationship between Christology and Ecumenism, see Dermot A. Lane, 'Ecumenism, Vatican II and Christology', *The Critical Spirit: Theology at the Crossroads of Faith and Culture*, Andrew Pierce and Geraldine Smyth (eds), Dublin: Columba Press, 2003, 135–58
111. An instructive account of this development is given by Anthony J. Godzieba in 'The Trinitarian Mystery of God: A 'Theological Theology', *Systematic Theology: Roman Catholic Perspectives*, second edition, Francis S. Fiorenza and John P. Galvin (eds), Minneapolis: Fortress Press, 2011, 131–99
112. 1 Jn 4:1
113. 1 Thess 5:19
114. Rowan Williams, 'Word and Spirit', *On Christian Theology*, Oxford: Blackwell Publishing, 2000, 125
115. *GS*, a.22
116. See *DI*, a.12
117. Acts 2:1-13
118. Jn 20:22
119. 1 Cor 12:3
120. 1 Jn 4:2
121. Karl Rahner, 'Jesus Christ in the Non-Christian Religions', *TI*, Vol. XVII, 39–50
122. Gal 4:6; Rom 8:15-16
123. 1 Cor 12:7-11; Eph 4:4-13
124. 1 Cor 12:7
125. Gal 5:22

VIII. THE JEWISH-CHRISTIAN DIALOGUE: A SIGN OF HOPE FOR THE FUTURE OF INTER-RELIGIOUS DIALOGUE

Nostra Aetate was a 'milestone'[1] and a sea change in Jewish-Catholic relations. This hard-won development at Vatican II has become even more significant in the light of the positive reception of *Nostra Aetate* since 1965. The key players in effecting this breakthrough at the Council were John XXIII, Cardinal Augustin Bea, and the Jewish French historian, Jules Isaac. The reception of *Nostra Aetate* has been promoted consistently by Popes Paul VI, John Paul II and Benedict XVI. The purpose of this chapter is to review the progress that has been made in Jewish-Catholic relations since the Council. The review will include reference to the achievements and setbacks as well as an outline of unresolved questions. It is intended that this report on Jewish-Catholic relations will stand out as a sign of hope for the future of inter-religious dialogue.

1. A BREAKTHROUGH AT VATICAN II

Any account of achievements would have to begin with the teaching of *Nostra Aetate*. In this regard it should be remembered that it took at least six different drafts to arrive at *Nostra Aetate*. We have seen some of the background to *Nostra Aetate* and debates surrounding its composition in Chapter Two. John XXIII wished to change the outlook of the Church in its relationship with Jews, especially the charge of deicide and the importance of God's covenant with Israel. Although we have already summarised *Nostra Aetate* in Chapter Two, it may be helpful to repeat some of that material here.

a. A Summary of *Nostra Aetate*, Article 4

In Article 4, the longest, the document addresses the relationship between the Church and Judaism. *The Declaration* notes:

- the 'spiritual ties which link the people of the New Covenant to the stock of Abraham';
- 'that in God's plan of salvation, the beginning of its [Christian] faith and election are to be found in the patriarchs, Moses and the Prophets';
- that 'the pillars on which the Church stands, namely the Apostles, are Jewish, as were many of the early disciples';
- that the Jews remain very dear to God since 'God does not take back the gifts He bestowed or the choice He made';
- that mutual understanding and appreciation, through biblical and theological enquiry, should be encouraged;
- that 'neither all Jews indiscriminately ... nor Jews today, can be charged with crimes committed during "the Passion of Christ"';
- that 'the Jews should not be spoken of as rejected or accursed as if this follows from Holy Scripture';
- that the Church 'deplores all hatred, persecution, displays of anti-Semitism levelled ... against the Jews'.

b. Documents Supporting *Nostra Aetate*

This singular teaching of Vatican II has been promoted by a variety of documents emanating from the Catholic Church since the Council. These include:

- 1974, *Guidelines and Suggestions for implementing the Conciliar Declaration Nostra Aetate*, no. 4, Pontifical Commission for Religious Relations with the Jews (hereafter referred to as PCRRJ)
- 1985, *Notes on the correct way to present Jews and Judaism in Preaching and Catechetics*, PCRRJ

- 1998, *We Remember: A Reflection on the Shoah*, PCRRJ
- 2001, *The Jewish People and their Sacred Scriptures in the Christian Bible*, Pontifical Biblical Commission

Add to these documents the striking gestures by John Paul II such as his visit to the synagogue in Mainz in 1980, the synagogue in Rome in 1986, and the placing of a prayer for forgiveness at the Western Wall in the year 2000.

Further, this breakthrough at Vatican II has been followed by a remarkable number of ongoing biblical and theological conversations between Jews and Catholics as recommended by the Council. These conversations have resulted in joint statements on both sides such as: *Dabru Emet – Speak the Truth: A Jewish Statement on Christians and Christianity* (2002) from the Jewish side, which was followed by a response from Christian scholars entitled 'A Sacred Obligation: Rethinking Christian Faith in Relation to Judaism and the Jewish People' (2002), to mention just two random examples in the English-speaking world.

2. THE UNREVOKED COVENANT OF GOD WITH ISRAEL

The key statement in *Nostra Aetate* is that 'God does not take back the gifts he bestowed or the choices he made.'[2] It is this specific teaching that must move to centre stage in the Jewish-Christian dialogue as the point of departure. This has been developed in the post-conciliar period, especially by John Paul II. During a visit by John Paul II to the synagogue in Mainz, he stated that God's Covenant with the Jews 'has never been revoked' (1980). This statement, recognising the enduring existence and validity of the Jewish Covenant, has profound theological significance for the Jewish-Christian dialogue and Christian self-understanding. This development goes back to St Paul's Letter to the Romans, especially chapters 9 to 11.

a. Returning to Romans 9–11

In Romans 11:29, Paul states that 'the gifts and calling of God are irrevocable'. The particular gifts of God to the Jewish people are, according to Paul, 'the adoption, the glory, the covenants, the giving of the Torah, the worship and the promise' (Rom 9:4). For Paul, 'the law is holy and the commandment is holy, just, and good' (Rom 7:12) and 'It is not as though the Word of God had failed' (Rom 9:6). God's covenant with Israel remains in place and therefore theories of supercessionism, substitution and replacement, which have been in existence since the second or third century, must now be put aside.

Further, if God's covenant with the Jewish people continues in existence, then this means that God continues to offer the people of Israel the possibility of salvation. The response of the Jews in faith to this divine invitation constitutes salvation for the chosen people. The enduring existence of God's covenant with Israel therefore implies the ongoing offer of salvation to the people of Israel. Once these theological truths are accepted, and it seems safe to say that these insights are now part of the teaching of the Catholic Church, then the relationship between Christianity and Judaism shifts significantly.

The real value of returning to Romans 9-11 is that it presents us with what James D. G. Dunn calls a conflicted Paul ' wanting to remain faithful to his heritage, but also (and primarily) to the revelation which has been given to him in Christ.'[3] Paul is also concerned about the possibility of a split between Jewish-Christianity and Hellenistic-Christianity. There is in Romans 9-11 a creative tension between Saul the Pharisee and Paul the Apostle. Paul does not wish to abandon his Jewish faith and at the same time he wants to be faithful to the revelation he has received from the Risen Christ. In Romans he seeks to go beyond the contrasting categories of Jew and Gentile to recover a focus on Israel, on God's enduring call to Israel, which now has been extended to embrace Gentiles as well as Jews (Rom 9:24-26). Paul is conflicted in these complex chapters of Romans as he seeks to be an Apostle to the Gentiles on behalf of Israel and Christ. Perhaps it is this sense of a dual loyalty to Second Temple Judaism and Christ that should inform Christians in their dialogue with Judaism?

b. From an Extrinsic to an Intrinsic Relationship with Second Temple Judaism

Prior to Vatican II, the relationship between Judaism and Christianity was perceived as extrinsic and after Vatican II, the relationship has come to be seen as intrinsic; a conflictual contrast was made between the Old Testament and the New Testament, whereas now there is an important degree of continuity between the two Testaments; emphasis in the past was placed on Judaism merely as preparatory to Christianity, now the focus is on the necessity of appreciating Judaism in itself in order to understand Christianity. Once this profound theological shift is recognised, past attitudes of Christians to Jews must change, the basis of supersessionism has been removed, and the source of much anti-Judaism and anti-Semitism has been eliminated.

John McDade, the UK theologian, summarises accurately in my view the implications of *Nostra Aetate* for the relationship between Christians and Jews in the following way:

1. *Nostra Aetate* marks 'the inauguration of a new Christian tradition in which a mature Church, by now long separated from its Jewish matrix, sets itself the task of relating positively to the Jewish religion and the Jewish people.'

2. The Church accordingly must 're-centre itself in relation to the continuing vocation of Israel as a condition of understanding its Christ-given mission *Ad Gentes*.'[4]

The challenge facing Catholicism, in the light of *Nostra Aetate*, is to integrate these developments since the Council into its self-understanding of its role in the world and, at the same time, it must seek to reformulate the uniqueness and universality of the Christ event within this new context.

Does the recognition by the Church of the ongoing integrity of God's covenant with Israel relativise the centrality of the new covenant in Christ, or does it perhaps purify and deepen the

Christian understanding of God's new covenant in Christ? How can the Church overcome the deeply ingrained Christian theologies of supersessionism, substitution and replacement embedded for some eighteen hundred years within tradition? How does the Church eliminate the seeds of anti-Judaism that these theologies have sown over the centuries?

The only way of addressing these questions and a host of other questions is through a re-examination and reformulation of Christology. Is it possible for classical Christology to renew itself in the light of *Nostra Aetate* and post-conciliar developments? The core issue, or as Paul puts it, the stumbling block between Jews and Christians, is Christology. It should be noted that a renaissance has been taking place in Christology over the last fifty years through the application of the historical critical method, literary criticism and social science criticism to the Bible. The fruits of these developments will help with any reconstruction of Christology in the light of *Nostra Aetate*.

3. DOING CHRISTOLOGY IN THE LIGHT OF *NOSTRA AETATE*

Part of the challenge facing Christology is to understand biblical Judaism as essential to a balanced understanding of the Christ-event. Christology must recover its Jewish roots and matrix. According to Johann B. Metz, we must begin to do Christology, not with our backs to the Holocaust, but facing the Holocaust, and this means developing what he calls 'a post-Shoah theology'. In the words of one Jewish commentator, addressed to Christians in the context of the Holocaust: 'No statement, theological or otherwise, should be made that would not be credible in the presence of burning children.'[5]

We must begin to look at the contours of Christology within this new context. This will require an understanding of the Christ-event

- that respects the ongoing validity of God's covenant with the Jewish people;
- that avoids supersessionism;
- that is constructed not at the expense of Judaism;

- that returns Jesus to his original Jewish context;
- that understands Jesus as the Christ within a Jewish matrix, even though the word 'Christ' has many meanings in Judaism;
- that recognises that the birth certificate of Christianity bears a Jewish address.

a. The Jewishness of Jesus

Within this new context and these new demands, the obvious starting point for Christology is the Jewishness of Jesus. Many Christologists today adopt a 'low-ascending' Christology, that is, a Christology that begins with the historical figure of Jesus and moves from there historically to a theological affirmation of Jesus as the Christ who is Lord, the Son of God, the Word made flesh – an approach that should not be confused with a 'low' Christology that fails to establish the theological identity of Jesus.[6] The overall context within which to understand the life of Jesus is Second Temple Judaism.

Accepting the Jewishness of Jesus of course begs the question: what kind of Jew was Jesus? Where does one locate Jesus within the variety of Judaisms that existed in first-century Palestine? For instance, among the Pharisees, there were at least two different schools, one being the Hillel school, which generally took a compassionate and humane approach to the Mosaic Law, and the other school of Shammai, which adopted a rather strict, legalistic interpretation of the Law. Alongside the Pharisees, there existed the Sadducees, who rejected the idea of a normative oral tradition and the doctrine of resurrection. Another group known as the Essenes rejected the temple worship in Jerusalem and believed in an imminent victory of God.

The US scripture scholar, John P. Meier, who has devoted much of his life to researching the life of Jesus, describes Jesus as a *Marginal Jew*[7] and by this he means that Jesus is marginal within mainstream Judaism, but not outside Judaism. The value of this understanding of Jesus is that it does not identify Jesus with any one of the above particular groups. Yet it is clear from the Gospels that Jesus interacted with the Pharisees without necessarily disassociating himself from the Pharisees as was once thought to be the case.

Meier singles out several distinctive characteristics about Jesus, the *Marginal Jew*. In the first instance, Jesus was seen and experienced as a prophet within the long line of prophets within Judaism and understood himself as a prophet sent to the House of Israel. In particular, Jesus the Jew appears as a particular kind of prophet, namely the eschatological prophet, that is, the prophet of the end of time announcing the reign of God and inviting the people of Israel to repentance and conversion within that particular context. As the eschatological prophet, Jesus appears as the last divinely inspired messenger, sent by God to the people of Israel.

A second feature about Jesus the Jew is that he proclaimed and performed the kingdom of God. Jesus announced the Reign of God not only as something in the future, but also as already present in his ministry. Through the performance of exorcisms, miracles, healings, the unconditional offer of forgiveness, and the initiation of a new open table-fellowship, Jesus inaugurated a new experience of the coming Reign of God. In some respects, the life of Jesus is cast in the role of Elijah or Elisha whose return within the history of Israel was expected as a herald of the final days to gather in the people of Israel. It is within this context that Jesus is concerned to assemble the twelve tribes of Israel.[8]

An additional aspect of Jesus the Jew is his moral teaching. Jesus issued ethical imperatives alongside his critique of the current interpretation of the Law (*Torah*) by the Pharisees. Much of his moral teaching is summed up in the Sermon on the Plain in Luke's gospel, and in the parable about the judgement of humanity at the end of time as found in Matthew's gospel.

Most of all for Meier, Jesus is distinctive in his knowledge and understanding of God. For example, Jesus had a strong sense of the Spirit of God as active in his life: anointed by the Spirit, empowered by the Spirit and sent by the Spirit. Further, the God of Israel is experienced by Jesus as intimate and personal in his life. This experience of Jesus is summed up in terms of a Father-Son relationship and is often described as the *Abba* experience. These distinctive features of the life of Jesus are developed by Meier at length in his four-volume work on *The Marginal Jew*. Meier sums up the life of Jesus in Volume Three in the following way: he spoke to the Jewish crowds, he gathered Jewish disciples, he selected twelve Jewish men to represent the eschatological gathering of the twelve tribes of Israel, and he appointed apostles.

This recovery of the Jewishness of Jesus, however, has not been to the fore among theologians, nor has it impacted sufficiently on Christology and ecclesiology. The Jewishness of Jesus is more than a historical accident and more than an incidental piece of sociology; instead the Jewishness of Jesus is of profound theological significance for Jewish-Christian relations.

Thus, the 1985 *Notes on the correct way to present Jews and Judaism in preaching and Catechetics* point out that 'Jesus was and always remains a Jew ' and that 'the Son of God is incarnate in a people and a human family (Gal 4:4; Rom 9:5).'

Further, John Paul II emphasises that the identity of Jesus 'is determined on the basis of his bond with the people of Israel, with the dynasty of David and his descent from Abraham'. Through immersion in the religious practices of Second Temple Judaism, Jesus 'became an authentic Son of Israel'.[9] In his book on *Jesus of Nazareth*, Volume One, Benedict XVI says that Jesus understands himself 'as the Torah', as 'the Torah in person', and as 'God's living Torah'.[10] This Torah-shaped and Torah-centred understanding of the life of Jesus prompts German theologian Hans Hermann Henrix to talk about Jesus as one who personifies and embodies Torah in his life and can therefore be referred to as 'Torah Incarnate'.[11] In this way an abiding reference to Israel is established in our understanding of Jesus and by implication in our Christologies and ecclesiologies.

This focus on the Jewishness of Jesus also prompts Henrix to highlight the Jewish specificity and concreteness of the Incarnation. We must speak not only of the Word becoming flesh but also of the Word becoming Jewish flesh in a Jewish Mother in an authentic Son of Israel. The Incarnation of the Word in the flesh of Jesus the Jew

279

irrevocably links Christianity to Judaism and all that Judaism stands for in terms of the Word of God, covenant, Torah, prophets and the Spirit of God hovering over creation and history.

In summary, this recovery of the Jewishness of Jesus establishes the impossibility of understanding Christianity without reference to biblical Judaism. It also reconnects the covenant of God in Christ with God's covenant with Israel. Additionally, it helps to locate an incarnational Christology within the religious practices, prayers and rituals of biblical and Rabbinic Judaism, especially in relation to the covenant theology of Israel and primacy of Torah for Jews.

b. The Jesus Movement as a Reform Movement within Second Temple Judaism

In this way, the preaching of Jesus attracts the attention of the Jews and draws disciples. A new movement of Jesus-centred-Jews comes into being, and this new group is best understood as a reform movement within Judaism. This new reform movement continued to exist after the death of Jesus as a part of Second Temple Judaism. Historians and scripture scholars are generally agreed that there is little evidence to suggest that Judaism and Christianity existed as separate entities in the first half of first-century Palestine.[12] The followers of Jesus during his life and after his death and resurrection did not see themselves initially as making up a religion separate from Second Temple Judaism.

Largely it was only after the destruction of the temple in Jerusalem in 70 AD and the establishment of post-biblical, Rabbinic Judaism that separation occurred between Jews and the followers of Jesus, and even then it is generally agreed that this separation was gradual over a period of centuries. The followers of Jesus saw themselves as a reform group within Judaism: dedicated to the Torah and continuing to worship in the temple with their fellow Jews while at the same time being devoted to the Apostle's teaching and 'the breaking of the bread' in the memory of Jesus.

c. A Gradual Parting of the Ways

While some form of separation and differentiation under the impact of the eschatological gift of the Spirit took place in the early decades, it is generally agreed that the destruction of the Temple of Jerusalem in 70 AD initiated a more marked but gradual parting of the ways, which, according to some, did not finally take place until possibly as late as the fourth century. After the destruction of the temple, Rabbinic Judaism began to disconnect itself from Jewish Christians. Some of the early followers of Jesus were excluded from the synagogues (Jn 9:22, 12:42), others were persecuted (Mt 10:17; Lk 21:12), and in a few cases some were killed (Jn 16:2).

In addition to the destruction of the temple in Jerusalem in 70 AD, other factors, theological factors, were at play among the followers of Jesus bringing about a parting of the ways. These include the extraordinary relationship between Jesus and God throughout his life and confirmed after his death through the resurrection and Pentecostal experiences, the deepening and developing understanding among the disciples of the full identity of Jesus, and the worship of Jesus and God the Father very early on after his death and resurrection.[13]

This God-centred character of the life of Jesus left a deep impression upon his disciples. There was an intimacy between Jesus and the God of Israel that manifested itself in various ways. Jesus was anointed by the Spirit of God at the Jordan and driven by the Spirit of God throughout his life. The religious experience of Jesus enabled him to talk about God as Father. There is evidence of a unique communion between Jesus and God throughout his life: in the desert, in prayer, in the Garden of Gethsemane, and on the cross.

This sense of the unity between Jesus and the God of Israel throughout his life informed and shaped the disciples' understanding of the identity of Jesus. There is, as with any identity, an historical unfolding of the full identity of Jesus. This unfolding moves from Jesus as a prophet, via the other Jewish categories such as son of David, a teacher of Wisdom, suffering servant and son of man, to a confession of Jesus as the Christ who is Lord, the Son of God, to the dramatic statement of Jesus as the Word made flesh in John's Gospel.

The New Testament evidence on the identity of Jesus suggests that this was a gradual, historical evolution within the understanding of the disciples of Jesus. There is first of all the Spirit Christologies, as seen in the last chapter, followed by the *Logos* Christology of John's Gospel. Most agree that the *Logos* Christology of John's Gospel is the climax of this unfolding of the full identity of Jesus and this particular Christology would have been a factor in the partings of the ways.

A further factor effecting a break from biblical Judaism was liturgical: namely the early worship of Jesus in the breaking of the bread after his death and resurrection. This worship of Jesus was also an important influence on the early Jewish-Christians' understanding of the identity of Jesus. Here we have an early example of the influence of prayer, in this instance prayer to Jesus, shaping what is believed about Jesus: *lex orandi, lex credendi*. Guiding this new self-conscious understanding by the disciples of Jesus was the action of the Spirit of God. Just as Jesus had been anointed in the Jordan by the Spirit of God, so the disciples were anointed by the Spirit of Christ at Pentecost; it was this same Spirit, who had been active in Judaism and was now personally embodied in Jesus, that enables the first disciples to recognise the messiahship, the divinity of Jesus and the personal presence of God in Jesus as the Word made flesh.

Other factors influencing the later parting of the ways from Second Temple Judaism into Rabbinic Judaism and Jewish-Hellenistic Christianity include the second Jewish revolt against Rome, the reaction by some Jews against the first 'Jewish Christians', the critique by some Christians (e.g. Stephen in Acts 6:14) of the Temple, the increasing need by the leaders on both sides to effect a clearer sense of self-definition, the teaching of the Council of Nicaea in 325 on the divinity of Jesus, the clash between Jewish Monotheism and Christian Trinitarian theology, and ultimately the Constantine settlement with Christians.[14]

Clearly, there are discernible layers of continuity between Second Temple Judaism and the first disciples of Jesus during his life and for some decades after his death and resurrection. Second Temple Judaism branched out into Rabbinic Judaism and Jewish (and eventually Hellenistic) Christianity. Equally, there are dimensions of discontinuity between Judaism and the first Christian Jews in the last quarter of the first century. This discontinuity came into sharp focus after the destruction of the temple in 70 AD and resulted from initiatives from within Judaism *vis à vis* the first Christians, and initiatives from within the Christian community *vis à vis* Rabbinic Judaism.

It is important to emphasise that this discontinuity should not be allowed to become a separation. This discontinuity only makes sense within the fundamental and irremovable continuity between biblical Judaism and Christianity. This is the import of the teaching of *Nostra Aetate* at Vatican II and the post-conciliar reception and development of that teaching. Early Jewish Christianity in its distinctiveness and in its discontinuity remained rooted in biblical Judaism and depended on that intrinsic connectedness to Judaism for its initial self-understanding.

Looking back at this thumbnail description of the life of Jesus and the emergence of distinctive early Jewish Christian communities, we are still faced with the question of how to understand the life of Jesus within the context of the new post-Vatican II Jewish-Christian dialogue. One area receiving attention from a variety of commentators is to depict the life of Jesus from beginning to end as a Torah-observant Jew,[15] which we have just seen as a key dimension of the Jewishness of Jesus. The life of the Jewish Jesus is driven by the demands of the Torah. He observes the feasts of Judaism, he proclaims the prophetic Word of God in the synagogues, he makes the annual pilgrimage to Jerusalem to celebrate the Passover, he visits the temple in Jerusalem. It is his fidelity to Torah and his unique interpretation of the Torah in the light of his call from God, and his prophetic proclamation of the reign of God, that led to his death on the cross. This fidelity to Torah by the Jewish Jesus implies that the disciples of Jesus also have a relationship to the Torah. It is when the Church forgets about the Torah as expressed and lived in the life of Jesus that Judaism and Christianity become separated to the detriment of each other. At the same time the early Christians saw in Jesus the completion and 'fulfilment' of the action of the Spirit and the Word of God in biblical history.

It is important to remember that nearly all of the first Christians were Jews and that the first layer of Christianity was made up largely of Jewish Christians. Quite early on, after much controversy, the Jewish Christians ventured out beyond the boundaries of biblical and post-biblical Judaism into the Hellenistic world. It is within this context of an emerging Hellenistic Christianity that a further break from Rabbinic Judaism took place.

By relocating Christology within the Jewishness of Jesus, by highlighting that the Jesus movement and the early Church as reform movements originating from Second Temple Judaism, and in remembering that the first generation of Christians were mostly Jews, we come to see that important grounds, historical and theological, exist for the re-centring of Christianity within biblical Judaism and for re-connecting the Church with Israel: the unrevoked covenant with Israel, the primacy of Torah, God's enduring election of Israel, and a shared hope in God's future.

With this re-location of Christianity within Judaism, an important question arises: how do Christians express the uniqueness and universality of the Christ-event alongside a recognition of the ongoing integrity of God's covenant with Israel? It is at this level of spelling out the particularity and universality of the Christ-event that a number of unresolved questions persist within the Jewish-Christian dialogue today which must at least be acknowledged.

4. UNRESOLVED THEOLOGICAL QUESTIONS IN THE JEWISH-CHRISTIAN DIALOGUE

The first unresolved issue within the Jewish-Christian dialogue is the horror of the Holocaust.

a. The Horror of the Holocaust
The memory of the Shoah in all of its pain and darkness and terror must be kept alive by Jews and Christians. A start has been made

by the publication by the Catholic Church of 'We Remember: A Reflection on the Shoah' (1998). This document in turn was followed up by an expression of repentance by John Paul II at the Mass of Pardon in Rome on 12 March 2000. At that Mass there was a request for forgiveness for Catholics who caused Jews to suffer, among other requests for forgiveness for other faults. That prayer, subsequently inserted in a crevice in the Western Wall in Jerusalem by John Paul II, states:

> God of our Fathers, you chose Abraham and his descendants to bring your name among the people. We are deeply saddened by the behaviour of those who in the course of history have caused these children of yours to suffer and, asking your forgiveness, we wish to commit ourselves to genuine fellowship with the people of the Covenant.

These are important steps on the road to the purification and healing of memories. Ongoing historical research in trying to understand the full extent of Christian and Catholic complicity in the Shoah will also help in the healing of memories.

Christians must seek to ensure that nothing they do or say could ever contribute to such a nightmare for Jews or indeed for any other religion in the future. We must learn – all religions must learn – that all that is required for evil to succeed is for good people to do nothing. We must also remember that a Christian faith that remains purely private is not truly a faith in the tradition of Jesus the prophet or indeed in the tradition of the prophets of Israel. There is also another side to the Holocaust that has troubled Jews and continues to trouble Jews and that is the deeper theological question: where was God during the Holocaust?

b. Where Is God in Human Suffering?

How can Jews talk about God's continuing covenant in the light of the Shoah? Where was God in the face of so much darkness and death in Germany at that time? These questions, however, are no longer only questions for Jews; they are also questions for Christians who now believe in the permanency of God's covenant with Israel. These questions cannot be avoided and should not be avoided, especially in view of the ongoing presence of so much suffering and death in the world today and in view of the increasing secular character of a disenchanted universe. The credibility of theological discourse about God's covenant with Jews and Christians is at stake in such questions.

Is it possible for Jews and Christians to work together on these unsettling theological questions? Questions about the presence or absence of God in the face of suffering continue to haunt humanity in the twenty-first century:[16] the Indonesian tsunami, Haiti, Somalia, Japan ...

The Jewish question about the presence or absence of God during the Holocaust is a question that has been asked before. It is also a question found in the life of Jesus, in his cry of dereliction on the Cross: 'My God, my God, why have you forsaken me?' It is also found on the lips of Job in his personal suffering and turmoil, and it is a question that pervades the psalms of the Hebrew Psalter.

In hinting that there might be some connection between the Cross and the Shoah, Christian theologians should be mindful of the existence of deeply ingrained negative attitudes among Jews towards the Cross. Many Jews continue to think that Christians blame them for the death of Jesus on the Cross, in spite of the repudiation of this view by *Nostra Aetate* and historical studies by Christian scholars on the death of Jesus such as Ray Brown and Gerard Sloyan. Further, Christians should not forget that during the first Crusades in the eleventh century under Pope Urban, thousands of Jews were killed under the banner of the Crusades and that the word 'crusades' is derived from the cross.

In spite of these ambiguous associations with the Cross in the Jewish mind, it may be possible for Jews and Christians to address together questions about the presence or absence of God in the face of darkness, death and tragedy. There is, for example, a tradition in the Hebrew scriptures that talks about the suffering of Yahweh found among Jewish prophets like Amos, Jeremiah and Isaiah. The Jewish philosopher and theologian, Abraham Joshua Heschel, talks about the pathos of God in the Hebrew scriptures. Heschel does not suggest that the prophets have received a revelation about the suffering of God, but rather in virtue of the close relationship between the prophets and Yahweh, they sense the suffering of Yahweh in the suffering of the people of Israel. Heschel points to Isaiah 42:14 which likens the sufferings of Yahweh to 'a woman in labor' (NRSV). Similarly, Isaiah 63:9 notes that 'in all their affliction, He [Yahweh] was afflicted' (NASB, KJB, ASB).

Dietrich Bonhoeffer, in struggling with the same question, came up with the statement: 'Only a suffering God can help.' Such language, as indeed all language about God, should be qualified and recognised as symbolic and analogical.

Another possible approach in this painful context of the Holocaust is the Jewish mystical tradition that talks about the self-limitation of God in history. This divine self-limitation follows from God's gift of freedom to humanity, a view also found among Christian theologians such as Langdon Gilkey and others. Alongside a theology of the self-limitation of God in history, there is also the Christian theology of *kenosis*, associated with the death of Jesus: a view that talks about the self-emptying love of Christ on the cross. Is it possible for Jews and Christians to join up these perspectives on God and to discern a pattern within Revelation which sees the self-emptying love of God as actively present in the first instance in the gift of creation, in the unique history of Judaism, in the personal life of Jesus, on the Cross at Calvary, and at the Holocaust? The silence of God in these events is not the silence of absence or rejection or withdrawal. It is the silence of a loving presence that limits itself out of respect for the gift of freedom to humanity; it is the silence of a loving parent watching her child taking the first faltering steps of freedom.

Another, somewhat different approach to this unanswerable question about the presence or absence of God to the suffering of Jesus on the Cross and the suffering of the Jews at the Shoah can be found in the words of the US poet, Theodore Roethke:

> In a dark time
> The eye begins to see

There is a sense in which 'darkness can be a special kind of light' and that the darkness surrounding the history of Judaism (e.g. 1 Kings 8:12), the Cross of Jesus at Golgotha (Mt 27:45), and the horror of the Holocaust reveal a kind of light on the hiddenness of God's presence in the world.

The Irish poet, Brendan Kennelly, in the poem, 'The Willow', describes how one night, shaken by a storm, the tree is transfigured by the same unwelcome storm. In the first part of the poem, Kennelly writes:

> But last night that great form
> Was tossed and hit
> By what seemed to me
> A kind of cosmic hate,
> An infernal desire
> To harass and confuse
> Mangle and bewilder.

Out of that terrible storm, there comes a new kind of peace and stillness which is experienced in a special way by the branches of the willow. Part two of the poem describes this new vitality. Before the storm, the branches had lived by 'roots ... lodged in apathetic clay' but now, after the storm, the branches, having felt 'the transfiguring breath of evil', realise

> That what a storm can do
> Is to terrify my roots
> And make me new.

There can be little doubt that apathy in our relationship with God is an issue facing Jews and Christians and that an apathetic theology generates an apathetic people. By working together, Jews and

Christians can generate a more passionate and compassionate theology that struggles to understand the question of suffering in the context of the covenantal presence of the Spirit of God to God's people.

c. Keeping the Memory of the Shoah Alive and the Williamson Affair

The importance of keeping the memory of the Holocaust alive came to the fore in January 2009. The lifting, by Benedict XVI, of the excommunication on four bishops of the Society of Pius X, a body founded by the dissident Archbishop Lefebvre, created controversy, misunderstanding and bad feelings between Jews and Catholics. One of the bishops in question, a Richard Williamson, turned out to be a Holocaust denier.

Within twenty-four hours, the Vatican issued a clarification denying it knew about Williamson's views on the Holocaust. Some days later Benedict XVI responded by pointing out that the lifting of the excommunication on these four bishops was a gesture of peace towards the dissident group, and was *not* intended in any way to offend Jewish sensibilities. Benedict went on to affirm the death of 'millions of Jews in Nazi death camps' and expressed his 'full and indisputable solidarity with the Jews'.

But that was not the end of the affair. Karl Lehmann, former head of the German Bishops' Conference, described the episode as a 'catastrophe', and the German Chancellor Angela Merkel asked Benedict to clarify the position of the Catholic Church on the Holocaust-denying Bishop Williamson. Walter Kasper, the Cardinal in charge of Catholic-Jewish relations, made it clear that he had not been consulted, and that the controversy filled him with 'great concern'. Cardinal Christoph Schönborn of Vienna spoke out critically about the incident, stating: 'Obviously a mistake has been made ... someone who denies the Holocaust cannot be restored to an office in the Church', and subsequently went on to criticise the Vatican staff for not doing their homework.

There are a number of issues that need to be untangled and named in this controversy. In the light of the teaching of the Catholic Church expressed in *Nostra Aetate*, the formal recognition by the Church of the atrocities against the Jews during the years of 1939–1945 in the 1985 *Notes on the Correct Way to present Jews and Judaism in Preaching and Catechetics*, the 1998 document *We Remember: A Reflection on the Shoah*, and the many references to the Shoah in writings by John Paul II and Benedict XVI, it is clear that the Catholic Church could not be at peace or make peace with someone who denies the Shoah. It is difficult to understand how the Church could enter into serious dialogue with the Society of Pius X, given the description by Archbishop Lefebvre of Jews as enemies of the faith in a letter to John Paul II in August 1985. Further, this antagonism towards Jews can also be found in statements among members of the Society of Pius X and some of the bishops released from excommunication.

The second issue is how could the Catholic Church enter into communion with an organisation that does not accept the teaching of Vatican II and the post-conciliar teaching? Lurking behind this question is the ongoing debate about the meaning and interpretation of the significance of Vatican II. There are those who claim that Vatican II changed nothing, that the Council did not teach anything new, and that there is a straight line of continuity between the pre-Vatican II and post-Vatican II Church. This particular group often invokes Benedict XVI to support this understanding of the Council, by quoting selective sections of his address to the Curia in December 2005.

In that address, Benedict XVI contrasts two approaches to the Council – those who see it in terms of a 'Hermeneutics of discontinuity and rupture' and those who see it in terms of a 'Hermeneutic of reform'. Benedict expresses dissatisfaction with the hermeneutic of discontinuity. Instead he favours a 'hermeneutic of reform' as the proper approach to the Council and justifies this approach by appealing to the opening speech of John XXIII to the Council and the closing speech of Paul VI in 1965. He notes: 'It is precisely in this combination of continuity and discontinuity ... that the very nature of true reform consists' and then goes on to talk about 'innovation in continuity'. Examples cited by Benedict XVI of this hermeneutics of reform concern the relationship between faith and modern science, between the Church and the modern state, between Christianity and other religions, especially Judaism.

There is a third issue buried within this controversy that also needs attention. In the light of the teaching *Nostra Aetate* at Vatican II and the theological implications of that teaching, the Catholic Church now carries within its own self-understanding a commitment to Judaism as a living and vibrant faith – not as an optional extra, not as an add-on, not as a piece of rhetoric, but rather as something that belongs to the very definition of what it means to be Catholic in the post-Vatican II era. Commitment to Catholicism carries with it a commitment to biblical and Rabbinic Judaism. So for example, when I enter into dialogue with another religion, I carry with me a special relationship with Judaism that must be a part of that particular dialogue. Likewise if the Catholic Church seeks to effect a communion with the Society of Pius X, then part of what the Catholic Church brings to that discussion is respect for and love of its Jewish heritage.

Another way of expressing these concerns can be found in a statement by the German Bishops on the Jews back in the late 1970s, which pointed out that 'He who encounters Jesus Christ encounters Judaism'. The way we do Christology in the light of *Nostra Aetate* is very important and therefore must contain key elements of biblical Judaism. This is something that flows from the theological implications of *Nostra Aetate* and the rediscovery of the Jewishness of Jesus. If this is the case, then it also follows that she who encounters the Catholic Church should also encounter Judaism as intrinsic to its ecclesial identity. Some progress has been made in this regard in the area of Christology, but little progress has been made in ecclesiology, and a good example of this lack of progress in ecclesiology is the row over the lifting of the excommunication of the four bishops of the Society of Pius X in 2009. While everybody, including Benedict XVI, agrees the Williamson affair should never have happened, it did highlight the importance of keeping the memory of the Shoah alive. The swift reaction from the Catholic Church and from the secular world against attempts to play down or deny that irremovable scar from human history sent out a clear message to all.

d. One or Many Covenants?

A further unresolved question that needs to be addressed in the light of relocating Christianity within Judaism concerns the covenant. The clear affirmation of the ongoing reality of God's covenant with Israel raises searching questions about the relationship of the First Covenant and God's new covenant in Christ. Is there one covenant between God and humanity with two unique expressions: one in Judaism and the other in Christianity? Or are there two distinct and separate covenants, one with Judaism and one with Christianity? Or might it be said that there are several covenants between God and humanity and that the Jewish and Christian covenants are two among many covenants?

In the light of *Nostra Aetate* and the clear statement by John Paul II in Mainz, Germany, in 1980, that the covenant between God and the people of Israel has not been revoked, it must be recognised that the new covenant in Christ does not replace or supersede or annul the covenant of God with Israel. Nor does the Christian claim that the promises of God's covenant with Israel find their 'yes' in Christ (cf. 2 Cor 1:20), eliminate or abolish the existence and the ongoing validity of the 'old', or better the prior covenant with Israel. What then is the relationship between God's covenant with Israel and God's new covenant in Christ?

The balance of debate appears to be tilted towards a one-covenant theory that has two distinct but different expressions, one with Israel which is Torah-based and the other with the new people of God which is Christ-based.[17] The new covenant in Christ is for some the outgrowth or concentration or crystallisation of God's covenant with Israel; for others, the new covenant in Christ is the completion or 'the final re-interpretation promised by the prophets of the old Covenant.'[18] The images most used to symbolise this connection between the two covenants are that of the relationship that exists between a seed and a plant, or the still more subtle Pauline image of the root of the olive tree representing Israel onto which the people of the new covenant have been grafted (Rom 11:16-24). Lest there be any misunderstanding, or any cause for triumphalism, Paul points out: 'It is not you [that is, the Christians] that support the root, but the root that supports you' (Rom 11:18). The Christian community is clearly dependent on Israel for its own life and self-understanding.

For some, however, the single covenant theory does not do justice to the uniqueness and universality of the Christ-event. Consequently, there are those who opt for a two-covenant theory, affirming the particular covenant with Israel through Moses and the unique covenant in Christ. In this way, it is presumed that the uniqueness and universality of the Christ-event is preserved. The problem with the two covenant theory, however, is that it seems to promote the old opposition or rivalry between the Jewish and Christian covenants, and thereby risks renewing forms of supersessionism. Further, a two-covenant theology which talks about Judaism for the Jews and Christianity for the nations seems to go against the unity of the economy of salvation.

Whether one opts for a one covenant theory of two different expressions, or two distinct covenants, it seems to me that there is a deeper theological question that Jews and Christians alike must address. That question is: how are we to understand God's action in establishing the First Covenant with Israel and establishing a second covenant in Christ?

Are these two different divine actions or are we talking about one divine action that comes to expression in two distinct moments and modalities in history? The difficulty with the two-covenant theory is that it gives the impression as just noted that God acts in one way for the Jews, and in another way for Christians. The unity of God's plan for humanity initiated in creation and the promise of completion in the *eschaton*, a view shared by Jews and Christians alike, implies a unity and consistency of divine action.

John McDade expresses the problem accurately when he notes: 'We lack a way of designating the co-presence of Israel and the Church within something larger than each of them, and so we seem unable to think of them together without subsuming one to the other.'[19]

One possible answer to this vexing question would be to suggest that the action of the Spirit of God hovering over creation, as outlined in Chapter Seven, is the primary covenant. This action of the Spirit is God's primordial covenant with creation and is the basis of God's covenant with Israel and God's covenant in Christ. Is it not necessary to begin with God's covenant with creation as the primary horizon in which God enters into covenant with Israel and with the Christian community in Christ?

The divine covenant with creation, the action of God in and with creation, is established through the agency of the Spirit of God 'brooding' over creation (Gen 1:1ff.), as seen in Chapter Seven. That same Spirit of God is active in bringing about the covenant of God with Israel and is personally active in Jesus establishing the new covenant in Jesus as the Christ. Of course, when the Spirit of God is active, so also the *Logos* of God is active in creation, in Israel and in Christ. These are not three different and distinct divine actions but rather one single saving action which is manifested universally in the gift of creation, offered in particular in God's historical covenant with Israel on Sinai with Moses and concentrated personally in the life of Jesus which culminates on Calvary. This single, unified action of a *Pneuma* and *Logos* continues in creation, in Israel, in Christ and in the Church. What is distinctive about Israel is the way the chosen people keep covenant with God through fidelity to the Torah. And what is distinctive about Christianity is the particularity of its way of remaining in covenant with God through commitment to the person of Christ and the Church of Christ as the eschatological community of the Spirit.

It is difficult to disassociate God's covenant with Israel and God's covenant in Christ from God's action in creation without once again giving the impression that God 'acts' in different ways, even arbitrary ways, in the world. While there may be different expressions of God's covenant with creation in the Hebrew scriptures such as the relationship between the creator God and the human family represented by Adam, and the cosmic covenant with Noah (Gen 9:1-17), this is not a reason for placing creation outside of God's

continuous covenantal action with the Israel of God and the C
of Christ.

There is a further reason why it is necessary to talk about God's
covenant in the context of creation and that is because the covenant
in Christ is described by Paul in terms that resonate with the
creation story, namely when Christ is described as 'the first-born of
all creation' (Col 1:15) and a 'new creation' (2 Cor 5:18-19) and the
'new Adam' (1 Cor 15:45).

What is at stake here is how do Jews and Christians understand
the unique action of the *Pneuma* of God and the *Logos* of God in
covenant with Israel, and the unique covenantal action of the *Pneuma*
of God and *Logos* of God in Christ? This is a theological question that
might be best answered by Jews and Christians working together.
In the light of a joint answer, they could then spell out their own
distinctive self-understanding of God's consistent covenantal action
in their own particular and unique situations.

As the UK Jewish scholar, Edward Kessler, suggests: 'An exploration
of the meaning of covenant in the Jewish-Christian relationship would
be of value' in shedding 'light on the way in which Christians can
witness through word and deed to their covenant with God through
Christ and likewise Jews through their observance of Torah.'[20] One
way of responding to this challenge is to locate the particularity of
God's covenant with Israel and in Christ within the wider, universal
covenant of God with creation. This proposal has the added value
of highlighting the unity of Jewish-Christian responsibility for the
healing of the world and the ecological well-being of creation.

5. OTHER DISPUTED THEOLOGICAL ISSUES

Over and above these unresolved theological questions, there
are other disputed theological issues facing the Jewish-Christian
dialogue. One such question is the issue of Mission.

a. The Question of Mission

What is the mission of the Church in the world today? Does it include
a mission to the Jews or perhaps a mission *with* the Jews? What are

the implications of the teaching of *Nostra Aetate* on God's unrevoked covenant and gifts to the Jews for the Church's understanding of mission? These questions are not only unresolved within the Jewish-Christian dialogue, but are also questions of some dispute within Church circles. Given the history of the proselytism of the Jews and even at times forced conversions from Judaism to Christianity, the chosen People of Israel, understandably, bristle at the mention of mission by Christians.

Alon Goshen-Gottstein sees mission within Christianity as the major obstacle to dialogue with Christians:

> Past history has made the Jewish psyche particularly suspicious of missionary activity. Suspicion of a hidden missionary agenda is probably still the greatest impediment to advancement in Jewish-Christian dialogue.[21]

The question of mission arose among Jews after the publication of *Dominus Iesus* in 2000 AD. In the context of inter-religious dialogue, *Dominus Iesus* talked about the evangelising mission of the Church towards other religions. The Jews responded negatively and critically to this un-nuanced statement of *Dominus Iesus*. In a clarification offered by the then Prefect of the Congregation for the Doctrine of the Faith, Cardinal Joseph Ratzinger pointed out in an article entitled 'The Heritage of Abraham'[22] in December 2000 that 'the dialogue of us Christians with Jews stands on a different level with regard to dialogue with other religions. The faith witnessed in the Bible of the Jews, the Old Testament of Christians, is for us not a different religion but the foundation of our faith.'

Some months later, in April 2001, Cardinal Kasper, president of the Pontifical Council for Promoting Christian Unity, suggested that: 'the term mission, in its proper sense, refers to conversion from false gods and idols to the true and one God.' In this particular sense, he went on to say: 'mission cannot be used in regard to the Jews.'[23]

In August 2002, a consultative document was issued by scholars from the US Council for Ecumenical and Inter-Religious Affairs and the National Council of Synagogues entitled 'Reflections on Covenant and Mission.' This document had a Jewish part and a Catholic part, with the Catholic part quoting Kasper on mission, and so calling into question the Catholic mission to Jews. This aspect of the document provoked an immediate reaction from Cardinal Avery Dulles, who stated that the document 'Reflections on "Covenant and Mission" is ambiguous, if not erroneous, in its treatment of topics such an evangelisation, mission, covenant and dialogue.'[24]

In November 2002, Kasper, now President of the Council of the Vatican Commission for Religious Relations with Jews, in a lecture at the Centre for Christian-Jewish Learning in Boston College, entitled 'Christians, Jews and the Thorny Question of Mission', takes up the question once again. Here he develops his views on mission. He argues that when you emphasise elements of continuity between Judaism and Christianity in terms of God's unrevoked covenant with Israel and the new covenant in Christ, then there can be 'no organised Catholic missionary activity towards Jews as there is for all other non-Christian religions.'[25] However, Kasper goes on to say that this emphasis on what Jews and Christians hold in common is 'only half of the problem'. Account must also be taken of the differences between Jews and Christians and how each reads the Bible differently. Christians, if they are to be true to their faith, cannot draw back from their faith in Christ as Saviour of all and the mandate from Jesus as the Christ to make disciples of all nations (Mt 28:19).

It is at this level that the question of mission remains a disputed issue for Christians in the dialogue with Jews. The question remains: 'How do we resolve the offer of salvation given in the covenant with Israel with the Christian recognition and faith in Jesus as the Messiah and the universal Saviour of the world?' Can these two statements be held together in a creative tension? For the Jews, God's covenant with Israel is the way of salvation and for Christians, Jesus as the Messiah and the universal Saviour is the way of salvation. However, this does not mean that there are two parallel ways of salvation. Instead, these two expressions of salvation are dialectically related and as much inform each other. Both Israel and the Church exist in covenant with the one God who saves, and both live out their covenant by relationship with God in distinct Torah-centered ways and distinct Christ-centred ways. There is a similarity but also a distinctness in the way they exist and relate to the one God.

For some commentators, the question of mission is: 'Why convert the saved?'[26] Instead of having a mission *to* the Jews, some hold that Christians should see themselves as having a mission *with* the Jews. In his 2002 article, Kasper summarises what this joint mission of Jews and Christians might entail:

- To point to a future that will be determined by God and God alone;
- To witness together to the incompleteness of the world and its 'non-completeability' by human efforts;
- To highlight the openness of history towards a new future;
- To protest together in a shared hope against the pessimism, scepticism and nihilism that is so much a feature of our modern and post-modern worlds.[27]

In his book *Jesus of Nazareth, Volume Two*, Joseph Ratzinger/Benedict XVI approvingly quotes Bernard of Clairvaux and Hildegard Brem who hold that the Church must not concern itself with the conversion of the Jews, since she must wait for the time fixed for this by God until the full number of Gentiles comes (Rom 11:25). In the same book he also notes that 'Israel retains its own mission' and is 'in the hands of God who will save it "as a whole" at the proper time when the number of Gentiles is complete.'[28]

The question of mission remains one of the challenges facing Jews and Christians in dialogue. And yet on this issue of mission to the Jews it should not be forgotten that it came up at Vatican II in discussions of the various drafts. The story is told by Susannah Heschel, daughter of Abraham Joshua Heschel, that her father met with Paul VI to object to the use of mission to convert the Jews, and that he had been told subsequently that Paul VI had crossed out a sentence in the draft relating to mission to Jews.[29] This is confirmed by a footnote in the Abbot edition of the documents of Vatican II which reads: 'A Reference to "conversion" of the Jews was removed from an earlier version on this Declaration [i.e. *Nostra Aetate*] because many Council Fathers felt it was not appropriate in a document striving to establish common goals and interests.'[30] Another issue, closely connected to the question of mission, which arose in 2010 is that of prayer for Jews in the context of the revised 1962 *Roman Missal*.

b. Prayer for the Jews

The background to this particular controversy is complex. John XXIII removed the word 'perfidious' from the Good Friday Prayer for Jews. Paul VI, in 1965, removed the negative language about the blindness of the Jews in the same missal. The 1970 *Roman Missal* revised the 1965 prayer by acknowledging the faithfulness of the Jews, in a way that reflects the spirit and direction of *Nostra Aetate*. In 2007, discussion began about the translation of the prayer for the Jews in 1962 *Missal*, and the view of most commentators, including high-ranking Church people and Jewish leaders, was that the best solution would be to make the prayer of the 1970 *Missal* the revised text for the 1962 *Missal*.

In February 2008, Benedict XVI issued a new prayer for the 1962 Tridentine Missal. This new prayer asks God to enlighten the hearts of the Jews so that they may acknowledge Jesus Christ and then goes on to say 'graciously grant that with the fullness of the people entering into your church all of Israel may be saved'. At the centre of this particular controversy is the question of mission. This newly constructed prayer for the 1962 *Missal* seems to imply a mission to the Jews. This new prayer provoked a negative response from the Chief Rabbi of Rome, Ricardo Di Segni, and from the Italian Rabbinical Assembly. The significance of this debate about prayer for Jews should not be underestimated. It has been and still is a principle of Catholic theology that the way we pray influences what we believe: *lex orandi, lex credendi*. There is something of a tension between praying for the conversion of the Jews and at the same time affirming God's unrevoked covenant with Israel.

c. Similar but Different Eschatologies

For Christians, the Messianic hopes and expectations of Judaism have been completed in and through the life, death and resurrection of Jesus and the outpouring of the Spirit. This is a core belief of Christian faith and it finds expression throughout the New Testament. These expressions include the healings and exorcisms, the unconditional offer of forgiveness, the introduction of a new table fellowship which was formalised at the Last Supper as the new covenant, but most of all through the death and resurrection of Jesus and the outpouring of the eschatological Spirit on the disciples of Jesus at Pentecost. This experience by the disciples of Jesus as the 'fulfilment' of messianic hopes within Judaism is articulated in different ways in the New Testament:

- Through the description of Jesus as 'the first fruits' of God's eschatological harvest (1 Cor 15:20);
- Through references to Jesus as 'the beginning, the first born of the dead' (Col 1:18);
- The account of Jesus as the 'new creation' (2 Cor 5);
- In the parallels drawn between Adam and Christ as the new Adam (Rom 5:12-21; 1 Cor 15:45-49);
- The different Christological hymns of Jn 1:11-14; Eph 1:9-12; Col 1:15-20; and Phil 2:6-11

This 'fulfilment' of Jewish hopes is an essential part of the Christian understanding of the uniqueness of the Christ-event. Jews, however, ask hard questions of Christians when they make these particular claims for 'fulfilment'. They want to know where is the evidence in history, in society and in creation for the 'fulfilment' in Christ of the messianic hopes of the Jewish covenant. Where is the peace (*Shalom*) and salvation that the promised Messiah was expected to bring? Jews point to the existence of widespread spiritual anxiety and selfishness within human beings, the presence of social and global conflicts in the world, and the enduring existence of political unrest and brokenness among the nations.

Christians respond by pointing out that the 'fulfilment' of the promises has taken place in the person of Jesus as the Christ. In particular, Christians suggest that on the cross, Christ has fulfilled the law once and for all as the representative of humanity (Rom 3:21-26; Gal 3:13; 4:ff.); that Christ is the goal and the end of the law (Rom 10:4; Gal 3:24-24), and that Christ has united Jews and Gentiles, slave and free, male and female, in his person (cf. Gal 3:28; Eph 2:11-22). Further, Christians claim that the Christ-event has set in train the inauguration of a new community endowed with the eschatological gifts of the Spirit. It is also noted that this new community celebrates the advent of the end of time in Christ in baptism, in the offer of forgiveness and in the celebration of the Eucharist.

Christians in more recent times are also careful to point out as Kasper does that this 'Christological focus and realisation of the new covenant as promised by the prophets for the Messianic end times is of course not an ecclesiological realisation.'[31] In relation to the Church, Kasper goes on to say: 'There remains an as yet unfulfilled balance of the prophetic promise.'[32] Awareness of this unfulfilled dimension of the Messianic promises is prominent also in the New Testament as seen in previous chapters. As already noted, the first Christian prayer, *Maranatha*, expressed in all probability at the celebration of the Eucharist, is an acknowledgement of this unfulfilled balance. This early Christian prayer is a statement that Christ will complete what he has set in train. A similar expression of what is still outstanding can be found in Paul's eschatology, which talks about what has already happened in Christ and what is yet to come, and goes on to acknowledge a tension between being 'in Christ' and becoming 'in Christ'. An additional statement of this outstanding balance concerning Messianic promises is found in the early Christian doctrine about the second coming of Christ (*Parousia*).

Jews will properly persist with their questions and further ask of Christians: where do these Christian claims leave the 'first' covenant? What are the implications of these Christian claims for the enduring covenant of Yahweh with Israel? Christians will reply that the promises of Yahweh have received a resounding yes and *amen* in Christ (2 Cor 1:20). Further, Christians claim that the new covenant in Christ embodies fully the first covenant and, prompted by the Spirit, they seek now to extend that covenant to all nations. However, this does not mean that the first covenant has been abolished: instead it suggests that the original covenant has been given a particular form and new shape in Christ – but not ended, not revoked and not eliminated. Further, in this regard Christians will acknowledge that it was in the second and third century, through Justin Martyr and Barnadas, that a shift from the Christological realisation of Jewish promises to an ecclesiological realisation took place and that it was this particular shift that introduced the Christian theory of the substitution of the first covenant with the new covenant, a point of view that has now been transformed by the teaching of *Nostra Aetate* and the teaching of post-Vatican II Popes which affirm the ongoing validity and integrity of God's original covenant with Israel.

Given this enduring validity of the Jewish covenant, Kasper asks the following question: 'Or is there still a balance of promise from the old covenant which has not been fulfilled in the new covenant, and can it be accorded any lasting significance?' Kasper replies to his own question by saying that:

> *Nostra Aetate* affirms the continuing validity of God's covenant with Israel and that Jews still remain most dear to God and that with the prophets and the apostles, the Church awaits that day, known to God alone, on which all people will address the Lord in a single voice and 'serve Him' with one accord.[33]

There is an important sense in which Jews and Christians together look to the future fulfilment of God's messianic promises. The Jews look for the first coming of the Messiah and the Christians await the second coming of the Messiah. For Christians, the crucified and risen Christ and the outpouring of the Spirit at Pentecost prefigures the future, giving it shape and colour and form.[34] The shape of the future is cruciform: the fulfilment of the future will be cruciform in the sense that the Cross is unavoidable. The colour of the future is one of a bright-darkness; the fulfilment of the future contains moments of darkness and light, elements of sorrow and joy. The form of the future is made up of a paschal pattern, involving dying and rising in Christ, a process of decentring and recentring the self 'in Christ'. For Christians, Christology is a concentration of creation;[35] that is, the drama of the life of Jesus, especially his death and resurrection, is a microcosm of what is taking place in the macrocosm of life. Jews and Christians live out of these similar but different eschatologies; they jointly witness to the future as God's promise and gift to humanity to be realised only in God's time; they believe that this promised future is not only about individuals, but also about history and society and creation in fulfilment of God's promises within both the first and second covenants. If there is a balance of promise from the first covenant which has not been fulfilled in the new covenant, it could be expressed in terms of the social and cosmic realisation of both the first covenant and the new covenant in Christ. The future for Christians has arrived in Christ in embryonic form, but the realisation of the implications of this gift in Christ awaits fulfilment at the historical, social and cosmic levels for Jews and Gentiles alike.

These developments at Vatican II in *Nostra Aetate* and in the post-conciliar period have given rise to a redefinition of the relationship between Judaism and Christianity. The covenant between God and the Jews remains in place and has not been substituted or replaced by the new covenant in Christ. Furthermore, in God's plan of Revelation, Israel has its own defining role to play.

These new perspectives are now an essential part of what it means to be Christian and Catholic in the twenty-first century. Consequently, as already emphasised, when Catholics enter into dialogue with other religions, they carry these new perspectives on Judaism to the table of dialogue. For example, for Christians, Judaism is unique among the religions of the world with a distinctive revelation in a manner that echoes the way that Christianity is a distinctive faith with a revelation focussed in Christ which claims to be final, unsurpassable and definitive.

Given these continuities between Judaism and Christianity, Jews and Catholics can give joint witness in the world to:

- The one God of Israel;
- The Messianic promises of God in Judaism and Christianity;
- The centrality of *Torah* for Jews and Christians;
- The importance of social justice as found in the prophets of old and in the person of Jesus;
- The call to work for the mending of the world (*Tikkum Olam*);
- The unique place of the Ten Commandments in the ordering of society;
- The disturbing memory of the Holocaust;
- The shared belief in the power of God to transform the individual, society and the cosmos which for Christians has been prefigured in the death and Resurrection of Jesus

To bring these reflections to a close, let me offer some images that might be used to describe the new relationship that obtains between the living faith of Judaism and Catholicism since the Second Vatican Council. We need new models to describe the new, unique relationship that now exists between Judaism and Christianity.

Up to recently, commentators talked about the relationship between Christians and Jews as one paralleling the relationship of a 'mother and daughter' or 'elder and younger brother' (used by John Paul II) or 'the good olive tree and the grafted wild olive branch' (employed by Paul in Romans and re-affirmed at Vatican II).

More recent images suggest we see Jews and Christians as 'siblings' (proposed by Alan Segal, a Jewish scholar) or 'competitive siblings' (John McDade). Another possibility within this category is the proposal to see Jews and Christians as 'fraternal twins'.[36]

This particular set of images emphasise elements of continuity and connectedness between Judaism and Christianity – to the neglect, according to some, of the equally important elements of discontinuity and difference that do exist between Jews and Christians.

A third image is that Jews and Christians might be understood as 'partners-in-waiting'. The value of this particular image is that it recognises that Jews and Christians share eschatological perspectives. Both point towards a shared hope about the world, about the origin of this hope, and its fulfilment. Both recognise that the fulfilment of the future is pure gift from God. The adoption of one or other, or a combination of these images may well help to promote a better understanding of relationships between Jews and Christians, and these images may also help us to watch our discourse and our actions in the presence of the other. In the light of Vatican II and subsequent developments, it can be said that Jews and Christians are partners, not rivals, in the work of justice and the promotion of the Reign of God in the world.

As David M. Neuhaus points out, it must be recognised that in spite of real progress in the Jewish-Christian dialogue over fifty years, Judaism is not Christianity and Christianity is not Judaism. There is a 'profound commonality and radical difference' between the two. 'Catholics and Jews share much and yet also differ greatly.'[37] The recovery of a new level of continuity between Israel and Christianity in the light of *Nostra Aetate* should put an end to 1,800 years of rupture between Jews and Christians.

The theological fruits accruing from the Jewish-Christian dialogue for Catholics are significant and should be proclaimed. They include:

- A new appreciation of the Jewishness of Jesus and the impact of this on Christology;
- A rediscovery of the Jewish roots of the Church and the importance of this for ecclesiology;
- A new understanding of God's unrevoked covenant with Israel and the challenges this poses for the proclamation of the uniqueness and universality of Jesus as Saviour;

- A re-centring of the identity of the Church within the living tradition of Israel;
- An end to anti-Semitism, supersessionism and mission to convert Jews within the self-understanding of Christian identity.

These are important theological insights for Catholicism. In brief, it must be concluded that the progress of fifty years of Jewish-Christian dialogue, despite setbacks, is an outstanding sign of hope for the future of Catholic inter-religious dialogue.

———

Notes

1. *Guidelines and Suggestions for Implementing the Conciliar Declaration* 'Nostra Aetate', no. 4, Pontifical Commission for Religious Relations with the Jews, 1974

2. *NA*, a.4

3. 'Preface to the Second Edition', *The Parting of the Ways: Between Christianity and Judaism and their Significance for the Character of Christianity*, second edition, James D. G. Dunn (ed.), London: SCM Press, 2006, xi–xxx at xxvii

4. John McDade, 'Catholic Christianity and Judaism since Vatican II', *New Blackfriars*, 88, 2007, 367–84 at 368

5. Irving Greenberg, 'Cloud of Smoke, Pillar of Fire: Judaism, Christianity and Modernity after the Holocaust', *Auschwitz: Beginning of a New Era?; Reflections on the Holocaust*, Eva Fleischner (ed.), New York: KTAV, 1977, 23

6. See Dermot A. Lane, *The Reality of Jesus: An Essay in Christology*, Dublin/New York: Veritas/Paulist Press, 1976/2008, 13–18

7. This is the title of a four-volume study (1991–2009) by Meier on various aspects of the life of the historical Jesus. A fifth volume is promised.

8. John P. Meier, 'The Jewishness of Jesus, *No Religion is an Island: The* Nostra Aetate *Dialogues*, Edward Bristow (ed.), New York: Fordham University Press, 1998, 24–55, 28

9. Address to the Biblical Commission, 11 April 1979, available at: www. vatican. va/holy_father/john_paul_ii/speeches/1997/april/documents/hf_jp-ii_spe_19970411_pont-com-biblica_en.html; accessed on 1 July 2011

10. Benedict XVI, *Jesus of Nazareth, Volume One: From the Baptism in the Jordan to the Transfiguration*, New York: Doubleday, 2007, 110, 111 and 169 respectively

11. Hans Hermann Henrix, 'The Son of God Became Human as a Jew: Implications of the Jewishness of Jesus for Christology', *Christ Jesus and the Jewish People: New Explorations of Theological Interrelationships*, Philip A. Cunningham, Joseph Sievers, Mary Boys, Hans Hermann Henrix (eds), Michigan: W. B. Eerdmans, 2011, 122, 134, 138

12. Daniel Harrington, 'Is the New Testament Anti-Jewish?: The Need to Develop a Sense of History', *Irish Theological Quarterly*, Vol. 63, No. 2, 1998, 123–32 at 131; and John Pawlikowski, 'Christology and the Jewish-Christian Dialogue', *Irish Theological Quarterly*, Vol. 72, No. 2, 2007, 147–69 at 158

13. See Larry W. Hurtado, *Lord Jesus Christ: Devotion to Jesus in Earliest Christianity*, Michigan: W. B. Eerdmans, 2005. James G. D. Dunn disputes the claims of Hurtado in *Did the First Christians Worship Jesus: The New Testament Evidence*, London: SPCK, 2010

14. These points are dealt with in more detail by James D. G. Dunn in his informative 'Preface to the Second Edition' of *The Parting of the Ways*, 2006, xi–xxx

15. See John McDade, 'Catholic Christianity and Judaism since Vatican II', 367–84 at 377–8; Benedict XVI, *Jesus of Nazareth, Volume One*, 110–11 and 169; Hans Hermann Henrix, 'The Son of God Became Human as a Jew'

16. On this complex question, see the significant contributions of Peter Admirand, *Amidst Mass Atrocity and the Rubble of Theology: Searching for a Viable Theodicy*, Oregon: Wipf and Stock, 2011; Terrence W. Tilley, 'Doing Theology in the Context of the Gift and Promise of *Nostra Aetate*', *Studies in Christian–Jewish Relations*, Vol. 6 (2011). Available online at: http://escholarship.bc.edu/ojs/index.php.scjr/article/view/1581

17. See, for example, Norbert Lohfink, *Covenant Never Revoked: Biblical Reflections on Christian-Jewish Dialogue*, New York: Paulist Press, 1991, and McDade, 'Catholic Christianity and Judaism since Vatican II', 367–84

18. Walter Kasper, 'Foreword', *Christ Jesus and the Jewish People Today: New Explorations of Theological Interrelationship*, x–xviii at xiv

19. John McDade, 'Christians and Jews: Competitive Siblings or the Israel of God?', *New Blackfriars*, 89, 2008, 267–79 at 275

20. Edward Kessler, 'Common Ground with the Chosen People', *The Tablet*, 21 October 2005, 10–11 at 11

21. Alon Goshen-Gottstein, 'Jewish-Christian Relations: From Historical Past to Theological Future' (1 January 2003); online at http://www.jcrelations.net/en/?item=1754; accessed on 13 July 2010

22. 'The Heritage of Abraham', *L'Osservatore Romano*, 29 December 2000

23. Walter Kasper, 'The Good Olive Tree', *America*, 17 September 2001, 12–14 at 14

24. Cardinal Avery Dulles, 'Covenant and Mission', *America*, 21 October 2002, 9

25. Cardinal Walter Kasper, 'Christians, Jews and the Thorny Question of Mission', *Origins*, Vol. 32, 19 December 2004, 458–66 at 463

26. See Eugene Fisher, 'Why Convert the Saved?: A Jewish-Christian Revolution', *The Tablet*, 30 March 2001

27. Kasper, 'Christians, Jews and the Thorny Question of Mission', 463

28. Benedict XVI, *Jesus of Nazareth, Volume Two: Holy Week: From the Entrance into Jerusalem to the Resurrection*, London: CTS, 2011, 44–6

29. See interview in *America*, 18–25 June 2007, 12

30. See Walter Abbot edition of *The Documents of Vatican II*, New York: Paulist Press, 1966, 665, n. 19

31. Walter Kasper, 'The Relationship of the Old and New Covenant as one of the Central Issues in Jewish-Christian Dialogue', 2–3, a lecture given at the Centre for the Study of Jewish-Christian Relations in Cambridge on 6 December 2004 and available online at http://www.bc.edu/dam/files/research_sites/cjl/texts/cjrelations/resources/articles/Kasper_Cambridge_6Dec04.htm; accessed on 7 July 2008

32. Ibid., 3

33. Ibid., 5

34. See Dermot A. Lane, 'Eschatology', *The New SCM Dictionary of Christian Spirituality*, Philip Sheldrake (ed.), London: SCM Press, 2005, 282–4

35. See Edward Schillebeeckx, *Interim Report on the Books Jesus and Christ*, London: SCM Press, 1980, 126–7

36. Mary Boys, *Has God Only One Blessing: Judaism as a Source of Christian Self-Understanding*, New Jersey: Paulist Press, 2000

37. David M. Neuhaus 'Engaging the Jewish People: Forty Years since *Nostra Aetate*', *Catholic Engagement with World Religions: A Comprehensive Study*, Karl J. Becker and Ilaria Morali (eds), New York: Orbis Books, 2010, 395–413 at 412

EPILOGUE

The report in Chapter Eight on Jewish-Catholic dialogue and the fruits of that dialogue are an outstanding example of what can be achieved through patient inter-religious dialogue. To be sure, more might have been achieved, but nonetheless there is an impressive record of progress for all to see that could not have been imagined back in the early 1960s. And of course, as seen in that chapter there continues to be deep, unresolved theological differences between Judaism and Christianity.

It would be unfortunate and against the spirit of *Nostra Aetate* if this progress in Jewish-Catholic relations was allowed to become a 'political ideology' against the diversity of other religions. Whereas one must welcome the new spirit of collaboration between Jews and Christians on the shared values of the Bible and the reign of God, this new Jewish-Christian alliance must not be stacked up as a united front against others who differ from the Judaeo-Christian heritage and its values. It would be ironic if the Jewish-Christian heritage became a source of division or confrontation with other religions, forgetting about the 1,800 years of bitterness and hostility between Jews and Christians.[1]

The real challenge for inter-religious dialogue in the present and the future is this: can the progress of the last fifty years in the Jewish-Catholic dialogue become a model for dialogue between Catholics and Muslims in the coming decades? There has been a discernible shift in the last number of years within the Catholic Church and among other Christian churches towards Islam. This shift began in late 2006, gained momentum through the publication of 'A Common Word Between Us and You' in 2007 (sometimes called the 'Nostra Aetate of the Muslim World'), and was given further traction through the establishment of an official Catholic-Muslim forum of dialogue in 2008 under the direction of Cardinal Jean-Louis Tauran. Add to these developments the Arab Spring of 2011 and the tragic events in Norway in 2011 by a political extremist with an anti-Muslim outlook, one must conclude that Christian-Muslim dialogue is not only necessary but in truth is now a cultural and religious imperative. While the relationship between Christianity and Islam is quite different to the relationship that exists between Judaism and Christianity, nonetheless there is an urgency for a Christian-Muslim dialogue to get underway.

A second challenge facing the future of inter-religious dialogue is the necessity for closer engagement and dialogue between the three monotheistic faiths of Judaism, Christianity and Islam. All three faiths profess belief in the one God, all name the one true God in different though sometimes complementary ways, all emphasise the importance of personal prayer and worship, all have a deep awareness of how much they do not know about God and that whatever names they do give to God are limited and fall short of the full light and glory of God, all affirm God as creator and have complementary as well as different theologies of creation, and all three faiths are prophetically alive in their critique of idolatry. These three Abrahamic faiths recognise that peace is a gift from God to be received in faith, prayer and praxis. This gift from God acquires greater effect in the world when all of the sisters and brothers of Abraham work together to promote respect, freedom and justice. Clearly there is sufficient theological ground for Jews, Christians and Muslims to enter into serious inter-cultural and inter-religious dialogue. A number of trialogues between Jews, Christians and Muslims have already occurred in places as diverse as Qatar in May 2008 and Madrid in July 2008. Further, there are academic, university-based centres dedicated to trialogue among Jews, Christians and Muslims. These include the centre for Scriptural Reasoning, located as a sub-unit of the Cambridge Inter-Faith Programme in Cambridge, England. This Scriptural Reasoning unit in Cambridge is headed up by David Ford who, with Peter Ochs and others, facilitate the reading and studying of texts from the Hebrew scriptures, the Christian Bible and the Qur'an in the presence of each other. Scriptural Reasoning is now an international movement generating new insights in the service of inter-religious dialogue. Another centre is the Institute for Advanced Catholic Studies at the University of Southern California, which has hosted and published the proceedings of three conferences on trialogues among Jews, Christians and Muslims.[2]

A third challenge is the need to intensify inter-religious dialogue among all major religions. It must be remembered that *Nostra Aetate* in Article 1 emphasises the importance of reflecting on what all religions have in common with a view to addressing the unsolved riddles of existence. Equally, *Nostra Aetate* in Article 2 calls for ongoing 'conversations and collaboration with other religions'. It also suggests that Christians should 'acknowledge, preserve and encourage the spiritual and moral truths found among non-Christians'. The Catholic Church is, therefore, called by *Nostra Aetate* to engage with the dazzling diversity of religions in the world in a way that no longer sees plurality as a threat to harmony and peace, but rather as a source of spiritual and moral enrichment. The real challenge for Christianity and the religions is to bring the voices of religion into the public square in the service of peace, justice and equality in the world. Is it possible that the voices of the different religions could become part of a new religious orchestra, making music in the public square in the service of healing divisions, transforming violence and bringing about peace?

If it is true, as the Catholic Bishops' Conference of England and Wales recently pointed out, that the basis of the Church's positive attitude to people and communities of other religions is its conviction:

> that the human race is one,
> one through its origin in the one creative act of God,
> one in physical descent,
> one in its predicament caused by sin and the need of salvation,
> and one in God's saving purposes,

then inter-religious dialogue is not just an option but an imperative for all. At present the unity of the human family and the variety of religious communities in the world are increasingly fragile. Part of the role of inter-religious dialogue is to support the unity of the world in a way that can serve social stability and political peace. Another part of the role of inter-religious dialogue is to reconnect people to the religious sources and the grounds of their existence.

One further and final challenge facing the religions of the world was clearly expressed at the end of the meeting of religions at Assisi in January 2002 after 9/11. In an agreed statement the leaders of the living faiths talked, among other things, about the renewal of a commitment by all religions:

- To stress that violence and terrorism are incompatible with the authentic spirit of religion;
- To educate people to mutual respect and esteem;
- To foster a culture of dialogue as a source of peace;
- To recognise that the diversity of religions can become an opportunity for a greater mutual understanding.

The agenda for inter-religious dialogue in the present and the future is indeed challenging and may be summarised in the following terms: prioritising the Christian-Muslim dialogue, promoting a greater engagement among the three monotheistic faiths, and intensifying the ongoing encounter among all religions of the world in a way that actively encourages mutual respect, peace, social justice and environmental sustainability.

NOTES

1. This concern and danger has been raised by David M. Neuhaus in 'Engaging the Jewish People: Forty Years since *Nostra Aetate*', *Catholic Engagement with World Religions: A Comprehensive Study*, Karl J. Becker and Ilaria Morali (eds), New York: Orbis Books, 2010, 395–413 at 405–6

2. See *Beyond Violence: Religious Sources of Social Transformation in Judaism, Christianity and Islam*, James L. Heft (ed.), New York: Fordham University Press, 2004; *Passing on the Faith: Transforming Tradition for the Next Generation of*

Jews, Christians, and Muslims, James L. Heft (ed.), New York: Fordham University Press, 2006; *Learned Ignorance: Intellectual Humility among Jews, Christians, and Muslims*, James L. Heft, Reuven Firestone and Omid Safi (eds), New York: Oxford University Press, 2011

SELECT BIBLIOGRAPHY

Invitations to Inter-Religious Dialogue

Nostra Aetate: *Declaration on the Relation of the Church to Non-Christian Religions*, Second Vatican Council, 1965

Dialogue and Proclamation: Reflections and Orientations on Inter-Religious Dialogue and the Proclamation of the Gospel of Jesus Christ, Pontifical Council for Inter-Religious Dialogue and the Congregation for the Evangelisation of Peoples, May 1991

Dabru Emet – Speak the Truth: A Jewish Statement on Christians and Christianity, September 2000. A document on the relationship between Christianity and Judaism signed by over 200 Rabbis and Jewish scholars, and first published in the *New York Times*, September 2000. This statement is available on the website of the Institute for Christian and Jewish Studies: www.icjs.org/programs/ongoing/njsp/dabruemet.php

'A Common Word Between Us and You', 2007, An open letter and call from Muslim religious leaders to Pope Benedict XVI and other Christian leaders, signed by 138 scholars, clerics and intellectuals, October 2007. Available online: www.acommonword.com

Meeting God in Friends and Strangers, Catholic Bishops' Conference of England and Wales, London: CTS, 2010

Christian Witness in a Multi-Religious World: Recommendations for Conduct, World Council of Churches, Pontifical Council for Inter-Religious Dialogue, and World Evangelical Alliance, June 2010. Available online: www.oikumene.org

Select Books

Barnes, Michael, *Theology and the Dialogue of Religions*, Cambridge: Cambridge University Press, 2002

Becker, Karl Josef and Morali, Ilaria (eds), *Catholic Engagement with World Religions: A Comprehensive Study*, New York: Orbis Books, 2010

Clooney, Francis X., *Comparative Theology: Deep Learning Across Religious Borders*, Oxford: Wiley-Blackwell, 2010

D'Costa, Gavin, *Christianity and World Religions: Disputed Questions in the Theology of Religions*, Oxford: Wiley-Blackwell, 2009

Cunningham, Philip A., Sievers, Joseph, Boys, Mary and Henrix, Hans Hermann (eds), *Christ Jesus and the Jewish People Today: New Explorations of Theological Interrelationships*, Michigan: W. B. Eerdmans, 2011

Dupuis, Jacques, *Christianity and the Religions: From Confrontation to Dialogue*, New York: Orbis Books, 2002

Edwards, Denis, *Breath of Life: A Theology of the Creator Spirit*, New York: Orbis Books, 2004

Fitzgerald, Michael and Borelli, John (eds), *Interfaith Dialogue: A Catholic View*, New York: Orbis Books, 2006

Gioia, Francesco (ed.), *Inter-Religious Dialogue: The Official Teaching of the Catholic Church from the Second Vatican Council to John Paul (1963–2005)*, Boston: Pauline Books and Media, 2006

Heft, James L., Firestone, Reuven and Safi Omid (eds), *Learned Ignorance: Intellectual Humility among Jews, Christians, and Muslims*, New York: Oxford University Press, 2011

Kärkkäinen, Veli-Matti (ed.), *Holy Spirit and Salvation: The Sources of Christian Theology*, Kentucky: Westminster John Knox Press, 2010

Moyaert, Marianne, and Pollefeyt, Didier (eds), *Never Revoked: Nostra Aetate as Ongoing Challenge for Jewish-Christian Dialogue*, Louvain: Peeters, 2010

O'Collins, Gerald, *Salvation for All: God's Other Peoples*, New York: Oxford University Press, 2008

Tracy, David, *Dialogue with the Other: The Inter-Religious Dialogue*, Louvain: Peeters, 1990

INDEX